Dictionary

of a

Family

GEORGIA R. THURMAN
SARA ELMORE
ANNE DIMOPOULOS

Georgia Thurman

Sara Elmore

Anne Dimopoulos

Llumina Press

Requests for permission to make copies of any part of this work should be mailed to Permissions Department, Llumina Press, PO BOX 772246, CORAL SPRINGS, FL 33077-2246

ISBN: 1-932560-96-3
Printed in the United States of America by Llumina Press

Library of Congress Cataloging-in-Publication Data

Thurman, Georgia R.
 Dictionary of a family / by Georgia R. Thurman, Sara Elmore, Anne Dimopoulos.
   p. cm.
 ISBN 1-932560-96-3 (pbk. : alk. paper)
 1. Rawlings family. 2. Thurman, Georgia R.--Family. 3. Elmore, Sara--Family. 4. Dimopoulos, Anne--Family. 5. United States--Social life and customs--20th century. 6. Petersburg Region (Ill.)--Biography. I. Elmore, Sara. II. Dimopoulos, Anne. III. Title.
CT274.R65T48 2004
929'.2'0973--dc22

                                    2003027416

Dedicated to

EMERY AND ELIZABETH WHO GAVE US WHAT THEY HAD TO GIVE.
AND TO THOSE WHO CAME BEFORE.
TO OUR CHILDREN, OUR CHILDREN'S CHILDREN
AND THOSE WHO ARE YET TO COME.

⤜⤛⤜⤛⤜⤛⤜⤛⤜⤛⤜⤛

TO LYNN HIRSCH
1937-2001

AND TO FRANK HIRSCH, LYNN'S HUSBAND,
WHOSE FRIENDSHIP CONTINUES TO ASTONISH.

Acknowledgements

This book could not have been completed without the support and help of some very special people. It began with Charlotte Kennedy who provided a magical retreat for us to begin this project. With fear and trepidation, we submitted samples of our early efforts to Nancy Cirillo, whose informed intelligence, experience, and passion gave us the courage to carry on. Bruce Felknor's reading of an early manuscript, and his heartfelt response, pushed us to get back to work. Our warmest thanks to Libby Geaslin, Lynn Koons, Bernice Sperling, and Kathleen Webster for reading, commenting, and encouraging us at various stages throughout the work. We are grateful to Cathie Boland and Connie Toenings, Petersburg natives and childhood friends, for reading the manuscript and for their enthusiasm and love.

To Georgia's daughter Dee and granddaughter Lizzy Hockman, thanks and love for their inputting of Georgia's work.

And hugs to Harry Dimopoulos, husband, brother-in-law, and general best guy, for cheering us on and for saying "That's the one" for the cover photo.

Table of Contents

Preface

The times are the 1930's, '40's, and 50's, from the Great Depression to the Cold War.

The place is, mostly, a small Illinois town 194 miles southwest of Chicago.

For better or worse, many of the attitudes and values described are disappearing, if not gone. In a few decades – 40 or 50 years – no one who shares these memories and experiences will be living. We think they are worth preserving.

But families are eternal, regardless of time, or place, or values. This was our family.

Georgia, Sara, Anne
The Rawlings Girls

Prologue

We are gathered here, three sisters: Georgia, the eldest, Sara in the middle, Anne, the youngest. Among us our ages total over two hundred years, our children total eleven, our grandchildren are thirteen, and Sara's great-grandchildren number four.

We have children ranging in age from 50 to 35, grandchildren from 33 to 1, and our adult experiences and histories span five decades.

We have met to consider our past, individually and collectively, to remember our roots, to understand, and honor, the family that created us, the environments that shaped us, the relationships that molded us. We are here to identify the forces that acted on us in the past and, to some extent, continue to act on us today. We wish to look at the values we hold, inherited or adopted, the abilities granted to us, the attitudes we have developed, the hows and the whys.

Here in a large sunny kitchen at a great wooden table, we talk and write. The kitchen is in the rear of a small, elegant log cabin, loaned for this purpose by a friend of Georgia's. It is early spring and, outside, around the paved patio, snow crystals melt on daffodils. Tendrils of ivy, not yet in leaf, climb the trunks of trees and overhead a hawk floats in the morning sky.

The loan of this retreat is a gift. So too is the subject of this writing — gifts we have received, gifts we have bestowed, gifts denied to us, or by us.

Each family has its own language, its own vocabulary, its own grammar. And yet each family, with a little guidance, will recognize the speech of another; the cadence will grow familiar, the phrases will meet with recognition.

This is the language of our family. As in most families, it reflects different memories, and memories remembered differently. It is remembered in code, in coined words and expressions, in meanings designed to fit our circumstances. Taken together, these definitions weave a story of a place and a time, about people loved and gone, about events trivial and momentous — events seen then, through a glass, darkly, but now more clearly. And soon, face to face.

A

Abet. Look it up! In the pages to follow, we three sisters want to "abet" all those of you who read this to do the thing that we have done here. From talking about "we should write a book" to actually finally making time and getting down to writing, has been an adventure without equal. We would like to abet you in your walk through *your* history. My sisters and I have laughed, cried, said "NO I don't remember that – really?" "You felt I did that?" "I just know it did NOT happen that way." "Oh yes I remember –how could I have forgotten that." "He told you WHAT?" "Oh, I am so jealous." And on and on as we remember, reminisce and write it down.

Some of the hurt of half a century is healing. The recognition of pain and joy and promise has been realized and acknowledged in these pages. The melting of resentment and guilt are in progress

If there are things that need to be said or exorcised from your family – do it now. Approach the unapproachable and say "sorry, let's talk – please listen" – do whatever it takes to get good with your family. Forget it takes two to make a war – sometimes a letter or a phone call will start the treaty process. Perhaps your history has a lesson we all need to hear. Our time here is so short we must not waste a second on unresolved issues. From our dictionary, get some clues and JUST DO IT. We are happy to abet.

~Sara

Ability. This is a strange word to put in our dictionary, as no one in our family was ever credited with having the ability to recognize a rainstorm out of which we should have come.

As I have written and read and reread these memories, I begin to realize how much ability we all had. Nannie and grandpa to start and what they handed to dad, innate as well as lessons in the living of life. I look at where dad's folks came from, hardy stock and of the earth. Nannie's folks built their homes from whatever material was at hand. Made barbed wire fences by hand, ran mules over the fields of their crops from sun up to sun down. No tractors in those days, nor could they have afforded one. There were no complaints, it was what they did.

Mom's folks were highly educated and maybe a bit shallow. That could be unfair, I only knew them from when we went to the west coast to visit as they rarely visited mom in Illinois. They seemed to give off an air that said dad might have been a bad smell under their noses. So even with their book learnin' they didn't hold a candle to what dad and his folks accomplished. I am in awe.

From the beginning of his working for himself, dad kept his own books, calculating his income and taxes to the penny. I have no idea about the Social Security System. I do know he paid into it from its inception and when he retired had a nice income due to THAT ability. I expect a lawyer customer helped him initially, but dad did the bookkeeping.

Speaking of which, I found his logbooks, many, many logbooks; long, slender volumes, reddish brown in color, all labeled with the year, hand written in his beautiful script. Each year he listed the cost of the steers he kept, from what he paid per head down to the feed cost and what it cost to slaughter them. He noted too, how he profited in the end by having them. He sold one and a half steers and had the remaining half quick-frozen and stored in a rented locker "down town" for his family to enjoy through the winter.

There were also logs listing his furniture customers. He kept track by name, date and "the job" he did for them along with his cost and the final price he charged. Often I would see a note, which read, "Did I charge too much on this" or "Henry seemed pleased," "now all Mary's daughters have a table," just some brief note to remind him about something or other. He made 17 gate legged tables for different folks. He listed who these people were and the type of wood (walnut or cherry), what they paid and how. Sometimes there was a trade of some sort. His logs were filled with facts about gardening, chicken raising, whatever the project of the time. All the logs were precise and legible.

Dad had the ability to turn most anything into a living for his family. From selling Togstad products door to door to turning a beautiful piece of wood into a bowl, a lamp, a gate legged table. When we sold our house, I donated his books and papers to the Illinois State Museum. How I wish I had kept them as they told a story of their own. The curator, though, was very excited about the documentation of the era. My father was actually an everyman. Many people in our town had regular jobs, went daily to them and drew a wage. My dad made his own job, kept his own hours and did something he truly loved to do. He made a living for us and we never knew if we were poor. How could he not know of his great abilities?

Momma was a chameleon, having the ability to change shape and color to fit into the fabric of her life with dad, a life so very different from her roots. I often wonder how she managed to come from her lively life in California, with a fun and easy family, to dad's part of the woods where everything was HARD. The life dad gave her, the people, dour – dour. The very earth she trod was hard and yet she managed. She seemed actually to thrive on what surely must have meant beating the odds of making her marriage stick. From that easier way of life, the more social and arty family on the west coast, to scrubbing clothes on washboard hardness - the ability to adapt to anything that might not suit us is something few of us can or even care to claim these days. To work that hard to fit into the life one's mate may provide – that too is awesome.

My sisters and I developed abilities from watching the patterns of our parent's lives. Though we HEARD a message of lack of ability, without even realizing how well we were being taught, we learned to push our talents, to be ourselves, to follow whatever we wanted to follow. Never mind the talents our parents had to make do, to make beauty, the ability to mold their kids into good citizens, with some truly fantastic abilities – well just read this Dictionary.

So without being told we could get out of the rain if we tried, we learned by example and are still working on whatever abilities we may possess. It isn't over, ya know, until it's over. ~Sara

Abundance - Joy - Rich.

Showers of blessing indeed.
Mercy falls down on God's children.
Oh, for the showers we need."

From an old Gospel Hymn

It's hard to write and remember the attributes of *abundance, joy,* and *rich* as three separate parts of the Rawlings family. In these pages you will come to know that our family was not money rich, we were not often joyful, and sometimes, maybe too often, refused to recognize abundance when it was right in front of us.

Daddy came from a hide-bound fundamentalist home. He left as soon as he screwed up his courage to do so, left high school, grabbed a train and rode away.

Momma came from a nomadic background, her father being a signalman for one of the big Pacific railroads: Northern, Central, Southern? We don't remember, but Momma had lived with her family in nine states when Daddy met her in Sacramento, CA.

Put those components together and it comes up ABUNDANCE – RICH - JOY? Well, yes, but in ways different from what one might expect.

"Abundance" translates into tangible wealth, stuff edible (mostly), saleable and coveted by people willing to pay for Rawlingsian abundance. That transfers to RICH?

5

Nope. "Rich" is a harder word to define in the Rawlings dictionary. Clotted cream was rich. Oh, boy! oh, boy! That's not what I mean. Rich is being wealthy in all ways but monetarily, at least in this dictionary.

Then there's JOY! For me, joy is a sudden happiness in a lack-luster place. Joy is never expected, is a sudden gladsome time not dreamed of, much less hoped for; it's even startling.

The old house we lived in was not grand, but with 10-foot ceilings and spacious rooms it certainly wasn't small and mean.

Our nearly three-acre property was abundantly managed. One acre we called the pasture. At first we had a milk cow and ran goats for a neighbor. The cow, a bony black and white critter, produced wonderful milk. In turn, we had milk for drinking or making into cocoa for breakfast. There was cream so thick a cat one time walked across a milk bucket in which the cream had risen. (We girls thought it was pretty funny, but Dad was very cross.) A dollop of cream on peaches or raspberries, fresh or home-canned, was pretty joy making!

Who has home-churned butter? The Rawlings girls did, and we had homemade cottage cheese as well, creamy and tangy. The neighbor's goats provided a milk supply for babies and toddlers who were lactose intolerant. Who had ever heard that phrase? And the baby goats were so <u>cute.</u>

At a later time Daddy decided to have sheep to keep down the grass in the pasture. Well, they did such a good job he had to discontinue that practice as they cropped the grass so close it stopped regrowing in places.

After that, Daddy got two or three steers every spring which were ready for butchering by late fall. They kept the pasture mowed, Dad hand-fed them from gleaned corn, and people begged for the beef we had. Even the hamburger was superior or do I mean rich?

With chickens filling the hen house at night and free ranging during the day, we had such an abundance of brown eggs that we sold them every week. We had plenty of eggs (and chickens) to eat from that pasture. Eggs "paid" for piano lessons and dental appointments. That was a rich pasture.

As if that weren't enough, there was the huge garden to the north of the house. How many rows of corn, peas, green beans, tomatoes, carrots, potatoes, onions and garlic were planted each year? It was liberally enriched by manure produced in the pasture. There were gigantic clumps of Chipman's Red rhubarb, red all the way through and much more sweet than any I've tasted since. Dad sold it by the grocery bag full. There were rows and rows of raspberries picked, sold, and/or canned every summer. Immense blueberry bushes, thanks to careful mulching with oak leaves from the big old trees in the pasture, gave us abundant desserts all year long. The robins helped us eat the excess berries.

We had a cherry tree, peach trees called "Polly," with white flesh, an apricot tree, and black walnuts to flavor Momma's divine divinity.

Does our abundance sound too much like an improbable grocery list? In the basement, the rows and rows of home-canned foods marching in brilliant jewel tones were sheer beauty, not a grocery list, but an artist's joy!

It was joy to see long drifts of narcissus in the pasture each spring. Someone long before us had planted them, and we loved the bouquets perfuming our home every May.

During the darkest days of the Great Depression, vagrants would come to our back door. By some secret sign, they knew they would never be refused. Sometimes they had a portion of what we were eating, and we had less. Even as children, we felt glad to share, and there was a certain joy in that. Sometimes the men had notions in their pockets: packets of pins, shoelaces, and papers of needles, occasionally lengths of bias tape or ribbon, spools of thread. They would exchange them for food, or Daddy would find chores for them to do

Fancy having grandparents kitty-cornered from our house. They had a big old apple tree I could climb and see halfway to the ocean. Their hill was superb for sledding in the winter. There was a path at least a block long down the middle of their garden. Our own private slope – JOY!

Nannie and Grandpa had a privy, as we did, but they also had a real porcelain toilet that <u>flushed,</u> and a bathtub that could be used if the hot water heating stove was fired up. That's where I took my bridal bath the first time I was married. At home there wasn't a tub for many years, only a showerhead in the basement, primarily used to slough off varnish remover in connection with Dad's shop.

"Rich" also included shampoos with water from Nannie and Grandpa's kitchen stove reservoir. It's a mystery as to how they had rainwater at their house but we did not. The Queen of England's hair cleansing methods are poor in comparison with the silky, satin refreshment of a shampoo at Nannie's using rainwater.

Growing up in our rather austere, depression-ridden time didn't give much space for joy, but how about a pair of bright red-dyed sheepskin earmuffs attached to red webbing over our heads and tied under our chins with woven red bands? Nobody – but NOBODY – had them except Sara and me, gifts from a favorite uncle and coveted by our classmates. We had rabbit fur mittens, too, with red leather palms. Maybe we just strutted at acquisition, but, with the wisdom of age, it seems like joy.

How about a swing next to the front porch, made of one-inch hemp and with a walnut wood seat? I still can see Daddy marching up the street with the coil over his shoulder. We had no car then, so he'd carried it from the lumberyard uphill several blocks to give to his girls. He attached it to a limb on the front porch oak tree, and when we "pumped" really high could almost touch the electric wires with our toes. Nobody else had such a swing. ABUNDANCE – RICH – JOY? Which? You decide.

After the war ended and life had returned to more placid living, one day the minister came calling. It had come to his mind that Emery and Elizabeth were contributing more money to the church than some others who had more means to do so.

He had come to tell them to give less. My parents were gentle with him. They continued to give as they saw fit. Maybe that minister found a different meaning for ABUNDANCE and RICH in later years, and, with that, found the JOY the Rawlingses knew. ~Georgia

Acceptance. Well, again, dad (you'll find him lots in these pages) never accepted himself, so of course, he couldn't accept much of his family. His mom's folks were "sod busters" – good, earthy country people the likes of whom shaped our country. He was ashamed of them and to a great extent I think of his own mom and dad as well. His father's people showed up from time to time. Grandpa's brothers were all over 6' tall, while grandpa was about 5'9." I have little memory of these people but in my child mind I remember them as quite nice and a bit awesome in their tallness. They were well dressed and well spoken. Dad had little to say about them, nothing really awful, so that was maybe a sort of acceptance.

Dad was fearful of what the neighbors would say, critical of what the neighbors DID! He would often tsk, shake his head and mutter that "just won't do." He was involved in the opinions of others and how they perceived him, never believing he was good enough and would "do." He was judgmental and vocal with it.

His work as a cabinetmaker was without equal. In many cases however, he would destroy a piece of wood because "it was not right" - not perfectly round, the burl was off center whatever, it wouldn't "do." If it didn't meet his very high standards, out it went.

He could not work for "the other guy" for very long at a time, as "the other guy" was unacceptable to dad's standards. Dad would see things clearly in a job situation, never cutting corners in order to finish a job more quickly, or using shoddy material to make more profit. These things would be unacceptable to him.

Dad had an awful time allowing anyone to do anything for him. I remember the largess of friends and his customers from time to time – in the manner of some THING, never money, and dad wondering to mom about "now why would he do that." There would be awe in his voice and more emphasis on the fact that the giver was a good person rather than HE was deserving.

Needless to say this non-accepting attitude washed over all of us including mom, and I at this advanced age am still working on my own thing re acceptance. Getting pretty good about my own self, but boy, all you other guys need to get it right! ~Sara

Anger. Sara was screaming, running through the house on her long legs. Daddy was chasing her, waving one of his heavy leather belts with a metal buckle. I don't remember anything else. I don't remember the outcome. I think the argument had something to do with the telephone. I don't know if he actually hit her, or if mother stopped it, or if I had hysterics. Only that single short memory remains.

Other memories: Mother, at her sewing machine, many days – mornings, afternoons, evenings, swearing like a dockhand at the machine, or a seam gone wrong, or whatever obstacle had arisen in her work. Venom in her voice, spitting the words, as though she would like to break something. Dad wandering by the sewing room door, stopping to sneer "Christian!" in a loud sarcastic voice.

I'm at the ironing board on a hot summer day, wearing very short shorts. I am fifteen. The edge of the hot iron grazes the top of my bare leg, and I curse, loudly. My father is up the stairs from the basement in an instant, one quick backhand across my cheek. "Never take the Lord's name in vain!" he shouts.

Rarely expressed, only a few short memories contain it, anger seemed to simmer as an undercurrent through certain days or weeks or months. As a child, I was frightened by it: these loving people, my family, transformed into dangerous, enraged, inexplicable beings. And then it would go away. Sometimes it seemed really to be gone, the problem was resolved, the family relaxed. Other times, it was smoothed over, controlled, but still, it lurked beneath the surface, ready to erupt again. I could sense these times.

Some anger seemed justified: I was visiting Nannie across the street. I was six. She was explaining to me in her sweet way the dangers of alcohol. Uncomprehending but wanting to please her, I wrote my name on a Temperance Union card, a vow that alcohol would never touch my lips. Later, my mother heard of this – either I showed her the card or told her about it. Lips tight, she rushed out of the house and across the street. I understood later that poor Nannie was fiercely scolded for this. I was a child, I had no judgment or reason at that age, I could not sign what I could not understand. Later, I was impressed by my non-drinking mother's sense of fairness and justice. Or perhaps she welcomed an opportunity to confront her (often interfering) mother-in-law.

Nannie would walk over to our house just behind the mailman. Bringing in our mail, she would begin, "Lib, here's the phone bill. Oh, here's a letter from Martha – wonder what she has to say? I see you have a postcard from the Greenes –they're in California, how nice...." At which Mama would shout, perhaps not the first time, or even the fourth, but eventually: Don't march over here and look at my mail! Well, Nannie was "interested." Nosy, some people thought, but that made her no less kind. Interfering, it was said, but only to try to make people happier, in her own way. It must have been so hard for Mama, two thousand miles from her own people, with parents-in-law across the street, the whole small town watching. No wonder she had to become a saint, Caesar's wife, totally above reproach.

I know there were angry times, angry scenes relating to my sisters. Sara's marriage, Georgia's divorce, Georgia's remarriage. I don't remember many details. I do know that Dad swore that Sara, after her marriage, would never "darken his door" again, nor would Georgia after her divorce. Mother, however, had other plans, and months later, each sister came home again and Dad grew softer. I was glad.

Anger came from both fear and grief: fear of what "people" would say, fear of consequences, fear of not being able to "hold one's head up." And grief, over lost hopes, broken promises, dashed expectations. Perhaps guilt, the eternal question of parents through the ages: what did I do wrong? What could I have done differently? The answers are always the same. Nothing. Nothing. So much. Everything.

And I was astonished at moments of grief without anger: Uncle Lynn, my father's younger brother, so talented and brilliant, a victim of alcoholism. I am thirteen, awakened at four in the morning by hushed, urgent voices. Uncle Lynn is in the throes of violent delirium tremens, imagining murderers creeping around the house to kill his parents. His panicked voice will not be stilled as he urges Dad to help him. "They're after our parents, our mom and dad! Get your gun!" And Daddy, voice quiet and soothing, "All right, Lynn. I'll come. I'll get the gun. You stay right by me." Mother is more disturbed, wanting Lynn to be quiet, to change, to be sober. But Dad takes care of it, goes out, and talks my uncle down until he falls asleep or passes out. Of course, the gun was never loaded. They explain to me at breakfast exactly what happened. I am old enough now, they don't try to hide it or conceal it. I remember nothing but grief about Uncle Lynn's weakness, no shouting, no anger, just sadness and frustration at the hideous waste of talent and goodness. Mother's youngest sister had the same disease. I think her family was not as compassionate as Dad. Now I can understand my grandmother's Temperance Union urgings. Mama should have understood, too. ~Anne

Artistic. Where did Daddy's ability to turn wood so beautifully come from? I don't see Nannie and Grandpa as being artistic, yet their two sons were both extremely talented artistically.

Dad designed his own table leg and bedstead turnings, and they were symmetric and gorgeous. He glued slabs of various woods together, creating multi-colored wooden lamp bases, picture frames and bowls, lidded ones and open ones. Cedar, walnut, and cherry picture frames with exquisite curves grace his daughters' and grandchildren's homes. There are clock shelves and pieces cut out with such intricacy that one might think there was magic in his jigsaw.

He was a machinist working with metal when he began using a lathe. His job then was to make wartime items – ship parts and submarine shells. It was a living and a good one. He hated it. Wood was another commodity entirely, and he loved what he could do with it. He loved the smell of the wood as his saw spun into it. He loved visiting the lumber company in Springfield to select wood for a gate-legged table or other project.

In the early days of living at 521 North 11th Street in Petersburg many of the appointments of the house were crude or even non-existent. There was little money for creating the beauty both Mom and Dad craved. They were desperate to replace the nasty cracked old kitchen linoleum. One day Dad found a rubber tile sale in Springfield and brought home stacks of floor samples of all sorts of colors. Together they designed, from bright yellow tiles, a two-foot five-pointed star in a periwinkle blue square for the center of the room's floor. Then Momma went to work creating an artistic kaleidoscope with the rest of the samples. It had a quilt-like symmetry when finished, even sporting a border. They received many compliments all the many years it was there.

The county fair provided an outlet for artistic abilities and Momma and Daddy collaborated on several occasions. One project comes to mind. Daddy had turned a round tray with a six-inch pedestal, made of walnut and some light wood, maybe maple. It looked rather like a footed cake platter. On it, Momma placed a container filled with clematis blossoms of various colors from her garden and streamers of ivy cascading down around the pedestal. Of course she got a blue ribbon.

Dad went to auctions and estate sales looking for furniture to repair and refinish to sell. Occasionally he would come home with pieces of walnut or maple stacked in his arms like kindling wood. Momma would ask, "What is that, Emery?" "Oh," he'd reply "It's most of a Lincoln rocker (or a sewing rocker or a nursing rocker) I got for a quarter."

Down in the shop it would go, emerging later as a beautiful piece for a bedroom or the living room, and placed where Momma could best show it to advantage for keeping or selling.

The time came when they could afford a gas kitchen stove and a refrigerator so the kitchen began to have a more contemporary look. There were counters and cupboards, as modern as any "House Beautiful" picture, but made by Dad. In one cupboard, Dad installed the flour bin from a Hoosier cupboard that had been moved into the pantry. This was pretty handy, since it held 25 pounds of flour, had a built in sifter, and Momma baked a lot.

Then, one day, Momma decided turquoise print curtains would be pretty in the kitchen (she ignored the floor). After they were sewn and hung, she thought the sink's metal front would look good if it were painted turquoise. No sooner said than done, and while Dad was painting the sink, decided to paint the refrigerator as well. Wow! How many turquoise refrigerators were there in the 1950's? Oh, maybe one.

Around the kitchen, about eye-high, was a small ledge from which Momma hung wishbones. Mostly, they were from chickens, but there were token bones from tiny Cornish hens, geese, ducks, and turkeys. It's an unusual sort of decoration, but apparently not unique. At least one of her granddaughters has chicken wishbones hanging around the window over her kitchen sink.

Momma could work magic with her sewing artistry. She never tackled men's suits at home, although she knew how to make them. But dresses, jumpers, shirts, slacks, children's coats and suits, formals, even Dad's boxer shorts – all were made by Momma. People in town said the Rawlings girls set style.

One motif in the big quilt I made years ago is a remnant from my Shirley Temple dress. Shirley Temple was a box-office rage in the mid-30's, with mugs and dolls and other commercial lures. I only had Shirley Temple paper dolls, but I dearly loved them. One Day, Momma picked up one of Shirley's dresses, looked at it, pulled out a dress pattern, modified it, cut out the fabric, and voila! I had a Shirley Temple dress. A few friends had dolls or mugs or lunch boxes, but I was the only girl in school who wore a Shirley Temple dress. Lots of artistic thought and practice in that dress. Thank you, Momma. Thank both of you for handing down such gifts. ~Georgia

Aunts. The aunts we knew best were not ours but our father's, Nannie's sisters. They were wonderful. The most memorable was, well let's see, Bessie comes to mind, but she was memorable for not such good reasons. Aunt Bessie, sigh. She played the piano at the Baptist

church and she played with an anvil hand. I'm not sure she really played she may have just chorded, but she really hit it. So here we have Ethel, Myrtle, Nannie, Uncle Ed, and Grace. I guess Bessie took the photo.

She had a husband named Harry, he was so placid and laid back no one could figure out how it came to be that he married Aunt Bessie. He died. But before he got away they lived in a big house in the country. The rooms were not used, some of 'em, and were full to bursting with mysteries. I loved to rummage in Aunt Bessie's house. Huge, unused upstairs rooms filled with wonders. I remember finding a carton filled with green rubber shoes in boxes. Never used. What were they for? I think her big house was to house her eccentricities. One never knew what one would find squirreled away in drawers, cupboards, and closets. I found dead teeth wrapped in wool batting, bits of silverware with no handles or tines. Reams of blank paper, books in foreign languages, Bibles with no spines, jigsaw puzzle boxes. No puzzles just boxes. Just "stuff."

We had many family reunions with dad's folks and many of them at Aunt Bessie's. Food? Oh, my gosh. People, yeah that too. BUT dear old Bessie would ALWAYS start an argument about something. Some fragments I remember after the dust settled were about wrongs of the aunts' youth–to each other and to her especially. One could not stay in Bessie's presence for more than a couple minutes without the fur flying.

I remember once driving with her up a very steep hill and her not being able to shift the gears. She became hysterical and began to scream we were going to die, the car would roll back and down the hill into traffic — with her hands in her hair and not on the wheel. Scared? But there was a fascination about her too.

After Uncle Harry gave up, Bessie bought another big house in town. This house was more normal as there weren't as many rooms and fewer drawers to stuff. She turned this house into a boarding house sans food and ran it very well. It being near my school, I would go see her on my way home now and then. I would ask her to play the piano (since there was little rummaging to do). She could only do hymns -- "The Old Rugged Cross" was a favorite of ours. There was another that started out "Jerusalem, Jerusalem, lift up your gates and sing." The two of us would yell out that one like we were going to glory right then and there. Too bad about Bess. From time to time Nannie and I would go to visit but before too long a time would pass, Nan would stomp out and away, dragging me by an arm, muttering something under her breath.

Aunt Ethel now, she had a twitch and was fearful of the color green. She wore no green, ate nothing green and probably would've killed the grass or dyed it could she have. She never took medicines either. All "worries" would go through the body eventually. She knew she was getting better when her feet hurt. She was good and kind and her husband Tom just lurked around doing what men did then. All these women were big and strong so the men folk were kinda wallpaper, just for decoration and working the farms and providing a baby here and there.

I liked visiting her, as we never had to eat peas at her house. She wore print dresses with cap sleeves and always an apron. She cooked and twitched and complained about her sister Bessie being so "peculiar." Yeah, right. But she was fun mostly to be around. Certainly more tolerant than where I lived. Peas, yuk!

Oh, now Aunt Grace. All Nan's sisters were big women, big boned, broad, not fat but BIG. Grace was over 6' with a laugh to match. Cooking was truly her forte. She made ---everything The reunions at her house were grand. Lots of singing, Uncle Frank played the fiddle and we sang and there were never lots of "no you can'ts" at her gatherings. There were kittens in the barn and hens flapping, even an old horse her husband Arthur kept because. She ate as she cooked and got teased unmercifully about it. Someone would say, "where's Grace?" And the answer would come "Oh, probably behind the door finishing up the mashed potatoes. " She would laugh with her teasers, saying " oh, you… no sense letting it go to waste!" And nothing much did.

At Aunt Grace's house we always made ice cream. There was a good sized brass strapped oak bucket that had a metal bucket set down inside that kept the sugar, flavorings, cream. Around that bucket was ice chipped into wee pieces. The crank was housed in a great gear housing whose teeth meshed into each other and don't get your fingers in there. We kids would get to turn the crank at the beginning, taking turns filling the

14

bucket with chips, emptying the chip water as it melted until the men had to take over because it was way too hard for little 'uns to do. The ice cream was almost always vanilla with fresh berries or nuts someone had shelled. Once in a while some lovely person would produce homemade chocolate syrup for those of us with that habit. Gosh, never since.

Aunt Myrtle was the littlest of them but had a big heart. She had, as I remember, a cozy little house near Nannie's. It may have been mean, but I did not know that then. She had tiny "things" in her house - figurines, dolls, vases - all my aunts liked stuff. Maybe the times. Anyway she NEVER said "don't touch." Never gave the impression she thought I would, no doubt, break her treasures. She seemed to enjoy my enjoyment of being able to play with her doll, sit in a tiny chair in the corner, an old child's chair I might have actually been too big to sit on. She had a wind up Victrola that she allowed me to play for hours! Never a no, never a be careful. She showed me how to change the needle and how to set it in the groove of the record. Amazing! I don't think this aunt cooked much, I don't remember ever the smells of baking or simmering, but she was another stop off on my way to my less accepting own home. She was always glad to see me. Such good memories.

Mom's sisters were not at all accessible – they lived west in California. But briefly, there was Kathryn who wore coke bottle glasses and had a pleasant face. I remember once having to go out to play in my boy cousin's shirt (all mine were either in the laundry or too good to wear). I fretted about people noticing that the buttons were on the wrong side. I was not at all happy about the situation and Kathryn just laughed like crazy. She said I wasn't important enough for people to notice me. Were all kids treated like this in my generation? It may have been they thought dad was not up to snuff ergo neither were his off spring. I dunno.

Aunt Marietta was an alcoholic and disappeared from view often, but when she was around she was lovely. Beautiful spirit, beautiful soul and beautiful to look at. She played with me and laughed and hugged me a lot. She always smelled good, as if just out of the bath.

Aunt Gussie (Sarah Augusta) was retarded and just a blessing. She smiled a lot and was always ready to have fun. Made up games with lots of laughter. My exposure to these aunts was very limited and when I was around them I was very young so these memories are not clear or near as vivid as the Elmore aunts. The Elmore aunts, however, more than made up for the lack. I'm glad I had 'em.~ Sara

Authority. One evening not so long ago, at my daughter's dinner table, I had a shock. Three of the four grandchildren were there, and their father. My daughter and oldest granddaughter were out of town and I was minding the house and family for a few days. Conversation was lively, as it always is there, reporting on events of the day, favorite books, and plans for the weekend. The children had been very helpful during my stay, helping with meals and clean up, doing chores, getting ready for school promptly, and the like, and I thought it a good time to pay them some compliments. I said I was really pleased, but also surprised, because I had heard from their Mom that such cooperation was not always the case.

To which Lauren, eleven, replied immediately: "That's because we're afraid of you."

My mouth must have dropped open; Lauren and her sister, Shannon, aged nine, nodded – smiled, but nodded. Andre, seventeen, growled teasingly "Yeah, Grandma, you're scary."

"Well!" I stuttered, somewhat flabbergasted. "Well…that's good!" And I thought, yes, it was good.

Now these children know I love them, without question. We play games, from hide-the-button to chess; we share books, we garden together, have birthdays together, do homework together, laugh together.

Yet, they say, they are afraid of me. And I say, "GOOD!"

After giving this some serious thought, my conclusion is not that they are exactly afraid of me, as in terrified. They are "afraid" of me because they know that I mean what I say. When I make a request/suggestion/demand (politely, saying please, in quiet tones) there are no responses such as "Pleeeeeese" or "But I…" or "But Mommie lets us…" or anything of that nature. When Grandma says it's time to cook dinner, or time to eat, or time to clean up, or put the laundry away, or feed the dogs, or whatever – then that's exactly what Grandma means.

Not too scary, is it?

This is how my sisters and I were raised. Our parents were the law and even when they were wrong, they were right – just because they were the parents. Our home was not run to suit the preferences or wishes or convenience of the children. It was the home of two adults who knew their own rules and values and who were not afraid to live by them, and demand that their children live by them as well. They were not afraid to say "No." They were not afraid to say "That's not how we act/talk/do things in this house." And the words "this house" carried great weight. This house was the home, the family, the core, the center and no matter what was happening in the houses of other people, "this house" had its own creed, its own dogma, its own purpose to which its members were required to adhere.

As a baby, I was loved, fed, washed, dried, kept warm, held, rocked, sung to, and played with. As a toddler I was kept from danger without childproof locks, childproof caps, or childproof plugs in the outlets. As a child, I was cosseted because of illness for a period of time, but once I was pronounced well, I walked to and from school in all weathers. I walked to and from piano lessons and to and from choir practice, sports events, play practice, club meetings. There was no question of being driven, of being chauffeured; we walked or we rode bikes or we got a ride with a friend (after friends started driving).

My parents were tired after their days full of work; my extracurricular activities were my responsibility.

Punishments were swift and certain. When I was a toddler, perhaps four, I wandered off the property and "went visiting." After two or three frantic hours, my mother located me at a house five blocks away and partway down our long hill, playing with two girls near my age. At home, I was switched with a limber, thin branch from a peach tree, then given tomato soup and told I was never – never, never – to leave the house or grounds without telling someone. I never did. I was spanked once for lying, slapped once for "sassing" and slapped once for taking the name of the Lord in vain. I was also smacked once for doing something (dumb) that embarrassed my father – but he later apologized.

My respect for the authority of my parents – my "fear" – did not come from fear of beatings or other physical punishments. Other than the above, I don't remember other punishments. I was never grounded, had no allowance to dock, did not suffer "time outs," and was not sent to bed without supper, nor deprived of dessert. My respect for the rules grew out of something deeper, some sense that Yes, we are the Rawlings family; yes, we do things this way and not that, we conduct ourselves in a certain way, we speak and act and do according to the family creed.

There was little money in our house for extras. We had a pleasant home, a large garden, two or three beef cows (called steers or heifers depending on gender) that we kept to keep the grass down for a season, then butchered around Christmas for meat for the winter – keeping one quarter or one half and selling the rest. Most of my clothes were made by my mother – skirts, blouses, jackets, suits, and dresses – summer dresses, dance dresses, recital dresses. I had few sweaters, however, because she did not knit. In those days, a straight skirt and a sweater were *de rigueur* for girls from 13 to 18, and my costume usually included a blouse rather than a sweater. I did not beg to borrow the family car; if my curfew was midnight, I was generally home by midnight or 12:10 in a pinch.

Nevertheless, I did not complain, I did not scream that my life was ruined, I did not pout or slam doors because my friends had more sweaters than I did or could stay out later. Such behavior wouldn't have even occurred to me. My parents provided what they could and I accepted it with gratitude or at least without complaint.

No, I was not a perfect child. My greatest failing was being buried in a book and not hear – literally – a summons to help or to come to dinner. I was awakened at five in the morning in the summer to pick berries and beans, to clean corn, to help Mama and Nannie with long hours in a hot, steamy August kitchen with the endless canning and freezing of the garden's bounty. I did not appreciate the bounty and would rather have been reading, or swimming. I screamed at the black worms I found occasionally in the corn, I suffered mosquito bites and sunburn – but I ate my share, and probably more, of the berries and cream, of corn dripping with butter, of peaches and green beans and tomatoes that graced our table during the long winter months.

Authority – my parents had it. My grandparents had it, my teachers had it. As children and young people, we acknowledged it. The majority of my friends and classmates had been raised with values similar to mine and we knew there was a line we should not cross. Yes, we sneaked cigarettes after choir practice; yes, we started at one point to (rarely) include beer or gin at our evening swimming parties and picnics; but we still gathered at each other's houses for slumber parties, chatted with each other's mothers and aunts and fathers and big sisters with ease and enjoyment, attended church with our parents – every Sunday, not just on holidays or when it was convenient.

It's a different world now, you say. Things have changed, children aren't safe on the streets, both parents have careers, children can't be treated as they used to be, they must keep up with their peers, we have television and the internet now, times are what they are.

Maybe I was an "easy" child, maybe times were unfathomably different then, maybe the relations between parents and children were hopelessly old-fashioned and things are far, far better now.

Only I know for a fact that neither my friends nor I could have had access to a stash of guns without our parents finding out. And I know, very definitely, that none of us felt a need for a stash of any kind. ~Anne

B

Baking. Mother did not love cooking – meals, that is. Now that I have prepared ten or twelve thousand meals, I understand. Her meals were usually good, often delicious, well balanced, but perhaps uninspired. No doubt this was because Dad would have not been pleased by an inspired meal. He liked his meals good, hot, plentiful, plain, and familiar.

But Mother's baking – ah, well, she won prizes. I have yet to duplicate her pineapple upside-down cakes that took the blue ribbon for years at the county fair, though mine are pretty good. I can't make a piecrust to save my life (though Georgia can), but Mom's were light as a feather, crusty and melt-in-your mouth, and of every variety: lemon meringue (another prize winner), cherry, apple, gooseberry, peach, raspberry, raisin, mincemeat, pumpkin, rhubarb, strawberry, blueberry, chocolate. Cobblers were a favorite of my father's in fresh fruit season, especially with ice cream.

The cakes, besides the pineapple upside-down ones, were chocolate and yellow and white, sometimes marbled. Special occasion cakes (at least for my birthdays) were nearly always angel food, made with 13 egg whites and pink icing. Sometimes the angel food had "rainbows" – swirls of pink and blue and yellow made with drops of food coloring. Layer cakes thick with butter cream frosting, cookies sliced or pressed or rolled and stamped, all from scratch, no mixes in this kitchen.

I was always fascinated by my grandmother's baking. While mother was quick and efficient, she always used measuring cups and spoons; Nannie simply grabbed handfuls of this and that, tossed them in a bowl, mixed them up, poured them in a pan, and put the pan into her old coal or wood-burning black stove. Her applesauce spice cake was out of this world – how did she do that?

But the best – the very best baking – was bread. Bread is made in Fall and Winter, when the air is drier. First, there are the images of Mother kneading bread – push, push, push, turn, fold, push, push, repeat. Even then I could tell that her mind might be elsewhere, but the motions were so familiar that her hands and arms never missed a beat. Into the big bowl with the warm dough and the magic of its rising, lifting the clean cloth off the bowl. Then the kneading again, then into the pans, and another rising. Then into the oven and wait – wait for the smell.

There is nothing in the world that compares with the perfume of baking bread. Unless, of course, it is the eating, hot from the oven, spread with butter, sprinkled with a bit of brown sugar. Two or three slices, and yet I'm ready for dinner two hours later. Well, it was a long walk from school, in the cold. ~Anne

Baptism. This subject is sort of an after-thought. When the three of us were reminiscing about so many "do you remembers" someone said, "I even remember being baptized." There were two echoes so I'll tell you what I remember.

I was six years old. The immersion ceremony occurred at night. The baptismal pool was up a few steps from the room where I'd first attended Sunday School. The man who baptized me may have been Faye A. Wirth or maybe E. L. Banta. Pastor Wirth was our minister but Pastor Banta had been associated with our church before he moved elsewhere to begin a radio ministry.

Anyway, I wore a long white nightgown Momma had made; it had a wide pale pink neck facing and sleeve facing and it was beautiful.

The really memorable part of that evening is that as we were getting into the car to go home, somehow my thumb got caught in the front door as it slammed shut. I expect I cried mightily but my mother's and grand-mother's cries and screams are what I remember.

"This is the Devil's doing!"

"This precious child is being tested on the day of her baptism!"

"The Devil's trying to snatch her back!"

There we were in the cold darkness, two people ranting maniacally, people I thought I knew. I could see blood dripping from my thumb by the car's eerie dome light. I was six years old and baffled by the whole business. I don't remember the cleaning up or going to the doctor and though I'm not six years old anymore, I am <u>still</u> baffled. So, yes, I remember my baptism. ~Georgia

Books and Reading. It's probably not true, but I think the summer between my junior and senior years in high school was spent on my back reading Shakespeare comedies all day. I do know that while I was reading (on the sofa in the living room) that I sucked on tomatoes from our garden.

Now, you try that! Your Momma is going to have a fit if you drip juice all over the upholstery. So, you find a technique in order to not drip, especially when you're laughing about Puck and the fun of <u>Midsummer's Night Dream</u> or Roz and Celia in <u>As You Like It</u>. Furthermore, Momma's in the kitchen, probably too hot with processing vegetables that you should be helping with, but she's not going to ask for help. Why? Because you're reading!

Reading in our house was on a different plane of importance than most other activities. We always had a reading lamp over our beds with adequate wattage so we didn't strain our eyes. Though all of us preferred lying down while reading, if we sat and didn't have the light over our left shoulders, we got told to move.

If we left a light on when leaving a room, we always were scolded that we were "wasting electricity." Never were we told we were wasting anything when we turned on a light to read on a dull, dreary winter day, so long as the light shown over our left shoulder, of course.

Flinging money frivolously about was frowned on at 521 N. Eleventh Street, yet there always was money to belong to two book clubs. We subscribed to "Collier's" and "National Geographic," magazines for the big people, and to "Jack and Jill" and "American Girl" for the girls. We had a set of Grolier Encyclopedia and the adjunct seven volumes of <u>Lands and Peoples</u>, published by the same company. Daddy made a walnut bookcase specifically for them. We had a big thick blue dictionary and when we didn't know the meaning of a word or how to spell it, someone would leave the kitchen table, where most of those questions were asked. The meal would continue while the questioner "looked it up." Everyone learned a little bit when the questioner read aloud what the dictionary revealed.

All families have their priorities. In some families, sports are the priorities, even if it's just TV watching. Hunting and fishing are the primary topic of conversation for some families, especially the males, but sometimes the females also enjoy the quest. There are other priorities endemic to some families. For Emery and Elizabeth, reading was a priority; they loved reading. That love was passed along to all of us.

"I'm bored!" In our family we didn't whine that dreaded sentence all parents despise, but if we had, we'd be told to go and read. We swallowed books like we swallowed food. When we were deprived of reading, life was hardly worth living.

One year I was given a book for my birthday that I'd wanted for a long time. I'd been given a pretty red pullover sweater and Aunt Grace Patton had made an angel food cake (from "scratch," of course) for my birthday. Unfortunately, I had a dry hacking cough that I couldn't control because I probably was "coming down with something." What I remember, though, is that Daddy would not let me read my new book until I stopped coughing. I wish I could forget that punishment. Somehow, being deprived of reading was worse than almost anything to my mind then – maybe that's true even now.

After I'd left home, Momma and Daddy learned that the State Library was accessible to them. When they went to Springfield twenty-two miles south of Petersburg, they always returned with a grocery bag full of books. They had to be returned in a month's time, but that was no problem. These books were windows to other times, other places, other ideas, and they were read quickly. Momma and Daddy were flawed as all parents are, but they gave us many gifts and one of their best gifts to us was giving us the zest for reading – all kinds of reading: history, biography, romance, sci-fi and fantasy, do-it-yourself, theology and philosophy. On and on through the whole spectrum of human thought that had been put to paper, they read and taught us to read as well.

Daddy's favorite fiction was <u>East of Eden</u>; Momma's was <u>Beau Geste.</u> What's mine? It's hard to say and it depends on my mood. My favorite author may be Madeleine L'Engle but I don't know what book of hers is my favorite. Rita Mae Brown writes charming mystery stories in which a Welsh corgi helps solve the mysteries and they are the only adult books that have pictures that I know of. Or maybe I haven't even read my favorite yet …so, excuse me, please. I've got a book I want to read. ~Georgia

C

Cards. I had a boyfriend my Jr. and Sr. years in high school who was 6'3" (he's the guy who took me to four proms in one season, he was the only person I danced with successfully as I was 6' tall at age 16.) Back to the point. Everyone liked Stretch, as he was called. Mom and dad were so approving of him, we spent many an evening playing canasta. Maybe rummy too, not sure. But canasta, remember canasta? My brother-in-law and maybe Georgia played as well. Mom was known for her clever moves some of which were not necessarily legal and often she got caught. We would get to laughing so hard with her! And her only response would be "what are you talking about I know more about cards than any of you." Such fun and joy I can remember. How did this happen?

Mom tried desperately to teach me cribbage. I think she and her sibs must have played this game a lot. Well, I was really young and it never took – two, six and a pair is eight? What? And those little tiny bits of wood in a long skinny board, beautifully inlaid with exotic woods and with CARDS? PLEASE!

Grandpa had made her not play solitaire under his roof when she lived in my dad's parents' house. Cards equal gambling, the wicked evil woman might gamble with herself at solitaire and maybe even cheat, ya know. She must have missed her card playing when she lived with her in-laws. Wicked evil woman taught me to play at least 3 types of solitaire when I had rheumatic fever. Saved her lots of time and kept me entertained. Grandpa never knew. Cards were a good thing. ~Sara

Cast Party. Now let's talk dichotomy. If you have read any of this book so far you will see that our dad, God bless 'im, was rigid, straight laced and altogether a tough guy with very little nonsense to him

This will blow your mind, as it still does mine as I write. It was the summer of 1950 and in New Salem State Park (three miles south of Petersburg) was to be a play called <u>Forever This Land</u> and I was cast in this extravaganza in some minor role. I was 16 and we were thrilled. There were thirty some folks in this play to say nothing of directors and sound folks, costumers and angels, just lots of folks, as I said. Anyway at the end of summer and the run of about 8 weeks, the question of a cast party came up. It would be impossible with all those people to have a really good party without it costing the earth so probably there wouldn't be one. Too sad. Well here's me with a huge house, a huger back yard, and the youngest thing in the cast. Always believing nothing ventured, nothing gained, I asked mom if we could have it at our house. The cast and I had prepared our speech and rebuttals before hand which went something like this—we will do all the work provide the drink and food and stay in the back yard and be gone by ten. Sounds good. Well, right off the bat ma says no. I say why? As if… She says your father would never allow it. Ok, but can I ask him and if he says yes can we? Well, you are just setting yourself up but go ahead. On the phone I asked him. Presented the promises: clean up, buy drink, not in the house, etc etc and quickly before he could get no out and hang up the phone.

So what does my wondrous pop say? "What kind of party can you have if they can't come into the house? They might want to see my shop. I helped make your stage ya know." Well, I'm speechless. Then he says "no drunken loud stuff and your mom can't have to do anything for this party but ok."

Dad set up saw horses in the back yard and put doors over the top of them. Momma draped the doors in sheets and the hoards came. Dad had a drink or three with the bunch and I think EVERYONE including Kermit Hunter, the playwright, was in "the Shop" finding dad the most fab of hosts. Go figure. Mom was a bit shadowy as always, but was, no doubt, lurking around shaking her head in awe as well. Everyone had the most excellent time. We must've gotten into the main part of the house as we had an old upright piano and that got banged some. No drunken loudness but they did not get gone till long after the cocktail hour. And nobody cared. Like I said, go figure. Baby sis has a memory of this too, where are ya Annie Roonie? Care to comment? ~Sara

Annie says: *I do remember (faintly) this singular and miraculous event. I was — seven? — and remember only a soft summer afternoon, still light; Dad and Mama rushing around, in and out of the house, setting up things in the back yard. A peculiar*

23

*energy buzzed through the air and through my parents, that I now think was excitement — even happiness. I remember tall Daddy, standing behind the white-draped, makeshift tables in the back yard, acting as bartender and host, smiling, talking, and laughing. Well, he was gracious — that's all there was to it. A gracious, gracious man. This isn't in my **Parties** story. This was Dad's party. His only one.*

Character. When I was a child in Petersburg, we occupied a peculiar position in our town — a position based entirely (as I see it now) on the character of my parents. My mother, a devout Christian and self-taught Bible scholar was, unusual for the time and place, a critical reader of and about the Bible and all religious dogma and teaching. We often had visiting pastors to dinner, including the local Catholic priest and now and then a rabbi, who sat for hours in discussions with Mother on histories and exegeses of the Bible. The adult Bible school group that my mother taught for a great while, the Women's Club, of which she was president for years, all seemed to be unable to function without her leadership.

For church or other outings, Mother was always dressed elegantly, impeccably, appropriately, as were her daughters and her husband. Her clothes and ours were nearly always her creations, sewn from carefully selected, beautiful fabrics, mostly on sale. I was told "never skimp on shoes or bras; it's a waste of money to buy poor quality." Dad's suits were handsome and fit well, though many of them were second-hand.

My father's reputation as a woodworker and painter, his skill with animals and gardening, his stainless honor, and his eternal, constant thirst for knowledge and truth in books and conversation, drew us into circles that, given his roots, might not have been expected to welcome us so warmly. Our position (I see now) was not based on our income, the car we drove, the trips we took, or the diplomas we garnered. Our car was old, there were no vacations as such, and no diplomas were framed on our walls. Our plain house, with its high ceilings and spacious rooms, was filled with beautiful furniture made or restored by Dad; adorned with handsome drapes and slipcovers and bedspreads made by Mama; with unique bits of glass, or vases, or chandeliers found at some auction or in some old barn, carefully restored and polished and set to good advantage. The couch, handsome and comfortable, was second-hand; so were some of the good firm mattresses. The grounds of our house were neatly kept, green grass mowed and smooth, the pastures kept clipped by the sheep or cows or steers that were allowed to graze there each summer. The fences were in good repair, as was the old house, freshly painted every few years, tall windows washed and sparkling, doors and steps firm and even.

These too were reflections of character.

Looking back, I see now that much of our way of life was based on more than one kind of pride. First, there was the good pride, that we could make it on our own, that we would owe no one, that we could live a pleasant, comfortable, dignified life based on hard work and little income. And the second kind of pride, a kind of vanity that, having less than the Joneses, we could still, in some ways, outshine them. There was another kind of pride, the Lord and Lady Bountiful kind that allowed us to give to those having even less than we did, the fruits of our labors from the garden or the kitchen. Or the pride that allowed Dad to give as a gift the work of his hands, a bowl of glowing cherry wood or a small walnut table, to someone who had much more than we, yet could not with all their money duplicate the unique handcrafted gift.

In spite of that, there were lessons learned: the sin of waste, the act of charity, the work of maintenance, the joy of beauty and order, the value of appearances. Beyond the usual edicts (tell the truth, don't swear, mind your manners, wash your hands, wear clean underwear, attend church, be kind), I recall no discussions in our family about honor, or truth, or how to live a worthwhile life. Our lives were the discussion. I think now about the lessons I learned, unspoken and unremarked, and I am overcome with a longing for things to be that way again. And I am unspeakably grateful for the time when they were that way. ~Anne

Chickens. One of the endeavors dad endeavored was "chickens." I can remember him preparing the brooder house for the baby chicks, which he brought home in huge boxes. The boxes were box colored, flat – about four to six inches high and three feet square maybe (I was very young during this era so everything seemed bigger and size could be distorted.) There were small round holes, about the size of a quarter, cut in the sides of the boxes so the wee chicks could get air. Dad would set the boxes on the floor; raise the lids and such a flurry you never saw in your life. The chicks were set free to eat and drink and rest under the big lamp, which was suspended from the ceiling for warmth. That's pretty much how it went, too. These tiny little furry bodies making bee-lines to the feed trays,

hopping onto the lip of these huge, round, galvanized feeders and then off to the watering pans and finally, bellies full, thirst quenched, asleep in the wide warm arc provided by the great hanging lamp. How did they know to do this? Takes me days to find my way in a new environment.

As these tiny chicks became chickens they were allowed into the pasture to peck at "stuff." Daddy allowed me to follow him around on his travels through the pasture from time to time. On one of our forages, he looked down at me and said with the straightest of faces, "if you drop your gum around here, don't pick it up, you might get hold of the wrong thing." He kind of waited to see if I "got it." I kind of waited to see was he serious. I kinda giggled and his eyes crinkled a little. I remember feeling so special that he made a joke with me.

Some of these chicken people became "layers." These ladies were the lucky ones. They gave up their prize once a day and were left to their own devices most of the rest of the time as they were a grand source of protein for the family table and an addition to dad's coffers.

The chicken house, which was different from the brooder house, had chicken ladders – roost bars and egg nests. The ladders would, of course, get full of bubble gum, as did the roosting areas where they slept. Dad kept these areas very clean as he was "that way." As the dark came, all the birds came in to roost and dad would close off the openings so the foxes couldn't get into the hen house. Literally.

Early a.m. and again around dusk, Dad scattered cracked corn and other goodies for the ladies (few gents as it's not nice to mix the sexes chick-wise; more on that later). This scattering was done from an old #2 coffee can as opposed to a large wire basket for egg gathering from the nests in the chicken house.

Some of the wee chicks weren't lucky enough to live long enough to become "layers." Many met with a very early demise as dressed chickens – "fryers" – sold to the community.

Now by "dressed" we mean undressed, actually. I'll share the drill. Momma would heat water to the point of melting fat, then either dad would "off with her head" via an axe blade or momma would wring the poor thing's neck. Even without their heads, the chickens flapped across the back yard for some time - kinda like "a chicken with its head cut off."

Then we – dad, mom, me, dunked 'em in the boiling water and plucked the chicken bodies free of feathers. This was usually in our base-ment with the chickens hung by their feet from a low ceiling beam after the dunk. I could strip a chicken with the best of them. The smell of wet feathers is pretty memory prodding even today.

The next move was upstairs to the kitchen with all these dead chick-ens – formerly known as baby chicks. I was but a wee lass, but was taught how to clean inside and out. I was very, very young and mom was very matter of fact about it all so it was just an adventure and I was happy to be included. The ugh of it all never seemed to be a factor; we just got on with it.

I learned to cut up a chicken in a most butcher-like way (we cut "country," so the wishbone was intact.) First the pinions or left over feathers were cleaned, oops, no the feet came off first - then the body search.

A nice big incision between the legs then reach in and pull out these long gray, glistening ropey innards. They usually came away in one bundle making a satisfying swooshing sound to let you know you didn't have to go in again. Once in a while one of us might accidentally cut the bile duct or something else equally as unfortunate. PU! Never you mind.

The gizzard, the heart. There were two pink spongy bits that I wondered aloud about and mom said they were its lights, actually the lungs. The heart was pretty much heart shaped, about the size of a prune. There was a small sack filled with gravel and undigested grain which I also inquired about. Mom said it was where the food was kept before going on to digest through the gray ropey things. She was always careful not to cut into this sack, as it was messy to clean up and unnecessary, in the big scheme of things, to open it. She did tell me that she had heard stories of people finding valuables in the sacks as chickens peck up anything. Stone, gravel, corn, diamond rings, you name it. I personally believed it would have been great to examine all the craws as they were called, we might find a fortune inside. Didn't work, mom made me leave them whole.

She taught me to cut away the fat and other gory bits on the gizzard and heart and liver as these, she said, some people thought were the best part of the whole chicken, she would tuck them carefully into the chicken cavity. I always thought it was a joke. Dress a chicken ok, eat its insides, I don't think so. The chick was reexamined for stray pinions and feathers, often necessitating singeing off these offenders over the open flame on the stove. Either the old coal job or later the new Roper. Aah, the smell of burning feathers – nothing like it. Folks bought these chickens – the fryers - and the eggs from the layers, thus once again keeping dad out of the "office" so to speak.

Now the reason we don't mix sexes, as I said, is twofold: our chicken biz was in the middle of town (almost) and baby boy chickens grow up to be roosters. We all know what roosters do at dawn and the neighbors (as well as our own family) wouldn't appreciate that cacophony each dawn, huh?

The other bit is of course – if young sexes are mixed and allowed to mingle freely, there will be hanky panky and eggs will be fertilized. Now in the chicken world one could say, so what, but fertilized eggs, believe me, are not a pretty sight with one's morning bacon. So that's the story of dad's chicken biz, mostly. The really gory bits I left out.

P.S. I can still cut up a whole chicken in six minutes, less with a sharp knife. ~Sara

Christmas. Mother was in love with Christmas. There were lean years when the holidays were celebrated mostly in the heart – as they always should be – and then there were the good years that I remember, when Christmas was a long season of excitement and preparation and making and baking and trimming and singing and things hidden in closets and drawers.

Mama started her Christmas preparations in January, when holiday items were bought on sale and stored away to await the end of the year. Sewing and planning started as early as August, or as soon as the canning and freezing of the garden produce was done, and by October, we were in full swing.

At some point, mother discovered candle making. There were months when the kitchen was filled with every kind, shape, and size of container to provide candle molds, and the kitchen reeked of melted paraffin and waxes, when my broken crayons were recycled to provide color – blue candles with silver trim, lots of red candles, sometimes with gold or white trim, deep greens, or plain white. Mama would whip the paraffin as though it were egg white, to make a solid fluffy mass to imitate snow that would be swirled around the edges of candles and sprinkled with glitter or little stars or sequins. Most of these creations became gifts, but some favorites were kept for us. There was a row of small red square candles that stood along the kitchen windowsill with a gold letter on each that spelled out "Christmas." There were tall thick rectangular blocks that wore on their fronts a scene cut out from an old Christmas card, surrounded with white whipped wax. When lit, the scene – usually a Nativity – would glow as though lit from within.

Some time in December, the tree would arrive to be carefully installed in the front living room, standing in a large bucket of wet sand, usually with thin wires running from the tree to the wall to provide extra stability. These trees were nine feet or more, the goal being to have the tree top ornament just grazing the ceiling, at ten feet, four inches.

Then the brown cardboard boxes would be brought from the attic, full of lights and ornaments. We would untangle the strands of lights – no matter how carefully packed, Christmas lights are always tangled the next year; it's the rule – and plug them in to test them before they were carefully placed on the tree. Properly spacing the lights so as to eliminate any dark spots or avoid having bulbs too close to each other was done scientifically, by standing back and squinting at the tree. Our original lights were the large but slender pointed bulbs of green, red, blue, yellow, and white, the kind that, if one bulb went out, the whole strand went out

— so much time was spent replacing bulbs in order to find the bad one. Later, we had bubble lights, which thrilled Mama as much as they did all the children who watched them bubble away by the hour.

We didn't have a star or an angel on our tree top, but one of those tall glass minarets — ours was red and gold, about twelve inches tall — that had to be perfectly arranged on the top of the tree so that it was straight from all angles. This sometimes happened immediately, but more often took ten or fifteen minutes with two people, one on a ladder, the other saying "a little right, now a little left, now back…."

After the lights were placed to our satisfaction, the ornaments were added — some from mother's childhood, some purchased over the years. The final touch was the silver tinsel, added painstakingly a single strand at a time. This was much more fun when my sisters were there to help. Some years we experimented by simply flinging the tinsel at the tree to achieve a "natural" look. This was not too successful. Much of this tinsel was saved from year to year, tediously removed at the end of the season and stored away in the boxes. But we always lost some and had to buy a new box of it every couple of years or so.

Once the tree was completely trimmed, a white sheet draped artistically at its foot to hide the bucket, the empty boxes removed, the carpet vacuumed, then candles were lit, the tree lights were plugged in, and the radio (later the stereo) was tuned to Christmas carols. And we sat in contentment and satisfaction to look at our tree in all its splendor for the rest of that evening and for most evenings thereafter, until the holidays were over once again.

Mother's sewing room was Gift Central from October on, and was generally off limits to me for a number of weeks. The room was filled with sewing projects in various stages, but its closet and bureau were also stacked with the presents that had been bought for family and friends. After the tree went up, wrapped packages made their way one by one to be placed under the tree and handed out as friends and neighbors arrived for seasonal visits.

Outside the house, there were Christmas concerts to be practiced and performed at school and church, angel costumes to be made, visits to be paid, a round of activities in addition to the usual chores. But my Christmas memories are mostly of our house, the simmering excitement, and the almost child-like glee of Mama as she went about her preparations.

Christmas Eve was quiet, a holy time, and from the time I can remember, Mama took me on her lap, in one of the big old rocking chairs, and read the verses from the Bible: "And it came to pass in those days, that there went out a decree from Caesar Augustus, that all the world should be taxed…. And she brought forth her firstborn son, and wrapped him in swaddling clothes, and laid him in a manger; because there was no room for them in the inn…And there were in the same country shepherds abiding in the field…And the angel said unto them, Fear not; for behold I bring you good tidings of great joy, which shall be to all people." No Christmas now is complete without hearing and reading those words again.

After all these months and weeks of excitement, Christmas morning was almost (not quite, but almost) an anti-climax. There was the year I had a washable baby-doll in a beautiful white cradle (large enough for a real new-born baby), the year I had a dollhouse, the special clothes and games and, always, books. The wrapping paper and some of the ribbons were carefully removed, and smoothed and saved for another year, the room was cleaned up, and dinner preparation began. Like the saying about travel, sometimes it is better to travel hopefully than to arrive.

Now for some reason – and this has to be said, because it was always part of Christmas – the happy preparations of the season made Daddy angry. Or grumpy. Or Scrooge-like. Anyway, he grumbled and complained and criticized from the beginning to about December 23rd. Once or twice, Mom and Dad had a major quarrel. Once was about the tree, when one of them threatened that there would be no tree that year. Well, I had tantrums only about really important things, so we always had a tree. Once or twice, Mama screamed and cried because Dad was depriving her of one of the important pleasures in her life.

Why did Dad do this at Christmas? I have no idea. He seemed to think that a major fuss and an unnecessary show was being made. I don't think he was worried about expenses as Mama was frugal to the core. Maybe it just boiled down to the fact that for about eight weeks, he was not the center of Mama's attention. Or maybe he was envious because he had never had such Christmases as a child. Whatever the reason, there he was, mumbling and grumbling and threatening, and we just learned to ignore him.

When I was 16 or so, some of my classmates – two or three boys – mentioned that they were going out to fetch a truckload of nice Christmas trees, and did I think my folks would like one delivered? Remembering the fuss about the trees in the past, I made my first executive decision, and said, sure – bring a good one, about 9 ½ feet tall. I can't remember if I even told my parents that one was coming. I don't think I did. One Saturday in December, the truck drove up; I said, oh, there's Bryce with our tree (oh, so casually). Dad looked like he was getting ready to fire up his grumble, but the boys got out of the truck, shouting "Hi, Emery!" in cheerful, confident, un-fearful voices, and stopped his grumbles in their tracks. So out Dad went, to supervise, and have the tree brought in, and fetch the bucket of sand, and there was some kidding and Dad may have slipped in some sarcasm, but the boys laughed him down – and he let them. "Merry Christmas" was shouted, and they left in the truck, and the tree went up, and it was beautiful. And not a word was said. I was waiting for some fuss to be made, but none came. As I remember, Dad even said that it was a nice tree. Well, that was Dad – unpredictable at every turn. And he made that doll's cradle for me. So that was Christmas at our house. ~Anne

Church. We went to public school from Monday through Friday. We went to Sunday school on Sunday – PERIOD. Our parents, and most of our friends' parents, felt Sunday was when we learned a degree of morality higher than we had at public school and, often, higher than we had at home. No whining, no arguing, no negotiating. We just went to Sunday school, as we went from Monday through Friday at First Ward School. It seemed so simple.

I can still remember my first Sunday school teacher, Irene Ahrenkiel. I wasn't in regular school yet, but I still know most of a song she taught us, complete with gestures:

"I washed my hands this morning,
So very clean and white,
And gave them both to Jesus
To work for Him till night."
"Little feet be careful
Where you take me to
For any acts of kindness
That little hands can do."
"I told my ears to hear
Quite closely all day through
For any act of kindness
That little hands can do
"I told my eyes to see what . . ..

and then my memory fails me. The memory of the classroom, though, the gestures, the sound of the music, still are quite clear. Occasionally, Momma let me sit with Miss Ahrenkiel during church. She let me cuddle close to her. What I really cuddled was her luxurious-feeling black sealskin coat – ah, what glorious softness.

There is a dim memory of a dark space near Miss Ahrenkiel's room with only a table and benches for Sunday school and, in the winter, we sat huddled around a pot-bellied stove with a wintry sun shining through the window trying to make the space warmer.

I don't remember much of those two classrooms (actually, they were just small spaces), but we did go to Sunday school, and if we begrudged being expected to do so, we went anyway.

During the years we lived in California, from July 1941 through October 1943, we were part of a big Baptist congregation in Vallejo. I went to my first church camp while we were living in California. It was high in the mountains, near Colfax. It was beautiful, crisp and filled with the beauties of nature. We counted ourselves lucky to be part of this setting, up and closer to God.

We moved back to Illinois, the war went on, and we continued to go to church. We helped teach Sunday school, we had Youth Fellowship meetings, we sang in the choir, helped served church suppers, and went to church camp one week each summer.

On one very memorable day, our Youth Fellowship group went roller skating at a rink in Springfield. Later we had supper at a Steak 'n Shake. While we were eating, word was received that Germany had surrendered – the place erupted! We dashed outside and down to the capitol square where we joined hundreds, maybe thousands, of others. We laughed, we yelled, people had horns and whistles and bells, there were streamers and confetti, what a jubilation that time was – VE day!!

And that memorable time was spent with my friends – my best friends from church. What a thrill to hug them, to shout our thanks and praise that our prayers were answered. ~Georgia

Criticism. Why, oh why was Daddy so critical? As a child, and even into adulthood, I was so afraid of him. I never found out why I was afraid; I just was.

I had to gather eggs, but the hens pecked me if I reached under them for the eggs they were sitting on. Daddy criticized me severely when I didn't want to get the eggs, making me feel small and stupid and <u>less.</u>

We had colds and coughs. Daddy got irritated when we coughed. "Trying to get attention," he would smirk. Keeping small pleasures from us for being unable to control our coughing was something he did and I still do not understand what he felt he accomplished.

If we slumped in our chairs and Daddy saw us, the edge of his hand, like a blade of metal, would slam into our spines. We learned to sit up straight early in life. I am glad I have a good carriage today, but why did he need to inflict pain to get his desired result?

When we were older, he hated for us to have teen-talk on the phone. "What was that about?" or "You didn't have anything to say" often was the comment after no more that a five minute phone visit with a friend.

This continued even in to adulthood and in our own homes, if he was visiting. He would point out that no one needed to "yak" on a phone so long.

If a meal was particularly good there never was a compliment. If, however, the gravy was lumpy, or vegetables not salted to suit, Dad always had a critical remark. "Did you run out of salt?" if not salty enough, or if too salty "Did you use all the salt you had?" And he never seemed to realize how hurtful his comments were. He just needed to have folks know he was displeased.

Dad had only to stand on our front porch and look across the street at the young folks who lived there and glare at them – too loud, too much makeup, too skimpily dressed. Oftentimes the kids would go out their own back door in order to avoid Dad's steely stare, that blue beam aimed at young people who did not meet his standards.

Criticism seemed to be Dad's most prominent characteristic and yet – well, there were signs that, with 20/20 hindsight, indicate he had few skills as a parent, maybe even as a social being.

A man brought a chair for Daddy to re-glue. It was a small job and took little time to fix. When the man came for the repaired chair, Dad didn't charge. "Oh, no, I want to give you something for it," the man said. To that, Dad replied, "Well, whatever you think it's worth." The man laid down a dime. Dad never again would accept any furniture for repair from that man – and he told the story about the man, over and over again.

I had straight A's from 2nd through 4th grades; my father's signature is on the report cards to prove he saw them, but I was never praised for them. Perhaps that's what he expected; I'll never know.

He had a need to be respected, and he was. Many a wooden bowl or picture frame or wooden cutout wall hanging went out the door as gifts. The garden produce and fruit harvests that were giveaways must have weighed close to a ton. Hot meals were transported at holiday time to folk living alone, delivered before we had our meal.

But there was that tongue, that mouth, saying critical and hurtful things to his children and his wife and to anyone else he thought needed his contempt.

It was to Sara to whom he was most cruel, but I want to believe he loved us all. He just didn't know how to show it. He didn't know how to respond when love was extended. When I would say, at the end of a phone conversation, "Love you, Dad," his inevitable reply was "Thank you."

When he was in the closing years of his life, we had a heated discussion about loving our neighbor as ourselves. I said I loved myself and was glad I did, because it helped in loving my neighbor. His final statement in this argument was, "Pretty arrogant of you, Sis."

Maybe I shouldn't have been afraid of him, and maybe I should have given him some of his own criticism. If he hadn't been Daddy, I might have done so. ~Georgia

D

Dad. My father – such a difficult man.

An early memory: Dad lying on his bed, freshly showered after work, fully dressed in clean, crisp khaki work uniform, his standard attire. He is resting before dinner, reading the paper. I am running down the short hall toward his bedroom in the front of the house, pulled by expectation, or the sound of his voice, or a whispered hint from Mama. I am three or four. I peek around the door and see his shaven, clean, ruddy face, his attention concentrated on the paper. He doesn't appear to see me, so I clamber up on the tall bed, near his legs, and creep, like a small animal, up his trousers to his chest. The smell of soap, of starch, of Bay Rum, and the clean man smell still lingers in the back of my mind.

Now is the time for our game. His shirt has pockets, with buttons. Abandoning his paper, he grins at me. We are both anticipating the goal, the prize. But first the dance – of hugs, of kisses, of teasing. Perhaps he holds me up in the air in his strong arms, or nuzzles my ear. Eventually, in a timeless time, but before we're called for dinner, I touch his pocket. I feel the lump. Small fingers struggle with the button, down into the pocket, retrieving the small hard circle with the magic hole. Red is the best, or orange, yellow shines like the sun, green greets my eyes like Spring. The evening Life Saver, permitted with indulgence before dinner, flavored with starch and love, from Daddy.

I was the youngest, the unexpected baby, happy and cuddly, and my sisters confirm that I had the best of our parents. Not only had they reached some relative economic security, the Depression over, the nation ready to enter the post-war boom of prosperity, but also they had mellowed into a comparatively peaceful contentment.

We had our house and our yard, our large pasture and garden, Dad was reaching his phase of being self-employed, a much happier circumstance for him and thus for all of us.

Some of the other memories are strange, confused through the mingled memories of childhood and of overheard comments and conversations. Dad's customers for his furniture shop were often friends, neighbors, people from church, town acquaintances, people we knew from other towns. He had been born and raised in this town of Petersburg, population 2000, and of course knew practically everyone in the county and beyond. Certain women would visit, often maiden ladies of uncertain age, handsome, corseted, and powdered in their summer dresses and careful hairdos – and Dad would squeeze their shoulders, tease them for a kiss, make inappropriate comments as to what might be missing in their lives, perhaps pinch their behinds. One of these ladies was our choir director and my piano teacher – I can't imagine what she thought, whether she was annoyed, intrigued, or amused. I know my mother was embarrassed and humiliated – but not enough to put her foot down once and for all. I don't know why.

To me as a child, it was just Dad, and adults fooling around. Other women were treated with respect, sometimes with affection, and I never knew what the distinctions were. Men were treated with disdain (fools) or respect and sometimes affection (wise men). Some men would come to the house, one at a time, and sit out in the back yard with Dad, and they would talk for an hour or so. Occasionally he would stop at someone's house to visit with one of these men, to talk away an hour between work and dinner. What they talked about, I never knew. Books, perhaps, or what was happening in the world or in the town, or other people's affairs. But it was clear these men respected my father, wanted to spend time in his company, to share their thoughts with him and in turn hear what he had to say. I never knew why. They were quiet, decent, civil men, men of affairs in town, men of stature. They did not add any luster to my view of my father, but his attention to them told me they were admirable people.

Dad liked to touch, and sometimes his touching hurt. An ear pinched or squeezed too hard, a rap on the head, a pinch on the bottom – when I was twelve, I did put my foot down and as I recall, he never caressed me in a painful way again. Sometimes he would sweep into the kitchen and grab Mama and give her the most amazingly graphic kisses, hugs, pats and squeezes you can imagine – she would protest, laughingly if the time was right, more strongly if she was in the middle of dinner preparation, but always ended up returning his kisses heartily – I think it was the only way he would let her go. That was nice to see, nicer to remember.

My parents came to sleep in separate bedrooms. Dad would drift off to sleep by 9:30 but Mama often read until midnight. To suit these preferences, after my sisters were gone, my mother set up one of the smaller bedrooms for herself. Dad made her a twin bed out of walnut, and she indulged herself with pretty sheets and a good reading light, and was content. They would begin the after-dinner reading or talking lying on Dad's big bed. I would usually join them for evening prayers. Then Dad would nod off, and Mama would move to her room for her private time. Dad got up first each morning, by 6:30 at the latest, with Mother up fifteen minutes later to start breakfast. One morning, I woke up to a quiet house, saw it was almost 7:30, no sounds of breakfast. I got up and peeked into Mama's room next to mine. There she was, and Dad beside her in that narrow bed, both still asleep. Hmm. I think they liked each other, most of the time.

You will read elsewhere in this book of not so happy times—of criticism and anger, of belittling and humiliation. Yes, they happened. I was told, and told, and told, not to play with the sewing machine. But I kept doing it and one day when I was four or five, ran the needle through my index finger, straight through the nail and all the way down. At my screams, Dad, out in the yard, walked by the open window in the sewing room, looked in, and said cheerfully, "Serves you right." And left me there. The sisters and mother rescued me within seconds and were appalled at his attitude. Well, I expect he might not have been so casual had I caught fire after being warned not to play with matches.

There are other little incidents like that here and there. Those are not the ones I remember the most. When I was ten or eleven, my appetite diminished and I developed some mild form of anemia. The liquid iron they prescribed for us in those days did not do the trick and turned my teeth gray besides. So Dr. Plews, in his infinite wisdom, said to my tee-totalling mother, "Try giving her a little wine before dinner – a couple of ounces." After recovering from the shock, my mother dutifully trotted down to wherever such things were purchased and bought a bottle of Mogen David wine, with no little embarrassment. A new evening ritual was begun: about 30 minutes before dinner was served, mother brought me a dainty little glass (not a wine glass – an etched juice glass, I think) two-thirds full of the ruby red elixir. I thought it quite pretty and not as bad as some medicines I had had before. It was about the third evening of this ceremony, when Dad, who had been watching me drink my wine, stepped into the kitchen, poured himself an equal amount of Mogen David, and joined me in the dining room, where we sipped companionably. Mother, hands on hips, came to the doorway. "I don't recall the doctor saying you have anemia," she snapped at Dad. His blue eyes twinkling, he drawled, "You wouldn't want the kid to drink alone, would you?"

It still makes me laugh, that scene. I think we all laughed. The wine lasted a couple of weeks and then was gone, my appetite returned along with a higher red cell count, and that was the end of wine tasting with Father.

Dad was critical; he was sarcastic; he did not often choose to be tactful, although he could be. Some people went out of their way to avoid him; others sought his company. He was painfully honest, had the highest integrity, avoided debt like the plague, did not suffer fools gladly or at all if he could help it, had no use for pretense or hypocrisy, was a perfectionist in his work, could not bear liars, cheats, braggarts, or those who cursed, would go out of his way to do a favor for a friend or someone in need, and would insult anyone and everyone equally, regardless of station, rank, gender, or age. His pride was extreme to the point of arrogance. I was mowing the front lawn one afternoon, wearing shorts and a halter top and hoping to get a tan that way instead of lying in the sun, which was boring. Dad came home from work when I was half-finished with the front yard, stopped the car in the front of the driveway, and yelled in anger "What do you think you're doing! Get away from that now!" And I was thinking he'd be pleased. He wouldn't even let me walk the mower to the back yard, but did it himself. Turns out he didn't want any of the neighbors or passers-by to think Emery couldn't take care of his own lawn but had to have his daughter do it. Quite a shock to me, and wrong-headed of him, but there was a tiny spark in my heart that said, how nice for a man to be so protective of his women-folk. But it wasn't me he was protecting of course – it was his pride. I think.

So many memories, such a mingling of pain and pride, of laughter and anger, of sentiment and sarcasm. The big black cat would leap from the ground to Dad's tall shoulder in one bound and they would go walking around the pasture together. Dad loved my canary and would tilt his head back and let the canary sit on his big nose, or laugh at the bird perched on his water glass at the dinner table, taking tiny sips.

So many memories---

--- his weeping – "Daddy, I'm pregnant" – no college for his baby, all hopes gone, holding his last child who now carried a child herself.

--- his final days, blind and disoriented, seeing visions, fearful of the end. Listening to us read the Bible, listening for words of hope, of peace, of forgiveness. We offered fumbling assurances, comfort and love, holding his hands, stroking his thin brow, trying to make it right for him, hushing his regrets. Mama's waiting. It is over.

These, only these things matter. Dear, difficult man who gave us what he had, our standard not of troubled love, but of honor, truth, and character, of pride and excellence, of beauty and wonder.

Somewhere, it is perfect now, and he is healed. Let us rejoice. ~Anne

Dad and Work. Dad had lots of jobs as I remember. He left home at 18 he told us, to go where the action was. A friend went with him and they worked side by side on many adventures. They rode the rails in the "blinds" - the blinds being the space between the passenger cars. Dad also spoke of the side-door Pullmans, which were the boxcars. He counted himself as the leader of the two "runaways" and was the bindle stiff for both himself and his friend. (You can look up that bindle stiff thing in that other dictionary.)

They worked the wheat harvest in Iowa and the apple harvest in Washington. Once they were to jump a boxcar but dad didn't as he was the bindle stiff and felt it was too dangerous so he and his friend got separated. He was to meet him in San Francisco but did not and I think he felt his friend abandoned him. He did learn later that his friend joined the marines and ended up in Hawaii. Had dad ended in the Islands I wonder what?

Dad was at some point working in San Francisco on the tourist boats, the Delta King and Delta Queen paddle wheelers, keeping the mechanics in good repair. The vessels took on passengers somewhere on what dad called the American River. One going up the river the other coming down, they would pass each other in the night, dispatch their passengers, get a new load after the mechanics checked everything and the trip would commence again.

As the story goes, dad went from there to work for the Union Pacific railroad. He worked on the great locomotives. He kept pictures of these huge engines showing various stages of righting a fallen train. Often they would derail in mountainous regions. The wonder of how these monsters were righted and pulled into the round house! This job was where dad apparently perfected his mechanical prowess, going beyond his actual job description.

He told me how he got all his tools for machine work, how he bought only the best ones from guys who left the job; some tools he found in pawnshops. He built a big wooden chest for all the bits and pieces he amassed over the years. And then one day, chest and all came up missing – no investigation – no compensation. Fifty years later, when he recounted this "thing" that was done to him, he was still angry, hurt and incredibly sad. One more reason not to believe in people.

Around this time Dad met and married Mom and came back to Illinois to settle in. It occurs to me the only things these two people had in common were the fact that mom's dad was a railroad man and momma was on the rebound from a love affair gone wrong. Guess it was enough.

Back in Illinois, Dad took a job selling Togstad, something like Watkins products, a line of household and kitchen items, spices, flavorings, what-have-you – from door to door. I remember one bedroom being given over to Togstad stuff. He left this job early – why I don't know. Probably people didn't or couldn't pay. He could never press people for what he was owed. This was in the early Depression era and things were really hard. He often took eggs or an occasional bauble in payment for his wares. Later when I cared for him I sold these small pieces of brass and pottery, glass – all sorts of bits that made up our household. Things used to pay my Dad for Togstad as well as later when he turned his machine talents to woodworking and he took payment in glass and the etcs. of other folk's households. All these things that were not considered to be of terrific value kept me and my dad in butter and eggs for a lot of time during his last years. Ah, how good the Depression era mind that could never discard a thing.

Dad had a stint with Caterpillar in Peoria, Illinois, doing, no doubt, mechanical stuff. He was in a horrific car accident early one a.m. breaking his face quite badly – his nose took the worst of it, never to heal properly. From his beautiful patrician nose to a bent and cracked knob. Gave him a rugged, rakish look – better to my mind. Not so blooming perfect. He was very stoic as I remember. He was even, I might say, funny about relating the accident saying there was one guy who kept saying over and over "oh, my neck, oh, my neck." This was to become a family expression over the years. Keep in mind folks I was wee when this happened but I can see and hear it even as I write.

I am not sure when he went to California to work at the Mare Island naval base/shipyard – '39 maybe? He repaired and built warships, he made shells for submarines. He also made bracelets for momma and for us girls. The material was catwalk steel with little elongated diamond shaped bumps on the surface. The bumps, he said, were part of the floor design of the sub decks, used in order to help the men keep their balance. There were twisted wire bracelets; flat pounded bracelets and a ring made for his mom. Beautifully crafted on his machine and set with an ancient coin. My grandson wears it today.

Mom moved us out to join him in California in 1941, leaving our big house for our paternal grandparents to live in. The grandparents rented their smaller house to –somebody. We were in Vallejo until the Easter after the bomb dropped on Pearl Harbor. We (my sis Georgia & I) went back east, driven by a couple the folks advertised for (not today though, huh?). We lived with Nannie and Grandpa for a while then Nannie took us back to the folks only to discover my mom with a fat stomach. The little interloper was on the way.

We returned to Petersburg in '43 with the interloper, the dog, and all. One thing here – before we left Vallejo, dad PAINTED our whole house because he didn't want to leave it dirty for "the next guy." Not only – he painted the kitchen TWICE as it didn't suit him. Not today boy! Probably not then either except by my dad. Anyway I was never a California kid and promised to do cartwheels when we hit Illinois soil and I did. Several. Which did not bother dad – hmm; he was usually bothered by any "display." He was an Illinois guy though so I reckon that's why.

He worked in an upholstery shop for about 27 minutes – never good at working "for the other guy." Dad could not abide shoddy work, short corners to save money so he quit, what else?

He was appointed to the New Salem State Park in the curator's workshop in charge of lots of folks to keep all the furniture in good nick in the village cabins. When the Democrats became the Republicans in Springfield, dad lost his job. Given dad's personality, he took this personally. I know he did an excellent job of work but politics is politics. He remembered this till his dying day, never missing an opportunity to say how he was wronged.

Although the war years were the best for us financially, his work on the A-BOMB job as he called it and actually part of the Manhattan Project in Hanford,Washington, seemed to haunt him; he felt guilt over helping to make such a thing of great destruction. Another layer indicating his sensitivity. He was inarticulate about so much. Men did not FEEL in that era and surely not MY dad. In later years though, as we did his oral history, he cried over even the smallest injustices. Injustices to the other fella as well as to himself.

Dad raised chickens, cows, steers, sheep, pigs - not at the same time. He grew popcorn, raspberries, rhubarb, asparagus and lots of wonderful other veggies, which we ate and which he sold, gave away and which momma canned. We had a black walnut tree in our back yard and sis and I would shell them. Only once did we do THAT without gloves. Left our hands first green then black with walnut stain. Did he sell the nuts? Can't remember, but he was always AT SOMETHING trying to make our lives better but still staying away from working for the other guy.

There was a time when he, his brother, Lynn, and their dad worked side-by-side painting and repairing houses inside and out. They were in high demand as their work was above reproach and I would imagine they charged less than other painters as well.

His final job the one where he stayed and where he did his best work–emotionally and where he had a consistent income, too--was in his Shop. I intentionally capitalize Shop, as it was so important a place in our lives. I think my dad was at peace in that space if ever he was at peace anywhere.

He turned an old Singer sewing machine head, now picture this, with its wheel on the head, into a lathe. He adapted a 2.5 hp motor to make the wheel turn. He did this with a heavy cord run through a hole in a yardstick fastened to the edge of the open table that kept the whole apparatus housed. He turned all this on by pulling the yardstick horizontally along the edge of the table. I know you can't even begin to picture it. But with that he began making and repairing furniture. His love of this work was obvious in the results. Finally dad was at home in his house and at home in his work. Settled at last.

As time passed and money grew he expanded his shop and his tools became more sophisticated, but the lathe stayed in the basement. It is probably still humming somewhere between reality and the shadowy world of Emery.

I am so lucky to have this background, this rural–ness, the extended families and now to have the ultra modern style of city high-rise living. Quite a wealth of information and knowledge. I love recounting the stories from that time. I am also grateful to have been witness to dad's virtues. He was honest to his core, his integrity was palpable. His work was his talent and his love of doing it all so well was lesson enough for the entire town. People may not have received much warmth from my father, but they knew where to go for fairness and workmanship par excellence. Also they were likely to get work done from Emery for a good bit cheaper than elsewhere. Whatever was missing in my life it was not the ability to soak up the lessons he was teaching, lessons he was unaware of teaching.

I wish there was one lesson I had not heard so well and that one is – not working for the other guy. Had I been more adaptable I might have had a wee bit better life… but on the other hand I most assuredly would not have had the adventures I have had. Life's a trade off. ~Sara

Dan. Dan was a beautiful lab/setter mix and for many years my best friend. Dad acquired this newest member of our family under great duress. At the time Dan came to us Dad worked in Peoria at Caterpillar and a man he was working with badgered him until Dad finally agreed to take the dog. From the beginning Dan and I were pals. He was a gift dad never knew he gave me.

For hours Dan and I would wobble together through our pasture, trod ever-new paths along the fence separating our property from the deep overgrown ravine, which led to the railroad tracks. A real railroad with trains that tooted through. It is still a family saying, "train a'comin." As kids we would all run to the window to see the great long freight trains puff through under the bridge at the end of our property. But I digress.

Dan and I ran, we rested, we visited. I told him my plans, he listened. Very rarely did he interrupt, oh, occasionally he would just get up and walk away, when he figured he'd heard enough, or perhaps from boredom, but he was never rude. Many an early a.m. momma or dad would find me in the basement curled up with the dog on his blanket. There would be some tisk, tisking, but I was never kept from my dog. He was gentle and patient – except when someone he was not acquainted with would attempt to come into the yard uninvited. An army could walk through if dad was in the yard, but if no one was in the yard to say OK, he would send up the alarm. I remember once, a neighbor came by with some meat scraps for Dan and dad held him off (would he have bitten? - who knows) anyway dad came from wherever, saying "just put the package down and many thanks." I wonder if that guy ever brought Dan another scrap?

At one point (more of this another place) we moved to California. Within a few months Dan joined us. Dad had my grandpa build a crate (of walnut thank you very much) put Dan on the train and voila – dog. In dad's oral history he referred to the moving of the dog as what WE wanted meaning the sisters – but I believe he wanted his dog (he just thought Dan was his, Dan and I knew better). For whatever reason my friend joined me in Vallejo, California and it was good.

He was in a whole other place, Dan, with little space to run or to have the kind of adventures we had had in Illinois but we found places to explore. He never offered to run into the busier street, or to go off on his own to explore, he just stayed in my presence quite happily, never knowing I was not other than just real special.

And when we returned to Illinois the crate was used again and we all rode home on the train. Dan and I picked up our adventures with a tiny addition, my baby sister, the interloper. We (Dan and I) had decided she was a keeper while still in Calif. I would play with baby sis Anne and Dan would be right there to help. Never once did he get frustrated with whatever I put him through, he tolerated the interloper with grace and dignity. Never can I remember him growling or baring a tooth.

As the years went on Dan got some nasty skin stuff including an awful case of mange. Dad made a sulfur dip in one of momma's washtubs. Whew did that stink and so did the dog. He was so depressed and dejected that dog. I just had to hold my nose and be there for him, making me stink too. Not easy to rid oneself of that smell let me tell you. And so it went – total acceptance from and for my dog, Dad never knowing of his gift and Dan never knowing how important he was to a young gangly girl who desperately wanted someone or some thing to just love her.

And then one day I came home and Dad's nose was red and mom had her hands in her apron wringing her hands and her apron into a tight twist. Dad looked at me and said "I want to show you something." He led me to the back of the house and pointed out to a small mound of freshly turned earth far into the pasture. "That's Dan under there." Well, I am crying now as I write this so imagine what happened back then. I was so angry, hurt, bereft. Gosh. I railed at him "why didn't you tell me? How could you do this to him, to me?" He tried to explain that the dog was old and sick I  could not, of course, hear him. All I knew was that my dearest friend was dead. There is a block in my memory of how this was ever healed, but there was never any question of another dog. Our dog days were done. ~Sara

Dishes. Sara and I always did the dishes. Of course that's a lie, because we usually only did the supper dishes. Momma washed up after breakfast because Sara and I went off to school. We didn't come home at noon, so Momma washed up then, too.

But, Sara and I <u>always</u> did the dishes. First, it was with warm water from the teakettle in the dishpan, and then rinsed with warm water from another pan. Homemade soap that didn't lather and a dishrag that I remember always being old peach-colored rayon bloomers that had lost their elastic, made the full complement of our dishwashing supplies. It's a wonder we said the dishes were clean.

Sara and I HATED doing dishes. We quarreled about almost anything, and then Momma's voice would threaten, "If you don't quit that, Sara/Georgia will do the dishes alone." I don't remember that ever happening, but it did make us hush.

Other times, though, we sang together. Maybe we weren't concert quality, but never were we told to hush. When Garrison Keillor has his audience sing "Tell Me Why" I always weep. I'm back in the kitchen, washing or drying dishes. Sara or I has said, "You go up, and I'll go down," meaning I am to sing soprano while she does the harmony and while she or I clean the dishes with a "sloomy," the peachish colored dish rag, or dries with a bleached flour sack... "and I will tell you just why I love you." Now I know why, and I know how much I love her.

The first kind of dishes I remember Momma having for "everyday," maybe for company, too, were kind of a departure from her "Baptist piety." They were burgundy, forest green and gray china. They were handsome, bold colors that I occasionally see in antique shops, but they aren't really antiques as much as collectibles and of course they are in that shop to evoke memories of our dishes and wonder, too, why any one would pay THAT much money for them. Memories have no price tag.

During that same period, Thomas Vincent Plews, our family physician, was dispensing medicines from his office. Some of his medicines came in deep amber-colored glass containers about 2 ½" in diameter, and either 5 or 6 inches and 8 or 9 inches high. For some arcane reason, either Momma or Dad thought they would be fine as drinking glasses. That may have been true, but they were also ugly! They certainly didn't "go" with the burgundy/green/gray dishes! I wonder what happened to them....

Later I remember everyday Prussian blue and white dishes with different Currier and Ives prints on each type of dish – dinner plates, pie plates, cups and saucers, cereal and sauce bowls, serving pieces of various sorts, even drinking glasses. I think they were "bonus" dishes, like the depression glass of a different era, but with a small price tag attached.

Momma loved those dishes because she was so fond of Currier and Ives lithographs. Her fondness expanded when an insurance company began using them on their give-away calendars. I see these dishes in shops as well. I guess there were lots of kids washing dishes and remembering them today.

Typical of Momma and Dad's artistic collaborations, she asked him to make walnut picture frames so she could hang the lithos in the living room with four favorite Currier and Ives calendar prints.

Again, typical of her, Momma found a cotton print fabric heavy enough to be used as draperies – the print? Currier and Ives scenes, of course, and it pulled the room together like a magnet. With a pleated valence, the whole project was a smash. Just as an aside, after she had died, her ashes were interred, having been placed in a soup urn with a Currier and Ives print on the sides.

During World War II, when money flowed freely for the first time in their married life, Momma and Dad made several purchases from Sears and Roebuck. One was an electric sewing machine labeled Kenmore, but made by White Sewing Machine Company, a venerable and most respected company. They also bought a plated silver table service for eight. It was a lovely pattern, but poorly designed with short fork tines and nasty short knife blades. One of my kids has it stored somewhere, but at least it's still in the family.

The china set they bought from Sears was white with delicately sprigged pastel flowers along the borders. The pattern was quite a departure from the more bold dishes they used every day. Momma and Dad were both quite pleased when she set the table for company.

It was summer time and we always had more chores, what with gardening, harvesting, canning and freezing. Momma said I could play in the pasture for a while with Sara and the kids from across the street, but that I'd have to come in to help with the dishes before long, though.

We were busy with our pretending – I was the queen, I remember– when I heard Momma call, "George, the dishes." We all groaned because we were kids and didn't want to work. "George, the dishes." Another groan. "George, the dishes (pause) are done!" It was a tiny thing, but she was as pleased with herself as I was glad to hear it.

Then there was the Great Uncle George plate that really was a humility object. Uncle George purportedly had money so when I was named, it was in his honor. For such an honor, he gave Momma a plate, hand-painted with daisies, and that was all. She had it for many years and then gave it to me as my inheritance from dear old Great Uncle George. I don't even know his last name, and besides, I broke the plate several years ago. So much for humility in this family. ~Georgia

Divorce. "You were always such a good girl. Why did you do this to us?"

"Well, you made your own bed. Now you'll have to lie in it."

"Oh, dear. Do you want to come home?"

All three of us divorced our first husbands. Each of us got different reactions from our parents. When Emery and Elizabeth married, divorce was shameful, even sinful. It most certainly was nothing that would happen in our family… the fact that we found evidence that Daddy had been married to someone before he met Momma didn't count but was very shocking to me.

Momma and Daddy both came from moral families; Daddy's perhaps was more fundamentally Christian. All of us girls saw and heard their quarrels. Both were dramatic in exhibiting anger with tears and stomping out and slamming doors.

Divorce

When I was little, Daddy rushed into the kitchen one day from being outside. He seized the teakettle of boiling water from the hot iron coal-burning kitchen stove and threw it on my mother. Momma screamed with the pain, I cried in terror. Years later, when I was an adult, Momma and I were visiting. I queried her about the only incident I remembered of Dad's act of physical abuse.

Her reply was quick and filled with laughter. "Oh, honey, don't you know what really happened?"

It had been a bitterly cold morning and there was a crisis in the chicken house because the water had frozen. Dad rushed in for a means to thaw the waterers the chickens vitally needed. As he grabbed the vessel, his foot slipped when water splashed out. Momma's anguished scream was followed by his enfolding her in his arms and crying for having caused her such agony. My tears had not been noticed. Nor did I understand what I was seeing.

Momma was the sort whose floor was so clean we could have eaten on it, as the saying goes. Neat, however, wasn't her forte, and her dresser drawers always were a loblolly. Daddy's drawers, however, were precisely arranged – if mom didn't get it right when putting his underwear and socks away he redid it for himself to suit himself. One day, he initiated a quarrel regarding clean vs. neat, or so I remember.

He began throwing his clothing around their bedroom, socks and underwear out of dresser drawers, landing on the huge brass chandelier and draping the seven-foot high walnut headboard of their bed. Pants and shirts flying from the closet were strewn on floor, chairs and dressers. Trying to prove a point about messiness and how hard it would to be to live with on a grand scale - yeah, a bit extreme.

Momma was horrified; so was I but, in retrospect it really was very funny. I can't remember the resolution to this or who straightened the mess (mom no doubt) but by nightfall they had kissed and made up. Their ground rules included a strong Biblical admonition: "Let not the sun go down upon thy wrath."

After I was grown, they came to visit on one of my birthdays. Momma was agitated about something Daddy had said. Something about the waste of Christmas (my birthday being right after so all the hoopla was still up and around) or perhaps too much TREE, whatever, anyway mom's first gambit to me was, "I think I'm going to just get a room in Chicago and I can have a Christmas tree all year long if I want it." Such funny little quarrels. Such different backgrounds. Such a strong feeling, though, of even if they couldn't live happily ever after, at least they did live together ever after.

46

When Momma was sick with cancer she came for one last trip to Chicago to see her children and grandchildren. One morning as I was working in the kitchen, she came to the doorway, and leaning her head against the doorjamb, said, "I miss my Daddy. I wanna go home." She was on the train that day. Such a true bond between such different people. Such work on her part to stick with her marriage and at the end of her life wanting only her husband.

When the call came to Daddy that his beloved Elizabeth was very close to death, he drove like a madman to the hospital twenty miles from their home, wrecking his car en route. He attempted a shortcut through a parking lot and got clobbered by a backing-up car. The story goes that the man was quick to help him on his way, not making great to-do about Dad's error. He made it to the hospital with some time to spare and he got to kiss his Elizabeth good-bye.

Theirs was a turbulent but strong marriage, and it was a true one, one I am in awe of even today. Divorce was never an option in this marriage.
~Georgia

Dr. Plews. From earliest childhood, Dr. Plews looms large; actually, I doubt he was much over five foot, 6 inches tall. His personality was big and he was pretty wide, too, so he loomed large. I suppose he had hair at some time but I always remember him being bald.

Doctor Plews' office was a small house downtown, squeezed between a garage and a filling station. His office smelled of the medicines he dispensed from his back room. He had a secretary/receptionist who had done our ironing till he offered her more pay and longer hours so we went wrinkled. No, not really, mom must have taken over. Anyway, how he and my parents became close friends, I never will know. I do know I called his wife "Aunt" Margaret, although they were Canadian and no relation. How did they come to our little town in the 1930's? I don't know that either.

Friends they were, though. Aunt Margaret had severe arthritis in her spine. Bending was painful so many activities were restricted. She and the good doctor enjoyed playing croquet and had a sunken plot behind their house for the croquet court. When her arthritis finally prevented her from playing, Dad made her a mallet with a longer handle. Both mallet and handle lovingly turned on his lathe made of beautifully grained walnut wood. So then she could continue her game with no bending over and with less pain.

When Momma was to have her breast removed (the first time, in the '30's), Dr. Plews and Aunt Margaret pleaded to let me stay with them. Their house was just across the street from my school playground. Dr. Plews was on the school board. I was a scrawny little girl in second grade, so Dr. Plews got board permission for me to skip recess. Instead, I skipped across the street to drink Ovaltine and vanilla ice cream in hopes that I might fatten up.

I didn't fatten up. I did, however, catch a glimpse of him taking a very early phone call in his long white night shirt. Outside of picture books, I'd never seen such a thing; I still haven't. Where do you suppose he bought them? What a magnificent garment.

When Momma still was in the hospital but feeling better, Dr. Plews and Aunt Margaret decided I should have a permanent. No consultation, no permission given, Aunt M. just took me, they did it, and Dr. Plews called me "Gorgeous George" when I was presented in the hospital to Momma.

She was not a happy Momma, but what could she say? They'd been so generous and sensitive to what they perceived to be my needs. With no children of their own they could pretend at being parents for a while. And hair grows.

Once, one of my sisters was listening while he and Daddy visited. Daddy made one of his outrageous pronouncements. Dr. Plews turned to my sister and made a pronouncement of his own: "Your dad has s… for brains."

On the other hand, he is the doctor who successfully brought Sara into the world under most extraordinary circumstances. Sara was born at home, breach, after an endless labor and weighing over 10 pounds.

More than once, when Annie was desperately ill, Momma called him in the middle of the night, and he came. He came to the house to care for his little patient and was glad to come.

While I was married to my first husband, my mother-in-law began exhibiting aberrant behavior. When she finally sought medical help, Dr. Plews examined her and sent her to a specialist in Springfield. He sent along his opinion, too: "Consider the possibility of a brain tumor."

The "specialist" treated her for stroke for four months. Through a complicated route, she eventually landed at Barnes Hospital in St. Louis where the surgeons removed a tumor the size of a small grapefruit from her skull. Almost immediately she returned to her normal self, doing needle work and playing her beloved piano.

Our family listened to Dr. Plews even if the "specialist" didn't hear him. Although I don't know HOW the Plewses and the Rawlingses became friends I have several clues as to WHY they were friends. Dad and Thomas Vincent Plews both had "rough cob" qualities. Neither suffered fools gladly. Each in his own way unstintingly offered help when they saw need. Furthermore, both of their wives were ladies.

The small town doctors of two generations ago are as scarce as buggy whips. If we reintroduce whips, would we also get house visits from doctors? hmm. ~Georgia

E

Eldest. I am the eldest and though my remembrances may not be the most fulsome, some are quite vivid. The first memory, recounted to my astonished mother years later, is of watching The Fire.

I stood on a windowsill, held from behind by the loving hands of an unseen person. I watched with horror and fascination as I saw the flames consume my home in Illinois and burn it to the ground. It was early December and I would be two on December 29.

I was born in Sacramento, CA, to two very handsome and unsophisticated people. I also was a prize for my mother's family. There were three aunts, three uncles; a set of maternal grandparents and even a set of my mother's grandparents and here was I, the first of a string of grandchildren. In those days, babies weren't planned; they just happened. And all that extended family thought that the fat black-haired and brown-eyed laughing baby was made especially for them. My mother told me that when she took me out in my carriage that her jaws ached from grinning at strangers as she strolled down the streets of the capitol.

Daddy worked at the railroad roundhouse as a first class machinist till he, like many others caught in the Great Depression, was without employment. Not finding any employment except to run bootleg liquor, which wasn't a swell idea and best he not do THAT, he moved his new family back to Illinois to live with his parents and paternal grandmother. Think of that! All those grandparents.

My Illinois grandparents became known as Nannie and Grandpa. Grandpa's mother may have been called Grandma, but I don't remember. I do remember, however, a family saying: "Mean as Martha." She was not a happy person and she <u>was</u> mean. She may have had some senile affliction but I can only remember her being querulous, demanding and prone to tantrums, throwing food, deliberately soiling her clothes for the satisfaction of having her daughter-in-law clean up after her—she was mean.

Where was my family the night of The Fire? They must have been close but I don't know where. We stayed at the Petersons that night. Dale Peterson and Dad had played together as boys and the families always were very good friends so we were scooped up without question and housed for who knows how long.

With all those adults to coach me, I spoke clearly quite early. Like a live puppet, I was taught all kinds of songs and poetry. By the time I was three years old I could recite the names of all 66 books of the Bible. I remember being stood up in front of the Baptist church congregation to do so. My parents and grandparents must have been so proud.

Because I was well behaved, I was allowed to spend overnight visits with Nannie's sisters and once, with her brother, my great uncle Frank and his wife, Helen. Uncle Frank lived at the Elmore homestead where Nannie had grown up. I remember it being an uncomfortable shabby and poorly furnished place and don't remember ever going there again.

When I was 3 ½ years old I remember standing on the bottom landing of the steps at the Petersons, where I'd stayed overnight. One of the Peterson girls told me, "You have a new baby sister." I had just become the elder sister on August 25, 1934.~ Georgia

Evenings. Evenings were for me a time of joy and trial. In winter I was made to go to bed much earlier than was necessary, way before, as I remember, I was tired. The folks needed us out of the way in order for them to relax, read, do—whatever—not be bothered? I should say here too that while bedtime was a chore and I hated going to bed, getting up was awful too—sometimes you never win.

In summer though it was better. We stayed out of doors later – ran, played hide-and-go-seek, said just like that – not just hide and seek. We were limited to the front yard as I remember as it could get pretty scary playing in the very dark dark of the back of the house. Olly olly oxen free. Gosh is that how you spell that? I can hear that call ring in my ears NOW. For us it usually meant time to come in and get ready for bed.

Sometimes the fog would roll in and make the streetlights hazy and magical, the poor silly old moths committing suicide right and left, buzzing against the bright bulbs. We played tag and aggravated the fireflies. Jars full of the poor things. I believe we wanted to see could we read by them.

On rare occasions, our folks would lie with us in the grass in our back yard and look at the stars. Dad pointed out the big dipper and the little dipper as well as other constellations - some of which I think he made up to entertain us. Lying on an old blanket in the sweet smelling grass listening to the night noises – katydids, crickets, the crunch of acorns as the steers walked in the pasture, once in a while we would hear the sound of a dog barking in the distance, or the hollow echo of neighbor kids calling out to one another as they played their own Petersburgish games - and finally the great bong of the Baptist Church clock chiming some curious hour - like 8 PM and off to bed we went. Except sometimes when mom had popped gallons of popcorn freshly drizzled with REAL butter and distributed it in big enamel bowls. Oh, yes we would scan the sky for shooting stars to wish on, too. We could not tell for what we wished as then the wishes would not come true. So many of mine have. I wish I lived now where the stars can be seen. I could use some new magic. ~Sara

F

Failure. What a sad word to introduce into the chronicling of a family. Certainly, though, there was a sense of it, a vague aura encompassing the feelings of failure we experienced. Perhaps the word wasn't used, but there always seemed to be more we should have done.

We includes all of us. Dad left home without a high school diploma, so his brother was the success with a high school degree. Uncle Lynn, however, got caught in a bootlegging scheme during prohibition times, so despite his high school graduating achievement, he was a failure, going to prison for his activities outside the law.

Dad, on the other hand, "rode the rails" with a school chum, following the wheat crop across the northernmost part of America – just a teenager! Eventually he landed in a railroad roundhouse in Colfax, California. There he was taught how to use a metal lathe, eventually becoming a card-carrying, first-class machinist. His mind was quick and he was curious to know more.

Many years later, I told him of my thrill at inspecting the famous "Mississippi Queen" paddle wheeler in Dubuque, Iowa. "Oh, yeah," he said. "It used to be called something else when I threaded the screw for it. It plied the river between Sacramento and San Francisco. Took a day and a half." Little did I know, and furthermore, he never spoke of it again!

But he was a failure, or so he'd tell the story. He lost his job. He had moved from Colfax to the Sacramento roundhouse where there were more opportunities. Well, lots of people lost their jobs. It was 1931 and no one cared that he was married and had an infant daughter. Of course, Dad cared, but nobody else did.

Tail between his legs, he went back to Illinois, dragging his lady-love and their 8 month old "Bide-a-wee," as the baby was called ... back to live with his parents and his paternal grandmother. Six of them in a small wooden house, privy in the back yard, wife separated 2,000 miles from family except for a thin thread of letters through the postal service. Failure!

Elizabeth's family did not come to visit. Elizabeth went to Sacramento to help bury her mother sometime in 1932. She didn't see her people again until 1938 and they gave her a grand visit. She brought Georgia, in 3rd grade and excused from school until she returned, and Sara, 4 ½ years old.

They visited all her family – Uncle Dale and his family in Elko, Nevada. Several weeks later, she went to Aunt Marietta and her family in Sacramento and stayed a while there. After that, she took the girls to Rio Vista to Aunt Kathryn's house. Gussie (Augusta) lived with them.

Gussie was second eldest and now I know she had Down's Syndrome, but then she was just fun. She played with us, took us to the library, read Nancy Drew Stories, and laughed.

While we were at Aunt Kathryn's, we got to meet the other two uncles: Jim, who was in college, and "June," really Ben Junior.

It was a gay and lively time, capped by getting to meet Grandpa Bell who lived in Stockton. He took us to the San Francisco Zoo, the Shriners' Circus, the San Francisco Aquarium, the seal rock, and made two little girls giddy with the thrills big cities had to offer. He also laughingly made us feel guilty when he asked if we'd seen the doughnut fish at the aquarium. We hadn't, of course, but while we were staying with him, he often went to the bakery to buy warm bear-claws or snails for breakfast. Why not doughnut fish? I expect I'd have enjoyed knowing him better.

All in all, Momma, Sara, and I were in California from before Christmas until March – a long visit by any gauge. In 1938-39, what an extravagance! Where's the failure there?

There is a letter Momma wrote, though, regarding her "selfishness in taking all the money just for herself" when there was so much need, etc., etc., etc. Maybe guilt is what she wrote, but failure was what was felt and projected. Who failed to tell her, "Go, Elizabeth! Have a great time! You deserve to spend three months with the family that you've missed since your oldest child was eight months old. Have a ball!"? Except for a funeral, no one saw the need for her to be with her family.

No one said any of those things. Instead, there's that letter. "I'm sorry to be having a wonderful time."

In the ignorance of the 1930's, when Momma discovered a lump in her right breast, the family doctor "prescribed" having a baby. "That might do the trick." Momma and Daddy had a portrait photograph taken with Momma in a pretty sweater to record forever the lovely breast line she soon might lose.

Despite the lack of money and no such thing as health insurance, Momma conceived. She gained 60 pounds, had only one maternity dress, and delivered her 10 lb., 2 oz. daughter on her mother-in-law's dining room table during a severe August thunderstorm. The doctor imported his niece, who was a nurse; there was a midwife in attendance, and Daddy helped, too, to deliver a breach baby with umbilical cord wrapped around her neck. Sounds barbaric, doesn't it?

But, but, but … Sara, the product of that nightmarish birthing, was a "failure." The reason for her being brought into existence did not work. By the time Sara was 3 years old, Momma had had her breast removed. "Sara didn't do what she was sent for to do," I was told. The failure wasn't Sara's, but she bore the stigma till Daddy died and finally quit reminding her.

Jump ahead a few years. Again, through the ignorance of the time, the high school principal told my parents what my I.Q. test results were. He was a personal friend of my parents and saw no harm in telling them.

I graduated high school in May of the same year Sara began high school. When Sara took her I.Q. test, the principal naively remarked that she had scored 1-3 points (who remembers?) lower than I had. Momma and Dad decided even more strongly that Sara was a failure. Incidentally, Sara is the only one of the three of us who has a Master's Degree (plus other academic accreditations.) Does that count? She's traveled to Europe so many times that Edinburgh, London, and Paris are as familiar to her as Chicago, where she's lived for 40 years. Too bad her I.Q. test wasn't as high as Georgia's, don'tcha think?

Circumstances were such that Annie did not use the fabulous scholarship she won to Denver University. She was the brightest student ever to graduate from that high school. (Again, the principal's gratuitous revelation.) The scholarship included four years' tuition, room and board, books, and even transportation to and from college each year. It was offered to 100 outstanding high school graduates to commemorate the University's 100th anniversary.

But Annie didn't go, so that was a failure. Instead, several years later, as a single mother with two small children, she went to work at Encyclopedia Britannica as a clerk in the credit department. When she retired in 1997, her career at E.B. had escalated to management and Vice President of Product Development. Too bad about her failure. Right.

But the failure film always was hanging there when we were growing up. In our academic successes, we kept tripping on it.

After we had left home, groping in our own ways to become satisfactory adults, we'd sometimes get what we called "idiot letters" from Momma. In them, she berated actions we had taken, beating her remaining breast at having been a failure in raising us, not teaching us Christian values because she'd set the example, ya-da, ya-da, ya-da. She fed us on the failure theme.

She died in 1967, when she was only 58 years old, her third bout with cancer. During our last visit with her, she told us, "I'm not afraid of dying, but I'm curious to know what's going to happen next."

I sometimes ponder how she would have evolved had she had more time to know how her daughters have matured. I wonder how she would have integrated our successes into her failure film of life. Would she have been as proud of her grandchildren and great-grandchildren's successes as Sara, Anne, and I are of ours?

When the younger ones fail, it's an opportunity to use the failure as a tool to attain the success they seek. I think all three of us have used the failure film to advantage in instructing our children.

> *"To laugh often and much; to win the respect of intelligent people and the affection of children; to earn the appreciation of honest critics and endure the betrayal of false friends; to appreciate beauty; to find the best in others; to leave the world a bit better whether by a healthy child, a garden patch, or a redeemed social condition; to know even one life has breathed easier because you have lived. This is to have succeeded."*
> Ralph Waldo Emerson

I feel gratitude that the sense of failure isn't a piece of my character-baggage; it's just a tool toward life's successes. ~Georgia

Flour Sack Dresses. If anyone remembers having their ma make a dress out of a flower sack and can prove it, I will buy lunch at a McDonalds of their choice. I think most flour sacks were used as dishtowels. My ma was much more inventive. We had a kitchen cabinet that in today's antique market would fetch $200 or $300 easy and it was the place were dad would periodically dump 50 # bags of flour. These bags were unbleached muslin. Some of them had " Flossie's Flour" or some such written on their fronts or they had big xxs on the front but some of them had wee sprigs of FLOWERS on them – all over. So momma would whip up something for us (George and me, Anne missed this). Now we were NOT this poor. I think mom just liked beating the system. She would take this rough cotton material, shrink it up, cut it out, sometimes putting rickrack or a beautiful piece of lace around the sleeves or neck. Such a genius, my momma. It tickles me now to even think of them. Look at **Swing** and you will see me in a flour sack dress. ~Sara

Food. There was a lot of joy about food in our lives.

When you grow up with meals that have homemade everything, and almost home-grown everything, and there is plenty of it, and no one has made up any rules or discovered cholesterol and spinach still has iron in it and there are no lima beans in the garden, how could you not be joyful?

Mother grumbled a little – just a little and not every day – about the incessant, relentless demands of dinner time, but we were so pleased at the dinner table, especially Dad, who grinned a lot, and paid compliments when he remembered, that it was, all in all, a good time of the day.

The summer bounty started early (sometimes too early, with Grandpa's peas and asparagus, certainly delicacies now but not my favorites then). Fresh lettuce, wilted with hot oil and vinegar dressing, then strawberries, raspberries, followed by the full glory of summer – green beans, cooked with a little bacon and onion and cooked, mind you, until they were nicely done and mushy – none of this al dente crunchy green bean stuff for us. Tomatoes and corn were the centerpieces and were often my lunch on a summer day – four or five ears of corn right out of the garden and a big whole tomato. We didn't grow watermelons or cantaloupes, but the melon man came in his truck and we picked out the special melons – the very best and tastiest in the whole truck – and kept the watermelons cool in a big washtub of water in the basement. Often we would each have a quarter of a large watermelon in the back yard after dinner. It was good that we had an indoor bathroom by the time I could eat that much.

Pot roast and beefy vegetable soups and white bean soup with ham bones (and cornbread); catfish caught that day (not by us) and brought to the table crusty with cornmeal and garnished with lots of lemon wedges; chicken, of course, fried for Sunday to a gold crunchy brown, with heaps of mashed potatoes and creamy chicken gravy (in summers, when all this was accompanied by ears of sweet corn and fresh tomatoes, dessert was an unnecessary frill). Steaks thawed from the freezer, from the poor heifers that had grazed in our pasture the year before – sirloins and T-bones and other cuts I didn't know, but all delicious, broiled and sizzling.

Winter brought forth the stores from the cellar – jars of tomatoes and beans, peaches and jellies, frozen berries and corn, enough for us and some to give as gifts to special visitors. There were potatoes in the cellar in bushel baskets, and baskets of apples picked in a nearby orchard late in the season to tide us through the cold months. We ate these in January and I forgot the hot steamy summer days spent in the kitchen helping to preserve the summer food for winter's use.

There were the not so popular meals occasionally; salmon patties from canned salmon I could live without. And liver, served every couple of months with bacon and grilled onions, was my worst nightmare – "Just take a bite, just a bite – now, that wasn't so bad, was it?" (Yes, it was.)

"Now take another bite, just two bites won't kill you." (Yes, they will.) Those bites must have worked, though, because I love liver today, now that it's gone out of favor.

There were the special dishes from other places. A dish of sorghum molasses at Nannie's, with bits of butter streaked through it and mopped up with home made bread or biscuits; cottage cheese from the Petersons' cows, made by them and never tasted since, tiny curded, mouth-wateringly sour. Nannie's sassafras tea, now known to be unhealthy – poisonous, actually, but then a delicious ambrosial treat. Gooseberries straight from the bush, never mind waiting for the pie.

We ate well and happily, innocent of the dangers lurking within the delicious tastes, sharing our bounty far and wide, and receiving bounty in our turn.

And we always, always said grace, the "Blessing." Not a gabbled formula, but a true prayer, made up from the heart, grateful for the gifts and for the hands that labored to provide them. We held hands around our table and said grace, and squeezed three times at the end, for I-love-you, and then we ate and we were glad. And we still do, and we still are. ~Anne

Sara says: See what we mean about different memories? I can only remember tenseness and stress at the dinner table.

Fragile. I think of me today and see my evolution. Fragile I ain't. But in my family growing up, well that's another story. I was so extraordinarily tall for a girl and for the times I caught lots of flack. I was teased unmercifully and no one at home thought it important enough to help me with it. You know the drill head back shoulders straight and fight your own battles. At 14 I was so fragile there were times I feared I would break. Slings and arrows in the world and no one at home to mop up the pain.

Momma was fragile, too. I reckon after living with dad and his folks she was totally brain washed into believing most of what she brought from the west coast was pretty evil. Solitaire and pongee pj's in the middle of the day was the surest way into hell, no problem. In order to save herself she hid herself and became part and parcel of the Rawlingses.

Georgia was less fragile I think, as she had a few years before the rest of us appeared, to get the best juice from mom and maybe had a better belief in her self-ness. Anne (the interloper) came along after there was some maturing and healing going on. The folks had some practice being parents so she didn't APPEAR to be fragile.

And then there's dad. He was certainly fragile, always worrying about what other people thought. Being afraid of not getting it right and agonizing over a tiny faux pas for not hours or days but years. He could revisit more mistakes than anyone I ever met. How do we get that way I wonder. Papa mine was so accomplished. He was self-taught in so many things it is awesome. He couldn't see it and he never knew himself as worthwhile. Why? Well, the world will always ponder these questions, there are no answers here. ~Sara

Friends. Of course we had friends. There were the close family friends, friendships that spanned decades and generations: Helen King and her daughters and granddaughter; the Petersons, whose only son was a childhood friend of our father and who had a wonderful farm with cows and geese and 25 cats; the Ennises, who lived 60 miles away in a beautiful old intriguing house with wood paneling and long halls and French doors between rooms, who had a boarder upstairs, an old lady who bribed me with sweets to come and sit with her for an hour at a time.

At one time, Nannie and Grandpa took in summer boarders in their house across the street. Some of these boarders became dear friends, returning to visit for a week or a month after they had moved on. I remember some of these kind people, who liked nothing better than to sit on the big front porch with Nannie, rocking an afternoon away, visiting and talking, or playing with a worshipful little girl who thought that the tall man with the thick brown hair was beautiful. I wanted to marry him, except I loved his sweet blonde wife just as much.

A lot of our friends were cousins of some kind, five and six times removed, or related by marriage to someone. Mom and Dad "went visiting" on Sundays, driving out in the country to spend an afternoon with friends on farms after a leisurely slow trip on narrow, pretty roads that wound through woods and fields. Friends would come calling, by arrangement or not, and would spend an afternoon or an evening hour after dinner, talking about whatever adults talked about.

My sisters had friends, girls who would come to the house and gather in a bedroom or the sewing room, brushing each other's hair, listening to records, talking and giggling – sometimes crying. Some of Sara's friends lived on our hill and would stop by of a morning to walk with Sara to school. There were boy friends, too, real boy friends or just friends who were boys. Sara would have boy visitors to the house, come to study or to rehearse for one of the high school plays, and these big boys would tease me and kiss me good night. These teenage boys and girls never shut the door on me, never chased me away when I wanted to sit with them, to listen to the older girl talk, to hear the music from the record player, or to laugh at the play rehearsals. They were kind back then, tolerant and generous and friendly.

I had friends, girls I walked to school with and boys I studied with, lots of pajama parties ("slumber" parties, we called them, though there was little slumber and we'd often see the sun come up and then go swimming). Friends on hay rides, friends in the school chorus or church choir, friends in 4-H and in French class, and friends who taught me how to draw girls in pretty dresses. I don't remember that there were a lot of cliques as there are now, groups of "in" girls and "out" girls. Certainly, we fell naturally into groups – the town girls who had been in school together since kindergarten, and the country girls who had been in grade school together out of town and came in to high school on buses. But there was a lot of mingling between the groups and we seemed to get along, by and large, without hurting each other's feelings too much.

It was different, in such a small town, different in that no one was anonymous. Not only did we know our friends from babyhood or childhood, our parents knew each other as well and shared a history often going back for generations. A lot is said about the lack of privacy in small towns, about the fact that everyone knows everyone else's business, about the gossip, the petty rumors, the uproar over a slight deviation from the conservative norm, the counting of months from the wedding day to the baby's birth. Less is said about the comfort of a small town, the help when trouble comes, food brought to the house, a hand lent to make a big job easier, a friend just sitting near, sometimes all night, to ease a burden.

These stories are about our family and how we lived and grew and learned as a family. But friends were the leavening, the yeast. They provided an arena where we practiced what we had learned within the family, tested our knowledge and skills against a wider audience, found what worked or what didn't, what was accepted or what wasn't. It's funny, but when I think of our family and our friends, we didn't step outside the family circle into a group of friends – the circle expanded to include them, and their circles expanded to include us. Friends, after all, those kinds of friends, were just another part of family.

Some of them are still friends. How remarkable. ~Anne

Furniture Shop Sign. When dad converted our basement to what he called "The Shop," we began to get many, many visitors to our house. In all his dealings, dad was known for his excellent work, and his fairness in business. He fast became a legend in our town and folks from as far away as Chicago came to get

58

furniture repaired and furniture made. It WAS far - we lived near Springfield, Illinois. It did not take long for momma to get pret-ty tired of monitoring the front door and the business of dad's shop. So, what to do.

At some point dad had taken a calligraphy course by mail, leaving him with the most incredibly beautiful handwriting and printing. Also in our front yard was a drippy old fir tree. And so, as ever, a remarkable thing occurred overnight. A hand lettered sign and not just any old sign, but one saying "FURNITURE SHOP IN REAR" appeared on the fir tree.

The sign was a large board painted white with very fancy black lettering. The board was firmly fastened to that fir tree at the beginning of the driveway. Voila, the cars would drive the ½ block long drive to the rear leaving ma to do her thing undisturbed and dad to mind his "Shop." It is such a blessing now to realize how he looked after her. ~ Sara

G

Gardening/Vegetables. "*I come to the garden alone, While the dew is still on the roses---*"

The beginning lines of an old hymn that Sara and I changed to the "dew is still on the raspberries."

Sara and I and Grandpa, and maybe others besides, filled homemade trays with handles that had the capacity to carry six one-quart berry boxes. The picking went quickly and Grandpa totted up each of our picking labors. If our baskets were not generously rounded, Grandpa dumped a few from other of our baskets till they met his standards, sometimes leaving us with less credit to our accounts.

Back we would go to the berries, not quite as energized as before. The sun was higher; the dew had burned away. The six baskets eagerly picked had been reduced to 5 ½ or even 5 quarts. We picked and ate till all the rows were clean and then in two days we came back to do it again. Grandpa's standards were high. His integrity was exemplary. Furthermore, the berries were delicious.

Orders usually had been made weeks before the berries were ripe. People came for their orders or sometimes we delivered them to the customers – wish I could remember how much we got for picking and how much people paid for them. Miss Lucy Flickinger, my piano teacher, was paid with raspberries in the summer and Dr. White, our dentist, was paid with them, as well. I don't suppose that makes a monetary equation but I loved my music lessons. As for dental appointments, well, I stand mute.

Each summer we engaged in a harvest dance. When we were young, foodstuffs from the garden always took precedence over other tasks and certainly over "fun" so our harvest was our dance. We canned, dried, or stored in damp sand or bushel baskets.

Early on a day, Nannie, Momma, I and later, Sara and I, and maybe even later than that, Sara and Annie would sit in a circle around a bushel basket or two of peas and, later in the season, string beans. We either wore aprons or had newspapers in our laps. We sat in the shade outside, on chairs dragged from the kitchen, our laps holding the vegetable we were dealing with. There always was a discard receptacle for pea-pods or bean ends and strings. There always was another receptacle for the shelled peas or the snapped beans. We listened as Momma and Nannie visited; sometimes we said something or other but we were not encouraged to be a part of the conversation.

When we got to the bottom of the basket, we girls "got to help" bring empty canning jars from the basement, take them to the sink, wash them, and scald them with boiling water from the big tea kettle on the stove. After that, we could go and play, or read, or play the piano or the pump organ. Momma and Nannie did the canning. I guess they divvied up the reap of the day.

Later, it was the tomatoes, or maybe the corn came first. Once, after I was married with a baby or two, I came home for a week's vacation. In came Dad, announcing he'd picked a bushel basket of corn for Momma to deal with.

She didn't want to can! She wanted to visit with me and enjoy the grandbabies. We went outside and shucked the corn together. We brushed off the silks and brought the cobs inside to cut off the kernels.

She pulled out the big breadboard she used for kneading bread. She whooshed the whetstone against her big kitchen knife to get a new keen edge. She picked up a corn ear from the bucket, angled it slightly and sliced a swath down that cob onto the bread board with the determination of an executioner cutting off a felon's head in medieval times.

Several times her knife viciously slashed to the board. I watched and then casually asked, "Do you want me to help?"

"No I do not!" she snapped. "You're on vacation and you shouldn't be working."

There I sat, mute and miserable. There she stood, mute, miserable and weeping as she martyred herself processing the corn for the canning jars, refusing help and hating her lot.

Incidentally, her canned corn was superb. I don't know what kind Daddy planted nor do I know what her method of canning was. What I do know is that, after canning, the corn appeared to be preserved in milk, and before being heated for eating, had to be drained and soaked in clear water for twenty minutes or it would be too salty to eat. Anyone with the recipe gets a free copy of this book. Boy, was that larrupin' good corn.

Garlic heads and onions were pulled, left in the rows for the sun to dry them a couple of days and then were tied with binder twine to hang on the porch till needed. Carrots were buried under layers of damp sand in big metal buckets to be unearthed – or unsanded, maybe – when we had creamed carrots and peas for a meal.

We always canned fruit but I don't remember Momma making jams or jellies, though Annie remembers her doing so. A quart of raspberries with cream made a fine dessert; a fruit cobbler was even better. Daddy grew Polly peaches, a variety with white flesh. They were smaller than the yellow ones but much sweeter and with a red blush on their cheeks that was an exquisite hue.

(When I was visiting in Belgium about ten years ago, one of the many experiences I enjoyed was tasting new foods. One morning a small plate of peaches appeared on the breakfast table. They were white ones from Spain. I burst into tears and my poor hostess didn't know what to do. I thought I'd never taste white peaches again, I explained; she had white peaches every day the rest of my stay, bless her.)

During the war years, when we lived in California, everyone had "victory gardens." Daddy planted along with everyone else but for us it wasn't a novelty. It was just what we'd always done, only we didn't have as much room for planting. The neighbors were impressed with his knowledge and asked much advice from him.

One year, word went out that the Del Monte orchards along the Sacramento River Valley were open to the public. The usual hired pickers were working in factories or were in the armed services. For a fee, we could pick peaches, apricots, black and Queen Anne cherries, and we did. Oh, boy. What good things we got to take home!

One of our neighbors had a car and enough gas rationing stamps to get us there and back. Then Momma and the neighbor lady pooled their sugar rations and, under Momma's guidance, together they canned that fabulous fruit. Oh, boy.

Imagine quarts of Queen Anne cherries (they're $5.99 a pound in the market this year) as a special treat. The peaches had to be cut in quarters to get them into the wide-mouth canning jars. When we moved back to Illinois later that year, the fruit was shipped cradled in towels, blankets and clothes to keep them safe. Not one jar got broken and Momma doled them out as celebratory Del Monte desserts that winter. She loved showing them off to all our Illinois friends and relatives, though when she did she always had to share.

After I had left home, other crops found their way into the garden, rhubarb, red all the way through, and blueberries as big as nickels come to mind. They came, though, after a freezer had been put in the basement. Freezing made life much easier for Momma, but the old ways of preparing and canning need to be remembered. We were blessed to have the space to grow and the hands to reap the harvest. ~Georgia

Grandpa. Grandpa Rawlings was a hard-working man who, though he scrambled for money, was enterprising in finding methods to find and stretch a dollar. He was born in November 1872 to Nathan and Martha (Cogdil) Rawlings and was one of seven children. He and Nannie had three boys, Daddy being the eldest, then Uncle Lynn, and finally, "Clarkie" who died of diphtheria at age six. Though Uncle Lynn was 6 foot, 5 inches, and Daddy was 6 foot 2½ inches, Grandpa wasn't much more than 5 foot 8 or 9 inches. He was slight of frame, and not as tall as Nannie when they were young, and shrank a great deal as he aged.

Grandpa could have invented the word "dour." Once, when someone caught him laughing in a snapshot, he became quite agitated that there was physical evidence of his having done so.

When he was young, he'd been employed as a tenant farmer. He was a trainman on a small interurban electric train line. He'd had a country general store and had been a mechanic and salesman after a Ford dealership came to town. By the time I remember him, he had become a house painter with a local man and, later, with his sons. He was even the janitor, for a while, at his church.

He had a huge garden. Their property was on a slope so there was a pretty grassy path down the center of the garden with rows of vegetables and berry bushes extending across the hill on each side of the path. Grandpa worked the soil with a hand-held wheeled plow, enhancing some of the crops with chicken manure from his hen house at the bottom of his hill.

Of course, onion sets were put out each spring. The easiest way this was accomplished was by crawling along the row on hands and knees. One spring he was doing that very thing. What he didn't realize was that his only grandchild was crawling behind him, industriously pulling up the carefully set bulbs. The dour characteristic of Grandpa was replaced by the VERY angry characteristic of Grandpa.

When I was a little girl there always was a supply of pink "peppermints" with four Xs stamped on them in the left pocket of Grandpa's jacket or sweater. He even smelled faintly of wintergreen. Whenever I smell that scent I think of him.

After The Fire we all lived in a little rental property Grandpa owned until their house was rebuilt on the same site. Grandpa was instrumental in Daddy buying a house diagonally across the street, thus ensuring a certain closeness, perhaps even a bondage, between himself and his older son.

This meant my mother lived nearly all her married life across the street from her in-laws. It also meant that the granddaughters had two homes, one as accessible as the other. Sometimes we got caught in the crossfire of in-law tensions. Other times we observed forgiveness being exhibited. We knew almost daily intergenerational give and take.

Someone was sick? Someone needed to be baby-sat? Plumbing needed repair? A basement needed to be dug? A tree of cherries needed to be pitted and frozen? A garage roof needed replacing? We always knew there were four adults who would fix things. They would take care of needs in ways that adults nowadays rarely can.

Grandpa always wore hi-tops. Not Adidas or Nikes – oh, no! He wore black leather high-top shoes all his life. When he got dressed for church he always wore a gray suit and in the winter he wore a U.S. Navy "pea-coat" for warmth, with his only shoes well polished and mended. He had a shoe last on his workbench, in order to repair soles and replace heels. Where did that skill come from, I wonder? He was always clean-shaven, using a razor strop to keep his old-fashioned razor in top condition.

I can still feel my hand holding his left index finger as we are walking to church on Sunday mornings. I don't remember where Nannie and my parents were since all of us usually were in church on Sundays. Maybe Grandpa and I were on our way to Sunday School.

Grandpa read the local papers but what he read the most was his Bible. Although not well educated he was sure of his authority when it came to biblical doctrine. No one laughed when he called "Stay-line" (Joseph Stalin) the anti-Christ. No one questioned his stating that his sister-in-law (Great Aunt Grace) probably was doomed to hell. Hebrew law stated in the Old Testament that a man must marry his brother's widow if there were  no issue. Either Aunt Grace or her husband, Uncle Arthur, had been widowed before they were married... thus, so Grandpa reasoned, there was the rationale for the damnation. This issue was endlessly debated as

Grandpa, Nannie, and Nannie's siblings and their spouses visited together after Sunday dinners.

I never heard Grandpa say he loved me, and Daddy claimed Grandpa never had said it to him. It was his dour way not to show affection but I know it was there in his heart. ~ Georgia

H

Helen King. One person who was important to me as a youngster was a friend of my mother's, Helen King. She was older than mom, but they were very close friends. Helen had a daughter a few years my senior whom I loved. We played for hours, inventing, exploring, writing letters, talking well into the night. She had a real playhouse in her back yard, almost too small for us to play in, but we managed until we could no longer get through the door without ducking.

Gloria had a big sister too. Her name was Ilavon spelled how I think. She was funny and quick witted. She would come home for visits from wherever with stories about roller-skating. I remember this was very important to her, skating; she carried her boots in a black leather case. She had detachable rollers of different kinds; she wore red pom poms on the toes of her boots. All very magical. She worked in a Catholic Hospital and a German nun called her skates, "boots mit rollers." She made it such a funny story we just howled.

There was a wasp nest in the chimney of their house of which I was terrified. Illy, as we called her, made up stories so plausible I forgot we might be invaded and stung to death momentarily (or so I thought). Illy had a daughter later in her life. She was called Becky, short for Rebecca Jane. She and Anne were playmates from their beginnings.

The Kings were big time farmers, well off for the times. I visited as often as I was asked and allowed. Helen called me "Softy." She would touch my face and call me pretty and her lovely Softy. I saw the shine of love from her eyes and felt it in her touch on my face. I stand aside and look at that little girl still able to feel her touch on that baby face. I could use some of that now, please.

They were all talkers and storytellers. The table was laden with fresh farm stuff – fried chicken the likes of which we don't taste anymore (I think she fried it in bacon grease – oh, boy was it good). Sliced tomatoes, peaches, mashed potatoes and gravy, corn on the cob, the table groaned with goodness. And this was lunch. All through the meal there would be stories about the day, stories about people, the past, plans for the day or the next day. Always there was conversation and exchange. There was lots of laughter.

Helen called Gloria and me God's wee ones – lots of strokes and pats and hugs just for being. I can't remember censure. There were things that were forbidden, though. The pump house was off limits as was the silo – though we did go once when the grain was very low. Gloria got an oat (I guess) in her ear and we were caught. Never again – too scary. The threat of drowning in oats wasn't very pleasant.

One time Gloria over-flowed the sink as we were washing dishes. Lots of water on the floor. I held my breath waiting – for whatever. Helen looked at the mess looked at Gloria and said "Well, we've got the water, when do we mop?". We all laughed harder than was warranted. Especially me for at my house lord knows what might have happened for that infraction. There wasn't much that was important enough to get upset about at Helen King's house.

We were allowed to go to the show when I visited. It was free and was shown on the side of a clapboard building in the little village where they lived. It was called Fancy Prairie; I think it had a population of 87 at the time. We sat on blankets and thought it was all pretty exciting to eat popcorn from a red and gold popcorn wagon while watching John Wayne with clapboard wrinkles on his gun These were idyllic times for a tall scrawny young and then not so young girl. One of the few places where I was just who I was and that was always enough. ~Sara

Home. It is winter, perhaps January. The last part of my afternoon walk from school to home is up a long, steep hill. The snow has been falling most of the day and the drifts are over my knees. Walking up the hill is a struggle for my ten-year-old self. I stop twice, panting, and near the top, feel overcome by fatigue, my knees shaking.

At the top of the hill, the first house is large, white, and ornate, to my eyes a mansion. It belongs to a friend of my family, a widower, a kind and brilliant man, and I have been in the house many times. Becky also lives in this house, as housekeeper/cook, but I have no concepts about hired help or servants – to me she is just Becky, a twittery, funny lady who is always glad to see me.

I struggle through the storm to the back door and knock. When Becky answers, I scarcely have time to give my rehearsed speech – "Please, may I come in for a minute and get warm?" – when she has pulled me in, whisked off my coat, boots, and other outer things, rubbed my hands, and deposited me in a chair by the stove with a warm drink, while twittering her concern. As I bask in the warmth, feeling safe, I hear her in the hall on the telephone, calling my mother, telling her that I'm safe and will be home soon. An aroma of Paradise fills the kitchen and I am wondering about it when Becky returns.

After more patting and chatting, she goes to the stove and removes from the oven an enormous baked ham – gleaming with glaze and studded with cloves. I mention shyly how good it smells, not expecting anything except a "thank you." Instead, there is instantly before me a plate with a slice of hot ham, pink and savory, a fork and napkin brought to the table, some milk or a glass of cider. In later years, I sat with Becky and wrote down her specific instructions on how to prepare a baked ham, and I have always followed her recipe to the letter. But the taste of that ham has never been duplicated.

When I arrive at my own house sometime later, my mother has hot chocolate waiting, with marshmallows – an unheard-of treat outside of the holidays, certainly not so close to dinner. But something has changed. Less than four blocks from Becky's kitchen to my own, yet my sense of the universe has expanded to include Becky and her kitchen, her caring, in my unconscious, evolving definition of Home.

Home: it is the place where baths are taken and hair is brushed, where laundry is done, meals prepared and eaten, prayers are said, beds are made and slept in and made again. Home is a place of murmuring voices, low laughter, and doors never locked at night. It is a symphony of smells – baking bread, soups or stews, frying chicken, peach cobbler, cherry pie, starch on ironed shirts, soap, and lemon oil.

Home has caves of secrets, closets and cupboards hoarding Sunday clothes and Sunday dishes, the good silver and linen. It is an attic full of old beds, old dolls, trunks full of old clothes and pictures, closets full of books, a musty smell of dust motes floating in thin sunlight.

Around the house stretch three acres, more or less. These, too, are home. Studded with great oaks and other trees, a fenced pasture, old sheds, sometimes spring lambs, it is a place where a child can ramble safely from corner to corner to corner, think private thoughts, learn to climb fences or trees, or just sit in a barn, with kittens.

Across the road live my father's parents – Nannie and Grandpa. Another home, another attic, cleaner and used for guests, but still full of treasure and mystery. Another kitchen with different smells, of spice cake or chicken with noodles, of sassafras tea or sorghum molasses. Outside, a huge old lilac holds a hidden room in its center, where I hide amid the fragrance of a thousand memories.

Below both properties, down a short hill, runs a railroad, across which runs the road via The Bridge. I can go *to* The Bridge, but not *on* The Bridge, and certainly not *across* The Bridge. No matter, these are home to me, seen through windows, approached with awe, train whistles punctuating the events of our day.

The roads to my school are home, the road to the Peterson farm, and the farm itself, are home – farm kittens and more smells of bread, and an old cabinet, glass fronted, filled with tiny crystal dishes, salt cellars and cups, twinkling in the sun for a child's enchantment.

Home was a big galvanized washtub filled with water from the hose to splash in on a hot July day. It was the melon man, driving up in his truck and cutting plugs in the watermelon for tasting before buying. Home was piles, hills, mountains of autumn leaves, raking for burning, but first for me to jump in, roll in, hide in, until my hair was tangled and I sneezed. The smell of burning leaves will always, always be home.

The county fair, in August, was most definitely home, with horse shows and a ferris wheel, with more friends visiting and eating and resting before the evening fair. It was my mother's peaches, perfect in their golden roundness, gleaming through the canning jar which wore its blue ribbon proudly before joining its lesser brethren in the cellar, stored against the winter. It was my mother  sewing, making pretty dresses, drapes and aprons, gowns and patched things, swearing at her nemesis, the cussed thing, her machine.

Home was when old friends came calling, turning my curls in their gentle hands. After the mid-day dinner, the murmur of voices sank into quiet when guests and my parents stretched out on beds and sofas for a Sunday nap. The house filled with a peace beyond silence, no dragons at the gate just now, the watchful guard could sleep.

Home was all these things, other things, other times, memories blessed or remembered wrongly or remembered not at all.

We carry it with us, of course, but home, and all it means, carries each of us through the days of our lives. ~Anne

House. Through this epic you read about our house. All of us have powerful and vivid memories connecting us to the physical structure of our house. I could never call 521 a home per se. To me a home is a place of warm fuzzies, hot chocolate with marshmallows, people and lots of laughter.

We did have popcorn, and though not often, there WAS hot chocolate with marshmallows, there was good food and sometimes there was a family thing and from time to time a streak of gaiety that left even my father giggling. What was missing for me was consistent human warmth; the connectedness of family taking pleasure in being and growing together was, to me, just not there. The house was my warmth, an entity almost, a living thing, something that shaped me.

I was born in the house I grew up in, left it when I was eighteen and returned to it in my forties to care for my dad till it wasn't feasible for the two of us to rattle around in the old barn.

Though we lived in town, our house sat on three acres of mostly pasture and garden. The house was enormous. Big rooms and lots of high ceilings. When dad bought the house it had been empty for many years.

I remember Momma's washing; it wasn't a happy day. We always had an electric agitator machine with a dangerous wringer, which I was taught to respect highly and at a very young age. The monster lived on our back porch before dad dug out the cellar. Two galvanized wash tubs hung on the porch wall as well as a copper boiler. (The tubs doubled as bath tubs – every Saturday night whether we needed it or not.) The copper boiler was filled with water, which was heated on the big black kitchen stove. Mom had to carry the water in smaller utensils to the washing machine, trip after trip. With each clean load we would go into the back yard and pin the clothes on the lines with wooden pins. I would pick up a piece of something clean, shake it out and hand it to her. We did the sheets together. Mom would take two corners and I would hold the rest in a bundle to keep it off the ground while she pinned her corners. Over and over trip after trip. Oh, momma, you had it so hard. She taught me how to sort and measure and rinse. How long to let clothes agitate, how to – carefully – feed things into the wringer.

When it was time to do the "sheers," curtains that were heavy cotton open work, mom made a huge vat of hot starch water. As each curtain became saturated with starch she would put it in a receptacle and take it to the back yard. We had a big curtain stretcher frame that could be configured into any size drape or curtain. Around the outside edge of the frame there were little tiny needle sharp tacks, nails, whatevers, that caught the material of the curtain and it was our job to get these fastened to the needly thingies without getting blood on the lace. We pulled and stretched and pricked our fingers until the fabric was in place and mom pronounced it good. The stretcher had legs that made it stand and mom would position it from time to time to follow the sun. I helped wash clothes as everything I did, as well as I possibly could. I believe now it was more for approval than because I really wanted to learn all that stuff. How glad I am that I did, though - learn all that stuff.

Although the big green monster moved to the basement one day where the water ran freely out of hose covered taps – one for hot one for cold - we never converted to automatic washing and drying. A succession of the monster's cousins came and went. Never another green one but each new one a bit fancier, a bit safer and a bit easier for mom to use - but never automated. While the method of cleaning clothes was truly hard, the sight of the laundry and especially the sheets, billowing in the wind, and the smell of the clothes after drying, remains a physical event - of burying our noses in a clean sheet as it was folded off the clothes line - that will be with me forever.

I remember the kitchen foremost – it really was big, bigger than some bedrooms. Heck bigger than the entire apartment where I now live. When dad bought the house for $1500 in 1931 with a loan from his aunt Bessie, he got a lot more (or maybe less) than he bargained for. There were few amenities in the kitchen. The sink was a big enamel number with only a big red pump (Georgia says it was black, wonder whose memory is real) that gurgled out wonderful cold water. On cold winter mornings one of the parents might have to prime this guy to get it awake- oh, the clunking and burping that came forth from the nether region when that happened. Then as the water began its rise to the morning, the sigh of gratitude that the pipes hadn't frozen in the night.

We had an old oak icebox that was fitted with brass hinges and got polished often in order not to ruin the finish from the wet. Our box was bigger than some as it had two doors. One side housed the huge ice block and the more fragile foods and the other was just for things that needed to be cool. A big square sign with 25 50 75 and 100 in big numbers on it was hung in our front window, rotating on ice day to indicate the pounds wanted for that week, the top number being mom's order. This allowed the iceman to drive right to the back of the house, grab a hunk of ice and bring it in. He had these huge ice tongs and he wore heavy gloves to protect his hands from the cold. He could swing a block of ice as if it were a cotton ball. This all went away when mom got her beautiful new refrigerator. In my antique travels I have never seen an ice sign, but boy oh boy are the iceboxes goin' for lots of money.

There was an enormous black stove that took coal and kindling and wadded up newspaper to get it going, coal bucket on the floor on the side of the stove at the ready. No pilot light for this fella. There were four "burners" which were not burners at all, rather flat round parts of the stovetop. They fit into the stove like big pot lids and were of different sizes. Mom had to lift these "lids" with a heavy wire handled lifter and poke around inside the stove in order to start and to keep the flame going while she cooked. As she needed to she added a coal lump. How the heck did she know how much and how often and what foods took what temperature. Mom ironed with huge heavy "flat irons" that were always on the back of the stove, ready to touch up a hem or collar. Why did they have to be so HEAVY? There was a reservoir for water (always tepid) affixed to one side of the stove. We used this water for dishes washing and face, neck and ear washing – other places too, I s'pose. Seems this water was rain water that dad caught in a barrel at the side of the house.

Over the top of the stove were warming ovens where mom kept plates to keep 'em warm. Nice warm plates to receive the scrambled eggs and wheat cakes fresh off the stovetop. She also would put the newly kneaded bread to rise in the warmth of these ovens. High puffy globs of shiny yeasty dough sending out vapors of the promise of new bread to come. No thermostat in the oven, mom cooked by instinct. Such very hard work.

There were long windows on the north side of the room. Our dining table sat between these windows and mom kept the salt pepper, sugar bowl and vitamins on the table. And usually a tiny vase of flowers. This table could be rolled into the middle of the floor, raise a spring leaf and voila seat six easy. Dad made the table for ease of moving. It was highly varnished and made of walnut. The casters were porcelain. They never squeaked. They rumbled, but they never squeaked.

Eventually the table went to the south wall. First came a cold-water tap then a hot water tap and finally dad built in a double steel sink and shortened the windows so mom could see out as she stood working in her kitchen. He bought a big Roper stove complete with thermostat and gleaming knobs. The new windows were very modern – wider than the old tall ones easier to make curtains for. So there went the pump. I've never had water like that since.

Mom would say something like: "I wish I had more counter space" so then came the cabinets. In the beginning of her housekeeping, Mom had a cabinet that had a roll up door with space for stuff behind it, like extracts, herbs, you know, cooking goodies. The cabinet part kept almost everything else. Just a few shelves on one side and on the other was a flour bin. There was an enamel surface that mom worked on when she cooked. Below were the pots and pans. That's it. So Dad constructed counters and drawers everywhere he could fit 'em in. There were cabinets from counter to ceiling. Drawers for everything, recipes, towels, odds and ends.

The old Hoosier cabinet went into the cold pantry after dad pulled out the mechanism for the retractable flour bin. He screwed it in place in mom's new cupboard. So now she had bright new cupboards with lots of counter space. Enough to leave things out of the cupboards if she wanted to and flour near her kneading board. What a life!

Then one day dad came home with a load of expensive linoleum scraps. The best in the land, but for which he paid little or nothing as they were all mixed colors and not useable ha ha. Well mom and dad put their heads together and designed the most beautiful floor including a really BIG yellow gold five-pointed star for the center of the floor. They cut and pasted colored construction paper pieces together in every conceivable pattern until it was as they wanted it. He cemented it into place so solidly and securely that the floor stayed in place till the house was sold in 1980 something. Can you imagine?

Then another day momma said she sure wished she could see through the big old oak door that connected the kitchen to the porch so she could see who was at the door and just yell come in to whoever it was instead of having to stop doing what she was doing to go <u>see</u> who it was. This was a hard oak paneled door not a hollow core of today. It must have weighed about a million pounds and was hinged with heavy brass cotter pins. Dad lifted it off its hinges, took it to the basement and, well, one day very soon after mom's wish she had her window. Dad had carved out the top, put in a glass and zip she had a door with a window so she could see clear to the outside stoop and didn't have to stop work – take her hand out of the dough, dry her hands, fluff her hair, whatever. She could see a friend and just call out "come on in" or call dad to see to a furniture customer.

In our basement there were many rooms eventually, but our basement/cellar had to have been very small originally holding only a big old furnace and a coal bin. Bit by bit it was dug out to accommodate mom's canning jars and the canned produce, a washing machine, things not in use. Dad needed running water in order to clean the gunk from the furniture skeletons he worked on so he rigged up a room to the south of the main basement. He moved mom's machine down stairs where she had free range cold and hot water. No more traipsing back and forth with hot water, waiting for it to heat. Oh joy. Also in that room in the corner was a showerhead. Not a stall, a head. Dad rigged up two pipes for water and affixed a huge plate sized showerhead onto the terminal. There were two commercial steel taps and dad marked the hot water tap in red enamel paint H so we knew what was what. There was an old chair with no back covered with old towels to sit on to dry if you waited around down there long enough to do that. It was an adventure to take a shower in our basement. One took bathrobe, towel, washcloth and courage to the basement, especially at night – the courage part. The dimly lit basement could help to conjure up all manner of things that might go bump in the night.

There were spiders and their webs, other basement crawlies and if we were really lucky a wee field mouse would be having a nap in the warmth of a washtub and jump up in a flurry of whiskers and tail as we shrieked bloody murder. Ah, wee sleakit beastie with a panic in thy breastie.

On the shelves of this room were canning jars of every shape and size some clean and ready to fill others groaning with the goodies dad cultivated for canning and stocking up for the cold. Momma may not have been enthusiastic about the work in all this canning and preserving but she never complained. Much. There were peaches, cherries, tomatoes and their juice and green beans, lots and lots of green beans.

We were blessed, but it was just the way we lived. I took all this so for granted, just knew there would always be green beans to eat. There may still be beans in that basement.

Some years later the old coal furnace went and the 20th century arrived with the event of the new furnace complete with thermostat. One more glorious day in an easier life for mom.

In the west end of the long room that was dad's shop he kept his extras. Clean rags for rubbing down finished work, dabs of paint for matching things, various grades of steel wool and sand paper. He always kept a huge carton of Gold something or other - soap. It was so strong he could use it as stripper for cleaning the wood he was working on. On the front of the box were the figures of two little —oh! I just remembered — the Gold Dust Twins! There were wee boxes in the carton. The boxes were bright orangey gold in color with figures of two little black kids on the front. By the time I came home to care for dad these boxes and their artwork were politically very incorrect. I took the boxes to various antique/flea markets and made a bundle - highly collectible memorabilia.

In the center of the room was dad's workbench, it had one leg and was set, braced against the short north wall under the windows near the best light. He kept nuts, screws and various other tiny bits of his trade in small clear glass jars that snapped into metal brackets. They hung in one of the windows, close to his hand. He could reach up and put his hand on the jar he wanted without looking. These wee jars may have been a spice rack in another life. Alongside this rack hung his hammers, drawknives, screwdrivers, wrenches, pliers – every conceivable tool and every size and shape. All lined up in graduated order. He had wooden blocks covered with of various strengths of sandpaper upright in a row leaning against the cement wall next to his bench. Over his head were small wads of steel wool tucked in crevices were he could just reach up to grab a wad as he needed it. He kept nails, brads, and washers of every size in tiny tin cans above his bench. He had rolls of gimp and beautiful gimp tacks at the ready in a drawer under his bench. He kept old nails that he drew out of pieces of ancient wood. He would use all these things to create new and restore old. He stood his brushes upright in coffee cans. After each use he would soak the brushes till every trace of paint or varnish was eliminated then he would spin them in his hands to dry the bristles. When they suited him he carefully wrapped them in newspaper and tied the bristles and placed it bristles up in its can. Dad was like this about everything in his basement. He could reach in his sleep and find the exact tool he needed for any job. Nothing higgledy-piggledy in my dad's basement.

Dad made his lathe from an old 2-horse power motor and a sewing machine head. The motor sat at one end of a long two-beamed open workspace. The sewing machine wheel started the motor when dad pulled a yardstick that hung across one of the beams about waist high. Gosh, I can see this so clearly. What I can't see is what the other end was. There was something attached else how could it have turned out such beautiful wooden art?

Even as the income grew and he was able to afford additions like a plane saw, a big table saw, and a joiner, his old lathe stayed. He had an ancient jigsaw from which came lovely intricate lacey shelves and what-nots. These were for family mostly. One in particular I remember he made for mom to hang over our big table for the Seth Thomas clock to sit on. It lives in my sister's hallway today. It sits under a mirror to receive the mail.

Dad had an old potbellied stove that went most of the time. He kept it going to keep his gluepot at the ready. He made the glue himself, meas-uring, stirring, smelling as it cooked. It smelled pretty bad, but I think he knew it was ready when the smell reached a certain crescendo. He learned early that some folks would claim his work was older than what was true so he designed a sticker to put on the underside of his work, his name and the date of repair. He glued on the sticker and covered the sticker with his glue. The sticker could not be removed. Makes it really nice today, as we have found in antique shops a few pieces he worked on.

In the last room that was dug out of the cellar, dad kept wood to be worked into tabletops and legs for chairs and plant stands. Also in that room was furniture he had finished and was waiting to be picked up. Bits and pieces of furniture in various states of disrepair were in this room as well, just waiting for dad's magic.

We had a privy until sometime in the forties – we can't decide on the date – when dad turned the cold pantry into a really spiffy bathroom. This pantry was a long narrow room that had held foods and odds and ends. Seasonal pans like the turkey roaster and the big canning pans. So the old

Hoosier cabinet became a catchall. I can remember one Christmas mom making a fruitcake, which everyone hated – but me. She stored it in the old steamer that lived on top of the cabinet. I would climb up on the shell of the cabinet, lift the lid to pinch off just a bite. I remember the ping of the aluminum lid hitting the side of the pan and fearing someone would hear me. I would quickly put my hand against the lid to stop the ringing. Silly me - they were glad I was eating that cake! I can still see me climbing up to reach that goody whenever I hear the ring of aluminum on aluminum.

Anyway the new bathroom. The tub was extra long with the taps in a funny wrong ended housing on which rested the lavatory basin. The other side of the basin rested on two long metal legs. Dad cut a window into the north wall and mom kept the window beautiful with homemade curtains. In one corner of this really tiny room dad installed a remarkable towel/medicine cupboard. He could reach into that cabinet in the dark and find his towel, aspirin. whatever. Such a luxury to "go" in the house on a toilet that flushed.

During dad's last years I was his caregiver and we lived off the "stuff" in the house. Our upstairs rooms were never lived in – no heat and unnecessary as there were four bedrooms on the first floor. There were two really large rooms upstairs, a wide hall and three closets – all to the brim with stuff. The attic, as these upstairs rooms were called, was the catchall for everything. Being of the depression era the folks found it hard to throw anything away.

One closet was full of books of every subject. Some of the books were left over from the folks who lived in the house before we did. Gosh, I'd like to be upstairs to look at those books today! There was Depression glass, rag scraps, dad's old ledgers, furniture bits, trunks, treasures without names. I remember bringing down a twig table some hobo had made and presented to mom for food. Dad said to me "What do you think you are gonna do with that?" Well, I took it to a flea market and sold it for $125.00. Ever hear of tramp art? Dad was in awe.

All us kids had many adventures in our attic. Make believe and dress up. Reading the old dusty books. Getting out of mom's way for an adventure "upstairs" was a favorite pastime (for her and us). Georgia has made quilts from scraps found in big cloth bags in that attic. It was really pretty empty of amenities in our attic, but it was full of wondrous adventure.

There were 30 years of Life and National Geographic and Readers Digest in our attic. I had movie mags to read in the quiet there. Glenn

Ford was my heartthrob. Dad would buy a case of Sweetheart soap, unwrap it all and put it in the attic to dry as he said. There was always the smell of soap in the rooms. Dad kept his old ledgers and paid bills in boxes and on pegs in the hall wall. I went to the absolute end of the attic rafters one day before we moved and found Civil War papers awarding some widow her pension for the loss of her husband in the war. Sold 'em to the state history museum. Wish I hadn't.

I can remember, and I may have told this story elsewhere, fiddling with an old gas fixture, which was affixed to the wall in our dining room. I asked dad what the hiss was when I turned the little knob. What it was, was GAS. He went through the house and dismantled all the jets with their hissing reservoir of gas – keeping the brackets and the glass etched shades – for another coup at a flea market years later.

There was a large, intricate grill in the center of our living room. This was to accommodate the warm air coming up from the coal furnace in our basement. We heated ourselves, dried our undies, and stood over it for comfort when we were under the weather. Dad rigged two pulleys that ran down the wall to the furnace, which could raise and lower the damper on the big old furnace without having to go to the basement to do that job. That grill went too in the later days.

There was beautiful wood wainscoting around the dining room with a lip of chair rail that NOW I realize was very special. I don't know the wood, but dad did a faux finish on it that could have been anything – oak, walnut – something really exotic. Later he painted it all white – sinful man. The windows in that room looked out into our back yard where from time to time we stood – watching seasons change, storms, snow or rain, squirrels, birds. In winter dad put out suet, corn, seeds of all kinds for the birds. The squirrels got field corn stuck upright on nails in the pasture fence posts. (sposed to keep them from the bird feeders – fat chance.) There was always a pair of cardinals. Year round, but in the winter with the red against the snow, they were beautiful to behold.

The windows in our sitting room faced east and they were very tall windows. Momma grew violets in those windows. And a hoya vine that almost overtook the room and which never bloomed after she died. Mom's friends came after she died, dad having asked if there was anything they might want of mom's. Many of her friends took violets.

Mom also had bits of colored glass on narrow glass shelves that hung in the long east windows. She collected glass slippers and there were many of different colors. She would fill an interesting bottle with colored water and set it in the window. On sunny days the colors would dance off the wall making watery rainbows appear. She made drapes of sheets and valances of a color or design to match. We could have instant change in our drapes as we pleased.

There was a rather modern chandelier in that room – modern as opposed to the antique one in the connecting room, which was through the square arch of the two great rooms on the front of our house. Often folks would not pick up a piece of furniture that dad had repaired and it would find its way upstairs. Mostly antiques – dressers, small tables. There were "Gone With the Wind" lamps in the sitting room. In the dining room was an enormous cranberry swirl globe over the light fixture. It emitted a lovely rosy glow and bathed the room with beautiful warmth until one day someone offered dad some really big money and that was the end of that glow.

Am I still talking about a house here? Yes about <u>MY house</u>. I have this slide show in my head and I can see the beautiful furniture, the odds and ends that we lived with that were really valuable and very much a part of how we grew up. To revere our things, to be careful of wood and to polish and clean so things would last. I can see myself curled up in bed with a Nancy Drew mystery, snuggled down in comfort as a storm raged around outside the long windows. I can smell the smells of mom's washing, fresh off the line, her cooking, canning – the heat of the kitchen in summer when she hung a heavy old army blanket in the kitchen doorway in order to keep out the heat from the rest of the house. I can hear crickets and "katydids," dad's saw rumbling in the basement, the rattle of mom's sewing machine. I can see the finished garments she made hanging and ready to wear on the occasion they were made to celebrate. So many images that flit around in my projector brain – these things that made up the memories of our house. These are really good things. And as I read and reread all these things about my HOUSE, I realize this was in the truest sense a home. We may not have used words to communicate, dad may have been a very hard person, but our home was stable, we were rich in the teachings by example of our parents. The lessons we were taught without lecture or fanfare have shaped us all in ways that I was not even aware of until I began to write. Such a fantastic revelation and how skewed our memories are. I may not have received the cuddly love I needed, wanted, but these memories are very warm and fuzzy so – I don't have any more words for this house thing. ~Sara

I

Imagination. Without it I would have died or gone really crazy. I was called odd, eccentric, strange and on a good day just different.

When I was ill as a child I imagined things and people in the folds of the bedding. Houses, churches and whole villages with loving families in them. I made drawings of things that didn't exist, talked to myself, to the radio and to things that didn't exist.

The rainbows created by the prisms momma hung in windows became a sure way to the pot of gold. Each time I moved the bedding the pot got closer or more far away, depending on my mood. Sometimes the prism lights were Christmas lights in the villages and would wink off and on as I moved the bedding. The colors of the prisms were magic for me, undulating across the bedding and up the walls. Never an end to what a sick kid could imagine.

I could see people and things in the knotty pine (still do), in the clouds (still do) and could entertain (I guess) my grandmother for hours with stories about things that never happened. When I was older and from time to time, late home from school, I made up the most fascinating stories about why. One being a man in a black cape and peaked hat stopped me to tell me that my folks didn't want me, didn't like me – big lie (at least the part about the man and the hat) but I was young and conjured up stuff to deflect the wrath of my folks for breaking the rules.

Our town was built on several hills, ours was called Irish Hill for whatever reason and I named myself queen of Irish hill for whatever reason – embarrassing my folks into the ground, you bet.

In our attic there was written the name of some girl. I made up story after story and told folks about the girl held prisoner in our attic long ago. Probably left to die and her bones would be found in the rafters of our attic if only dad would look.

I dismantled dolls that rattled, clocks that stopped ticking. I never could get things back as they were but I tried to find the answer to why. In my imagination it was always some exotic reason.

Of course this behavior was pretty scary to the elders (except my grandmother) – lies all, doncha know. And destructive – terrible child what are we to do? Well, when I was a senior in high school, I fooled 'em all by entering a literary contest, which required me to write an original monologue. I did and it was about people and things that never happened and – yep, I won that contest all the way to the finals.

Momma must have had imagination as well, as she lived with my father in an atmosphere that could not have been nice for her. She surely had a way with the sewing machine, making dresses from matching prints for George and me. Making skirts I designed and drew and she whipped up seemingly with no effort. She did ruching, tiny tucks, and covered buttons – where did all that come from? I remember one coat I loved so much I ate it. Long after it fit me no more I wore it still. I discovered the collar point and gnawed it to the nub. Mom took it away from me.

My mom was Martha Stewart before Martha was. She made soap poured into wooden frames. She made rolled bees' wax candles for our holiday tables. Tiny Christmas trees and strings of new ornaments made from old "stuff." I still have three tiny bells strung on rickrack my mom made. Dad had no fetters on his imagination either as he used every method known and then some to keep us "off the dole" – various adventures in farming and animal keeping – turning a nickel into a quarter. Oh, yes, as you read through these pages none of us lacked imagination. Just imagine all these diverse folk – mom from California, dad's folks so very bright and clever, with less than grade school educations, dad and his ability that seemed just to be – just imagine – it takes some doing ~Sara

Ivy. Our dining room was in the center of the house. It was a dining room only on special occasions – holidays and the rare actual birthday party or other celebration.

The rest of the time, it was where we lived – what might be called a family room today. It was good sized, at least 16 by 20, with a linoleum floor covered here and there with rugs braided by hand by our uncle Lynn. The register above the coal furnace took up a large amount of floor space, a black heavy metal square grill about four feet on each side, with a central circle through which the hot air rushed. We would stand on that circle in winter after our baths, the warm air rushing over our damp bodies, until we were warm enough to enter the cooler bedrooms for  dressing. Secured by heavy wire, a bucket hung below that circle, into which we poured water every day to add humidity. In the summer the register was covered by a rug, usually braided, and sometimes beautiful.

There were two cupboards in this room – an antique walnut pie cupboard that held mostly linens and the silver chest, and a very tall, massive corner cupboard of cherry in which were kept all the 'good' dishes, china, crystal, and other precious things. An old daybed used to be against one wall, but was later replaced with a regular sofa. The telephone was in this room, near the wall next to the kitchen door, with a rocking chair beside it. The wide gate-legged cherry table that my father made stood beneath the tall windows and opened to seat ten, or more if we squeezed.

The room had white wainscoting up to a chair rail, and above that was wallpaper, and the wallpaper was always ivy. The room must have been repapered eight times or more in the decades we lived there, and the specific design might vary, but Mother always had her ivy wallpaper in the dining room. Sometimes it was small dark leaves with tiny red berries, other times there might be large and small leaves of different tones of green. There were rolls of leftover wallpaper up in the attic and we could trace the history of the room by looking at the old patterns, green against white, sometimes with a coordinating border that ran along the top of the walls.

Later on, Mom got a set of china, just a casual luncheon set for four or six, but the white plates had green ivy leaves on them, and I could see how they pleased her every time she looked at them.

I can never see ivy now without thinking of the dining room, and Mother. We use ivy for decorating at Christmas – the holly and the ivy – with leaves curved around candlesticks or trailing through a centerpiece. I have ivy plants in my house, two or three different kinds, that sit on the piano or the mantle and when I set the table, the plates are ivy plates – white with leaves of green, twining through my memories.~ Anne

J

Jeans. One cannot begin to imagine the amazement and delight a young gangly pre-teen can experience when serendipity crosses her path: The quickening of the pulse, the flushing of pleasure. I must have been 13 when, after watching me in his dry goods store idly flipping through racks of way too short slacks with a look of longing on my face, Mr. Robbins said to me, "Sara, have you ever tried on our work jeans? Lots of women wear them on the farm to work in. They come in all sizes to match your middle and your height. Why don't you ask your dad can you try a pair?" Well, right then and there I tried a pair. The waist was too big, but the legs were long enough. I could even turn them up a couple times! Oh joy, no high waters. The next hurdle was to convince my folks, blue jeans (as they were called "back then") were the answer to my long unfitable legs. As I walked home, I rehearsed many a dialogue to present to my family. Mom could be freed up to sew other, more glamorous garments, they would last a long time, the jeans. I could set a trend (that one I quickly abolished as surely we weren't gonna spend money on trends, for heavens sake.) I met very little resistance, amazingly, and they bought me two pair on sale. Thus began my freedom from the tyranny of legs that were too long on a girl that was so young.

I did set a trend and soon all my "set" was wearing turned up blue jeans everywhere except to school. We were not EVER allowed to wear slacks of any kind to school. Except once I did when I had a really bad ankle sprain and needed to elevate my foot. That was high school and I was sent home to change, but that's another story. One not really about blue jeans. ~Sara

K

Knives. We could have done other "K" words – knowledge, kindness – but those concepts are covered elsewhere, and Knives is (are) unique.

From the time I can remember (probably for many years before I was born even), my mother's favorite piece of equipment was what we called the "butcher knife," a long, heavy, deadly looking tool, not as wide as to-day's chef's knives, used for the big cutting jobs of chopping up a chicken or cutting corn from the cob. Dad sharpened this knife periodically, and over the years, it began to shrink. By the time I left home, the blade was only five or so inches long, if that, but still useful and still very, very sharp

That's how all tools were kept around the place – clean, oiled, sharpened, ready for service, and in their proper place. There were no muddy or dirty garden or farm tools hiding in garage or barn – they too, were kept in fine form.

Mother's sewing scissors, specialized kinds of knives, all were preserved in their original boxes when not in use. God help you if you were caught cutting paper with any of her sewing shears as nothing dulls an edge quicker than paper, I was told repeatedly. Mom's Wiss pinking shears, those scissors with the zigzag edges used for finishing inside seams, were sent off every year or three to be professionally sharpened. As I child, I thought these were simply called wiss-pinking-shears, as mother always referred to them. I think I tried cutting my hair with them once, with blessedly forgotten results.

The real knife story, though, has to do with what happened two weeks before Georgia's wedding. It was to be an early June wedding, and I was five years and two months old. I was playing with my pal, Butchie Halper, who lived across the street from us. He had a grand sandbox by his back door and we were digging away in the sand under the warm sun. At some point, he fetched from the house two table knives, not sharp ones, just the butter-your-bread kind. I don't know if his mother knew, but at any rate, we dug away quite happily in the sand. After a while, Butchie said, "Come in the front yard – and bring your knife."

Now I know I was only five, but I remember this day as though it were last week. He went 'round the house to the front yard, I trotted dutifully behind – knowing full well exactly what he was planning to do. There were two trees in the front yard, about 30 feet apart, and he planned to stand by one tree and throw his knife at the other tree to see if it would stick in it, like the knife people do at the circus. *I knew this.* I knew this as certainly as if he'd told me (which he did not).

And what did brilliant little me do? As he positioned himself by tree A, I positioned myself just as carefully by tree B – right in front of it, facing tree A full on. What was I thinking? What was Butchie thinking? Do kids think? Obviously not.

Well, he threw the knife. What a throw! It landed point first right below the bridge of my nose, about half an inch from my left eye – and stuck there, quivering. I forgot who pulled it out – I think I did, but it was stuck and it <u>hurt!</u>

Oh, the screaming! Oh, the blood! I had on a green sunsuit with white dots - with the red blood streaming down its front, it was quite Christmas-like. Poor Butchie was yelling louder than I was. His mother, my mother ... good Lord. I did scream that Butchie was not to be punished, that it was my fault, too, but I'll bet he got it good that night, poor guy. So there I was with a blip on my nose, like a small raspberry stain, at Sissy's wedding - the little flower girl in her yellow dress and curls. And in every picture, my little gloved hand is held daintily up to my nose so no one can see the mark. Silly us. Very lucky little girl. ~Anne

L.

Love. This piece falls almost in the middle of our dictionary, but it is among the last to be written.

It is last because only now, looking back over the memories we have brought forth, do we understand that this is a love story. So we suggest that you skip this for now, and read the rest, and then come back and read this one, as it was written.

But I'll bet you won't.

Love is a peculiar word and an even more peculiar concept. In four letters, love is meant to encompass the strong, often overwhelming feelings we all have – for our parents, our siblings, our friends, our lovers and spouses, our children, our country. We use it for our feelings for ice cream or pizza, for a sports team or a flower, a color, a movie, an actor, a pet.

The Greeks got it a little more right, differentiating as they did among philia, eros, agape. There are adjectives that can be helpful – maternal or paternal love, that mixture of ferocity, tenderness, laughter, tears, anger, frustration, and pure joy over those small humans produced from our loins. I know of no specific name for the love we bear our parents, or those who stood as parents to us. One speaks of filial "obedience" – the duty of a child toward her parents, a mingling of respect and obligation – but in our modern minds (unlike the thinking of the Middle Ages and further back), duty and love seem unable to coexist happily. One forgets, or never knew, that mingling of duty and love, each enhancing the other, felt by a knight toward his lord or his lady fair. Honor comes in there somewhere, another concept ripe for rebirth.

In the Rawlings family, love was there – hovering. Sometimes it got shut in the closet, or put in the attic with out of date clothes for a time, and forgotten. We find now that we always knew it was there. It had gotten misplaced, or hidden behind some old pictures or books, somebody forgot to bring it out, tack it up, and dust it off. But it was there. It was rolled up in the leftover wallpaper, and in the back of the closet underneath the sheets smelling fresh from the summer air. It was in almost every jar of canned green beans or peaches, and certainly pieces of it got sewn into our jumpers and coats. Love flavored the bowls of popcorn and oiled the wheels of skates and scooters.

I suspect it hid under the bed when sarcastic words were spoken or when hurt or shame or fear were felt so strongly. Maybe then it took a little trip, to the next county or the next state, for a day or a week, for a month or a year. It always came back. It stuck to the shoe like bubble gum sometimes, or got into the making of a bowl or a table along with the stain and the varnish. Certainly it was in every load of coal that kept us warm and in tubs of water that kept us cool in the summer.

Love grew outside with the corn and the roses. The wrens and the sheep knew it was there all along. Love stretched its thin elastic line from our house across the road to Nannie's and Grandpa's, and even further down the road to the Peterson's, and miles out into the country, to Helen King's.

Every kind of love was in our family – the love of community and neighbor, the charitable agape that would not let a family go hungry or cold if we could help; by extension, the love of country and the fears brought by the war years, the willingness to live with the deprivations, the participation in seeing that the blackouts were observed. We saw the love that is filial "obedience" – a two-way street with our parents and grandparents working together to support each other in the endless work. We saw maternal love, with our mother caring for her babies and the babies of neighbors and friends.

Much to our shock, though, what our memories and stories have exposed for the first time is the love story of Elizabeth and Emery. Two passionate, wounded, beautiful people, drawn together from wildly different cultures and experiences, yet able to forge common bonds stronger than anything they could have found alone.

A memory: one day when I was twelve or so. Mother was in the kitchen, Dad was in the basement shop, I was in my room. I heard nothing – until mother gasped, dropped her pan or broom or whatever she had and ran for the basement. Up the stairs came Dad, then Mother running for rags, ice. I saw blood everywhere, Dad sitting on the steps, mother beside him, Dad's hand in a bowl of ice. He had, on one of the electric saws, cut off just the tip – the very tip, about a third of an inch – of his left index finger. Oh, how it bled! Oh, how it must have hurt! But all I could see was Mama, her face drawn as though she felt the pain herself, and Dad, near fainting, leaning on her shoulder.

They bandaged it and mopped up the blood and the finger healed and life went on. I said to Mama later "How did you know what happened? I didn't hear anything – he didn't scream or yell." And she said, "I heard him swear under his breath. Nothing would make him take God's name in vain unless he was really hurt. And he prayed for forgiveness later. Poor Daddy." She had heard him. Her ear must have been constantly tuned to her husband as he worked among his dangerous tools in the basement.

This is one, only one, of the thousands of events and scenes we still see in our minds. Some of them are in this book. Many of them are only in our hearts. Most of them are only between Emery and Elizabeth, lovers until her death, drawn to each other, not as moths to flames, but as flame to flame, each burning brightly for the other, each feeling quenched and dimmed without the other. How could we not have seen it? And yet it was there, always there, and grew richer and deeper with the years. This is their love story, but only the smallest part. It is, I'm sure, still going on.
~Anne

ᛉ

Mama. Yes, we all spell "Mama" differently. And yes, we all think of her differently as well. This work, as I read over what has been written, is dominated by our father. In part, he dominated us because Mama permitted him to do so. If she had once put her foot down – no, that's not right. She often put her foot down; if she had *kept* it down, had kept after Dad to alter his behavior, his perceptions, his beliefs, if she had nurtured his sweet side, his good side, life would have been much, much different.

Because Dad would have followed her lead. Because he adored her, and because he wanted to be "better." If ever a human being existed who was frustrated by his own inadequacies, it was Dad. And he was eager to change. He adopted habits that were alien to his upbringing and his experience, such as using napkins at dinner, having "company" china and silver, holding doors and chairs for women, taking his hat off indoors. And he took pride in his Elizabeth and what she brought to his life.

But this is about Mama, not Dad, about whom much is said elsewhere.

My mother told me, when I was old enough (or young enough) not to be too appalled, that I was almost aborted. She was 36 when she became pregnant with me, and her doctor recommended an abortion because of "female troubles." (Not too long after my birth, she had a hysterectomy.) What was needed was another doctor's signature. Mama's doctor gave her the name of another doctor who would sign the papers (in August of 1942). Mama dutifully called the second doctor's office and was informed that Dr. X had just enlisted in the Army. "A sign!" she exclaimed. "This child will be born." And so I was.

I was supposed to be a boy, after two girls, and my name was to be John Ross Rawlings. The fact that I was a girl delayed my naming and I was nameless for about 48 hours after my birth. Despite that disappointment, it was apparent that I was a cherished, adored, unexpected, late-life baby to both my parents.

Mama loved to tell me stories of my babyhood. I was born a chubby, 9-pound plus child with a mop of bright red hair (no reasonable explanation for that has ever come forth). Almost from birth, she would place me, totally naked, in a window where the sun shone (in California, this was most of the time). So from a few months old, I was a red-haired, tan, fat baby. (I blame her for thus using up all of my natural pigmentation, since all I get now are freckles.)

There must have been a remaining streak of Victorianism in our family, since they seemed enamored of pictures of naked babies. Even more shocking, the local paper published a picture of me at six weeks old, full frontal nudity, spread legs, sleepy eyes, and all, announcing the glory of a new child on earth. While it was a much-needed relief, no doubt, from the screaming war headlines that had begun three months before, it is difficult to imagine such a picture being published in today's culture.

In a trunk in the attic of our house were beautiful old things – some of Mother's 1920's dresses, an old blue velvet, floor length gown trimmed in gold, and a billowy, pale blue silk baby dress. I wore that blue dress when I was not quite two and broke my collarbone by falling down the back porch steps. So I had a little sling, and that blue silk dress. Imagine dressing a baby in silk! And we were – not poor, but not silk-dress class, either. Such a reward for a broken bone.

Mother loved babies, and occasionally supplemented the family income by child minding. A local doctor's wife became ill after her third child was born, so we kept little Helen with us for a few days at a time, off and on over a couple of her toddler years. I called Helen "Little Bubbles" because she loved the bubbles we put in her bath (in the kitchen sink). She was the one who christened Mama and Daddy with the names they were called by all the grandchildren – Mama-Bet and Uppy-Dad.

The Mama-Bet part happened this way. Helen started to call Mama "Mama." Not wanting that, Mama (being Elizabeth) trained her to say "Mom-Betty," but that evolved to Mama-Bet. Perfectly logical.

The Uppy-Dad part was a little more involved. When Dad came in from work in the evening, he would swing little Helen up and sit her on top of the tall refrigerator. From there, she learned to leap into his arms with a shriek and a laugh and a call for more. And the call was, "Uppy, Dad!" Well, I know this is about Mama, but I had to explain Uppy-Dad, didn't I? And if that doesn't sound like the Dad described elsewhere in this book, remember, I softened him up with my adorable self, and then, Helen was the most beautiful baby imaginable – the Gerber baby personified, with a blond cap of hair, round dimpled face, and enormous blue eyes. A bubbly cherub.

Mama was quite the girl in her day, from the stories she told. With three brothers and three sisters, life was busy, giddy, and social as she grew up. There are pictures from a desert camp-out, with twelve or fifteen young people, her brothers and various friends, all riding out into the desert, lighting campfires, sleeping overnight. Having older brothers to chaperone her gave her enviable freedom and when the household chores were done (or sometimes when they weren't), the "gang" would go off in a pack to entertain themselves.

She loved to dance and regretted that Dad was not a dancer. She could dance the Charleston like a champ, of course, and tried to teach me but I always had two left feet or more. She prided herself on being "double-jointed" and would occasionally sit on the floor and put her ankle behind her head (and if I remember this clearly, she had to be 45 at least). But her favorite "thing" was to kick the top of the kitchen doorway, like a chorus girl. I don't know how often she did this in private, but she certainly did it every morning before preparing a holiday meal. So one Thanksgiving, about 5 in the morning (when the turkey had to be prepared and put in the oven), she kicked the top of the doorway, slid on the floor, and fell on her tailbone. She had forgotten that the floor had been very freshly, heavily waxed the day before, in preparation for company. She was 52 and felt old for the first time in her life, she told me.

Mama loved to fix things, electrical things, dangerous things. She re-wired lamps and light switches, fixed irons and toasters, and would have fiddled with car engines if we had had a car.

Well, we eventually got a car. I was ten or so, so it was 1953, and Dad got an old maroon coupe of some kind, probably early 1940's vintage. It got us to Chicago and back several times, often in ice storms, to visit Georgia and Sara. Then he traded that for a 1948 black sedan (Ford, Chevrolet?), from which he could remove the back seat and thus carry his ladders from paint job to paint job. But it was also the family car. And then, around 1955, he surprised Mother with a 1952 Chevy, red and white, clean as a whistle, cute as a bug's ear, for her very own. Mother cried and laughed and cried and laughed until she wet herself. She loved that car (but I learned to drive, somewhat, on the old black sedan, gearshift on the floor, mother braking in the passenger seat every three yards – an adventure).

When I was thirteen, I was staying with the King family out in the country, the annual summer visit with my friend Becky and her grandparents. It was usually a visit of three or four weeks, but the day Mother was due to come pick me up, Helen King told me that I would be staying an extra day or two, making up some excuse to which I paid no attention. The next day, she told me that Mama had been in an accident ("Now, don't cry." I cried.) Then we went to the hospital to see Mama ("Now when you go in her room, don't cry." I cried.) There was my poor, invincible, indestructible mother, laid up in a white hospital bed, all bruises and stitches and stiff and bandaged. Oh, I cried. It was a terrible accident, and they didn't find out until a week or two later that her jaw was broken – so it had to be rebroken and set, and wired shut with those silver wires, like braces, only worse. Six weeks with only liquid food – two or three times she choked when swallowing, and I thought she was going to die, trapped behind those wicked braces, choking, not able to open her mouth and breathe. To this day I swear I'll never get my jaws wired shut, no matter what.

Now the reason she had the accident on the way to the King farm was this: Mother did not like cats. She had a phobia about them, like some people have about snakes or spiders. (Incidentally, she had no problems with picking up snakes with her bare hands, which I saw her do several times.) But touching cats, or thinking about touching them, gave her the cold willies. This is why we had no cats in the house (except once in a while, when I was sick and a kitten was brought in for an hour or two).

During that particular summer, Dad had made the tough decision that he could no longer tolerate the black tomcat, barn resident, who had the interesting habit of dragging eggs out of the hen's nests onto the floor, then lapping up the delicious mess. So his solution was to box up the cat, put the box in the back of the car, and have Mama dump the cat somewhere out in the country on the way to pick me up.

Well, this was not a swift idea. A half-wild tomcat in a box, clawing to get out and wailing, Mama driving but significantly distracted by this creature behind her. So she lost control of the car and ran into a cement abutment (one of those cement pilings that begin and end a bridge).

About three months after Mama got home from the hospital and things were going nicely, wires gone from the jaws, back to normal, the black cat returned – scrawny, flea-bitten, battle-scarred. Mama came out to the back stoop and up strolled the cat. She screamed, Dad ran from wherever he was and immediately threatened to kill the cat – with an axe, a shotgun, his bare hands. But Mama swept the cat up in her arms and declared, "As long as I'm alive, this cat has a home here." And he did, Black Tom, until he died or wandered off to where the chickens' eggs were less closely guarded. Mama fed him at the back door every evening, petting him and murmuring whatever one murmurs to a fellow survivor of a near-tragedy. She had laid down the law. Her cat phobia seemed to have disappeared as well.

Mother was a seamstress. She did not simply know how to sew, she knew how to Create. What Dad could do with wood, Mother could do with fabric. My junior prom gown was created with no reference to me – she chose the fabric and pattern and made the gown and when I made a slight protest, well! this was what I was going to wear. I was Mistress of Ceremonies, after all, and a Rawlings girl in such a role must be dressed appropriately. So I wore a dress that no teenager would ever choose – a gold brocade top, v-necked and sleeveless, embroidered with tiny red and green flowers all over, and an attached skirt, yards and yards wide, of pale gold chiffon, painstakingly gathered and hemmed by hand, with dark green high heels and red roses on my shoulder. I got to choose the dress for my senior prom, watermelon taffeta with a wide skirt and spaghetti straps, and it was cute – but Mother's dress was by far the more elegant, as I know now.

(That junior prom was a great event, in spite of the formality of the dress and the ceremony. My friend Connie and I, having no steady boyfriends at the time, invited two boys who had graduated high school the year before. One of them had a spanking new Impala convertible, white with red interior, and I think the guys were intrigued by the idea of returning to a high school dance with the freedom of new graduates. We were all buddies together and I hope the boys had as good a time as Connie and I did. Small towns are too much fun. I mention this under 'Mama' because it was just the kind of outing she enjoyed so much in her youth.)

Oh the clothes! Of course, she made drapes and bedspreads, often made boxer shorts for Dad and repaired everything, but the clothes she made for herself and her girls were exquisite. Wide corduroy circle skirts of gold or blue or red, with matching gingham blouses, straight skirts of fine gray wool or green tweed, summery dresses for church or dates, elegant jumpers of gray or green or blue with matching blouses underneath, sheath dresses with three-quarter coats, suits of muted patterns. When I began to buy my own clothes, it was a considerable shock and a gigantic step down in the world. Unfortunately, Mama's sewing machine, an old White electric, jammed constantly. So this good Christian woman could be heard, swearing like a sailor, as she sewed, and sewed, and sewed.

Mama loved flowers. We did not have many flowers when I was very young, all extra money and energy being devoted to vegetables and fruits for survival. But by the time I was in grade school, rosebushes began appearing – one or two at a time – or a clematis vine, or a bed of pansies. How she would croon over her flowers – they were living things to her and another group of her children. (These were obtained by Dad from mail order sources, when money allowed, to surprise and please his sweetheart – but this isn't about Dad....)

My mother was the victim of Disappointed Love. When she was eighteen, she was engaged to a fraternity brother of her brother Dale, an apparently gorgeous hunk nicknamed Swede. Big, blond, exuding animal appeal and high spirits, by all reports. He was the first true love of Elizabeth Bell. Sadly, one evening Swede drank himself into a stupor and woke up married to a little dolly he met on the party rounds. Mother's heart was broken and she retreated into gaining 20 or 30 pounds at the ice cream shop where she worked. This is where Daddy met her, fell in love with this buxom, wounded, but fun-loving brunette, and wooed her until she said Yes. She wanted babies, she wanted a nest, and she was, since Swede was gone, not particular as to the means. But once wed and committed she acted the part, if not at first of a devoted and loving wife, at least a dutiful one and one who knew how to scrimp and save, to make the best of things and to make do, to put meals on the table and clothing on her family.

She told me at one point that Swede would probably have made a terrible father, might not have wanted children at all. She said this with a little sigh, and until I left home at seventeen, she seemed at times to still mourn her lost love.

Now, during the writing of these pages, we have realized that Mama really was in love with Dad. He may have caught her on the rebound, but from old letters and notes and cards we've looked at, she was most definitely in love with her husband. There is a note in her hand from the 1930's, apparently written during a visit to California, which reads in part "I can't wait to get home to my Daddy." Home was definitely where her heart was, and where he was. I'm glad I know this now.

When I married and left home, she told me in about these words: "You're a grown married woman now, and your place is with your husband. Of course, I will love to see you whenever you want to come home for a visit, but don't think that you can just move back home if things don't work out. This time now is for your father and me, and I want to spend time with Dad, just the two of us, now that all of you girls are gone." As young as I was, I faintly understood what she meant, and I never moved back home.

Now, the words I remember the most are the ones she said one evening when we were washing the supper dishes. I was sixteen, and gabbling on about school and friends—"then he said, and then she said, and then I said!" And Mama made a sly comment that made me gasp or laugh, or both, and I was slightly shocked. And she looked at me from her wise, loving, beautiful brown eyes, and said, "When you look at me, you see this aging, gray-haired lady – but inside, I'm still sixteen."

Yes, Mama – me, too. ~Anne

Manners. "Excuse me, please."
"Thank you, Nannie."
"What do you say, Georgia Lee?"
"Have you written your bread-and-butter letter?"

Change the names to protect the innocent and what have you got? A wide void between yesteryear and nowadays. Today's parents, many of whom were taught "manners," don't seem to think they are important.

Today's supermarkets have more commodities on their shelves than any three grocery stores would have dreamed of during the depression years. Back then, we asked the proprietor or manager, "May I have a half pound of rat cheese, please, Mr. (who ever)?"

After Mr. (who ever) cut the sharp cheddar, he would wrap it and say, "Is there anything else, please?" To that we replied, "No, thank you," or went on with more requests. Today, we pick up the pre-packaged cheese, take it to the clerk, and are lucky that we get correct change, much less a "thank you." Oh, I'm being cynical; some clerks whine, "have a nice day" because their employers tell them they must be polite to the customers.

Manners are a little different from being polite to the customers, I think. Somewhere along the line, someone told me table manners were not so much for us as for those who ate with us. You know, "eat with your mouth closed – don't slouch over your plate – keep your elbows off the table –don't hold your fork in your fist – break off only two or three bites from your dinner roll – put your napkin in your lap." The list goes on, or at least it used to. When I look at my dinner companion as he or she scarfs down his grub, I can't help calling to mind what Momma and Daddy kept yammering at us: MIND YOUR MANNERS!

Despite what you may think, Daddy expected us to mind our manners as much as Momma did. When we finished a meal, Daddy usually was the one who left the table first. If, for some urgent reason, we had to leave before he did, we always asked to be excused from the table.

We didn't interrupt when grown-ups were speaking, unless the soup was boiling or the cake was burning, or some other emergency. And even then, we excused ourselves for interrupting. Nowadays, when I telephone someone with small children at home I sometimes get kind of crazy. I compete with some child who wants whatever he wants while his parent tries to respond to him while trying to respond to me, too. It's rude, rude, rude.

When Momma and Daddy were dating, they were out for dinner one evening. Another couple Momma knew approached their table and was introduced to Daddy. As he later told the story, "There I sat like a rube and didn't know enough to get up." He told the story several times over many years, still chafing with chagrin at his being gauche. He felt such embarrassment I think he'd have apologized to those people if he'd ever seen them again.

As kids, we were reluctant to write our Christmas thank-you notes, but write them we did. That was part of the Christmas ritual. Nowadays, I write small checks to all my children and their spouses at the time of their birthdays. I rarely get a thank you; maybe that's a ritual I just don't understand. Darn it, they were taught manners, just as I was. Times are really different. Maybe it's not times, it's "time"-- we don't make time to mind our manners.

Life's too busy, time goes too fast, but I'll go to my grave feeling manners make for graciousness and thoughtfulness toward others. I'm glad I was taught by people who felt the same way. Thank you very much. ~Georgia

Manners, Again. "Say Please."
"Say Thank You."
"What do you say?"
"Elbows off the table."
"Say how-do-you-do."
"Come and say goodbye."
"Use your napkin"

How many times did they say these things, and hundreds of others? A thousand? Five thousand? Didn't they get tired?

I never remember the tone of voice being other than quiet – a gentle reminder ("You know this; you just forgot"). I was a shy child and had to be prodded into the social graces – hello, how are you, I'm fine, thank you, goodbye, thank you for coming, thank you for calling, thank you for the present, thank you for inviting me, thank you, thank you. All the compliments had to be acknowledged: what a nice poem! (thank you); how well you read! (thank you); your dress is so pretty! (thank you).

As a little girl of three, or not quite, I had a lovely outfit with a dress, a coat, a hat, and (wonder of wonders) matching panties. So on the church stairs after services one bright Spring Sunday (it may have been Easter), when someone said "What a pretty dress!," I proudly said "Thank you! And I have panties too!" and whipped my skirt up high to show them.

Perhaps that's when I became a little more socially shy.

"May I be excused?" From the table, from company. "Excuse me, please." When coughing, sneezing, burping, interrupting, bumping into, walking around, for breathing.

"I'm sorry." For bumping, for dropping, for hurting (accidentally or deliberately, physically or emotionally), for sassing, for forgetting, for being late, for being early, for leaving early, for breathing.

Oh, we were polite. And I am so glad. We could use a little more politeness today, or a lot more. It makes the days more pleasant and the nights more peaceful.

And I am pleased to report that our children – and especially our grandchildren – are also polite. Some years ago, I brought a little potted flowering plant home from the store one day, bought for myself to cheer a winter month. When I brought it out to show the visiting family, saying, "Look what I got!," four-year old Lauren cried, "Oh, Grandma, *thank you!*," her face beaming, her hands outstretched in joy. Well, what could I do? She got the plant. Manners are very useful.

But no one can remember how the silverware goes on the table. Forks go on the *left*, my dears, forks go on the left.~Anne

Marriage. Each of my sisters and I left the family of our birth in the same year we graduated from high school, to enter into the state of matrimony. Georgia, the eldest, who always did everything right, was the only one who had a grand wedding. In a formal photograph, she is dressed in a cousin's white satin dress with flowing train that spreads before her feet in a perfect circle, a shimmering lake from which she rises – straight, stern, and lovely as a queen – facing without fear her new life as a young matron.

The rest of the wedding party wore dresses sewn by mother, long, lovely, summery gowns – pink for the maid of honor, green for our sister Sara, yellow for me, the five year old flower girl. Soft pastels, Easter egg colors in June, a rainbow of youth and expectancy. In 1948, in the country, some medieval attitudes remained that encouraged and celebrated such marriages of children. I hear now, as I write this, that Georgia held two scholarships for college. No matter – she would only end up married anyway, why bother with all that expense.

Sara's wedding was secret, and was known to our family only after the fact. I was nine, and was led to believe that her choice was so poor, her judgment so faulty, that it was likely I might never see her again. They thought my tears were of grief, and were satisfied; it was an occasion, for them, of grief. But my tears were of anger and rage that covered a determination that if I did not see my beloved sister soon, I would run away, and find her, and stay with her forever. Those who refused to keep her would not keep me. Fortunately, after the early emotional storms had settled, my mother did take me to see her, thus saving me from a runaway childhood.

My own first wedding was a gray, lifeless, cold ceremony. I wore a new, but dull, dark green dress, attended by my parents and my father-in-law (all so stern, so disappointed, with false cheer and brave smiles). The only gesture of kindness or of romance came from the minister in the Ohio town who performed the ceremony. He was not our minister, so we had no connection to him, but he provided a dozen red roses, long-stemmed and lovely, from the only person present who saw a young, white-faced bride with no flowers.

Like all marriages should and must be if they are to survive, my parents' marriage was an evolution. Being the youngest, I saw the best of it. I remember some spats, some quarrels, over things of not much importance. The scarier times were those hushed talks, urgent whisperings, behind closed doors. Later, I understood that these concerned scandals or tragedies concerning relatives, uncles, sisters, friends, and were not quarrels at all in the true sense.

By and large, what I saw were scenes of amity, of pride, shared excitements, small private jokes, and kind services. Late on a hot afternoon, my father home from work in his paint-stained white overalls, relaxing under the elm in the back yard, my (non-drinking) mother taking him a Tom Collins or a cold beer and sitting with him to share the small events of the day before our early dinner. Or one calling the other to see a spectacular sunset, or watch a flock of migrating geese honking high through the sky. Or stopping together to gaze in awe at the first opened rose of the season – or the last. There were readings aloud, from books or articles, to share a thought, to incite laughter or tears, to add knowledge.

They planted corn or beans together, working up and down the rows of our long garden. Dad would stare in pride, smiling, as Mother demonstrated that she had repaired a toaster, or an iron, or a light switch.

I remember – Mama holding a wooden bowl, a thing of beauty, made by my father from a tree now gone, once loved. The bowl, rubbed by my father's hands to a shine of walnut or cherry, brought to her as a gift, to please her, to say, "I love you." And her face, gentled beyond a smile, a kiss offered through tears.

We were a sentimental family, whatever else we were.

I remember – Mother grumbling in the kitchen, stirring and mixing. It is evening, after dinner. What are you doing, I ask. I'm making sugar cookies, she snaps. But, I say, you told Daddy that you were tired, that you weren't going to make them, that all he thought about was his stomach. Your father wants sugar cookies, so I'm making them, she replies. Someday, you'll understand.

And, finally, now I do.

And *that* wedding was lovely. ~Anne

Middlest. I was young when I was born, not little, but young. It didn't last long, being young. (Or little.)

I was heavy, over 10 pounds and I was breach. I was dropped upon entry (or exit, as you wish). I tore my mother badly, of course, and that was my fault. Being 10 pounds was my fault and being dropped was my fault and that breach business was my biggest sin. As time went on and depending on the day and the mood I was lazy, arbitrary, contrary, defiant, stubborn or all and others to boot. Ergo, unable unwilling to "get into position" that's what I heard anyway.

My father was poor, my mother may have been, but I didn't know her as well. Because dad was poor, I was born at home on our dining room table that could seat eight with all the leaves. A mid-wife attended, that's who dropped me before I made my entire entrance into this world. I was badly bruised for several days and I cried a lot. Actually I cried pretty much continuously till I was very old - like last week.

I probably had a lot to cry about.

I can remember from the dawn how much I wanted and needed to be loved.

When I had my tonsils out (the first time at almost three) I tried to die by hemorrhage. At this advanced age I can still see my mom and her panic when the blood began to roll from my mouth. She scooped me up and ran to the hospital elevator screaming to get her back to the O.R. During the years after, I was often sick and some of that I can "see." There were many things going on in my kid brain. Perhaps I thought, "moma does love me, she's worried I'm sick" some sense of caring as compared to the nothing that happened when I wasn't sick.

Moma told me when I was grown that during my sick and coughing times she kept me in the "cold room" a lot because dad couldn't stand to hear me cry or cough. We had two large rooms on the front of the house that were closed and never heated. This would be helpful for a kid with a bad cough, huh? "She coughs to get attention," he said. I was really pleased to hear this as it pretty much cemented my feeling of worthlessness. That and the fact that she prayed for me to die, she said. So try and figure – was mom worried because dad was irritated when I was sick, or worried just because I was. Did she want me to die just to get the hell out of the way... what? Just stress I guess.

There were times when ma may have been proud of my accomplishments and me. There were inklings, but she never ever, that I remember, said, "I love you." She may have, but didn't want dad to know so she kept quiet.

My mother was, to me, an enigma. She is long dead, but I still l have not figured her out. She was smart and beautiful; she was raised well and with humor. Lots and lots of humor. She had 6 sibs, she, too, was middle. Out of the seven only one was an idiot as dad said – Downs' Syndrome probably, I was never told. They may not have known. I was named for her.

Moma wanted babies – not toddlers or teenagers, but she really wanted babies. There was no rhyme or reason to her childrearing – she used a switch a lot on Georgia. When she punished me it was really severe.

She beat me one time with the <u>edge</u> of a hardwood yardstick. I had embarrassed her by being unable to say sorry for passing in front of a friend who was visiting. I was very young, but I can STILL remember being totally tongue tied and unable to speak. It was not from being hardheaded or defiant. She didn't get it. But boy did I! Dad was scarier but he seldom hit - just to see anger in his eyes was threat enough. Eyes. Hard and blue. I think moma married him for his looks. He was truly a gorgeous devil, as they say (true in his case) black hair and turquoise eyes and when his smile reached his eyes your heart could stop.

He never smiled at me unless it was some sarcastic thing he said or did to get me. Poor ole me.

I remember a picture of my older sis and me – a big one, 9x12 maybe, sitting on the piano. I would sneak a look at it every once in a while, looking for the ugliness I was told was that baby. I never found it.

I can't believe how bad it was for me, thank God for my rescuers along the way, nor can I really think dad knew how bad it was or how damaged I was to become. Surely he would have tempered his treatment of me.

I was an end of the depression, planned kid. The only planned one of three girl types. To relieve a lump in her breast, which might be cancer, mom's doctor prescribed pregnancy. My job was to dissolve the lump. Already that little fetus was dead in the water. Had the prescription worked this story regardless of middle would be different. The lump remained, the breast was removed, and mom died of cancer – when I was 32. I don't know how mom felt about this very bad trade but dad pretty much hated me from conception and never let me, or anyone who would listen, forget it. All I ever heard my entire life was I could never get anything right – not even the job I was sent for to do. One of dad's very favorite things to say was "we should have thrown her out and raised the afterbirth" - was this funny? Doesn't sound too funny to me.

Over the years I tried to win dad's approval. Couldn't be done. I was very good at lots of stuff, dramatics as we called it in school. As an elementary school person I won highest honors for the delivery of a humorous monologue.

Went as far as the contest went and won an AA++ rating never heard of in the land. I even made the paper in our little town. Mom took me to the state finals on the school bus and dad's witticism upon our triumphant return was "Well, she'll cough for a week, now." Once I won an art contest, second place: "What only two entries?" There, that feels good even today. From the time I can remember, I excelled at something artistic, acting or writing or painting.

Each award was THE one that was gonna make my family and in particular DADDY proud. Well, it never happened. It NEVER HAPPENED. Can't remember ever feeling I got it quite right for my family

Dad did call me names as I grew older – taller than many high schoolers and most of the teachers, skinny – no lumps anywhere except, as he mentioned, my nose looking like a glob of putty on a shingle. My personal favorite was animated windmill. He liked Butch, which was the name of one of the local dogs. A long legged black and white setter type. I was made fun of a lot because of being tall. And that was my fault, too. I was never given solace by my parents, just "learn to stick up for yourself." I could have used some lessons on how to. At nine.

I can remember spilling my milk at the table, turning over the glass three out of five times that we sat. Yep, every time we would sit down to eat dad would say, "Well, I guess you'll spill your milk." Being a dutiful and fearful child I heard this as some kind of twisted command and – I spilled my milk. Now I don't think my father deliberately set this up to cause chaos in my tiny mind but – you guessed it – it made me CRAZY. We didn't talk or, God forbid, laugh at the dinner table. All I heard were these peculiar orders from my father – things that I thought I was to do, did them, and then discovered I got it wrong once again. Meals were not fun for ME. Even when I was grown up, when we had people to dinner he would comment about how many gallons of milk had been spilled over that table over the years lest I forget.

I remember our cow and pre-pasteurized milk, the leather-like sweet cream and black raspberries from our very own garden. Only I was not allowed the cream – "better to put it down the sink as waste it on some skinny kid" and he did – pour it down the sink. Just some, to make his point.

I reckon I didn't know my mother because she was such a shadowy figure. She needed to please, too – she was a martyr and a wimp for dad. I betcha had she stayed west with HER family she would've been herself instead of this other person who snuck in. Mom's sibs often asked who she was and why she married dad. Maybe nobody saw his eyes. Some way I learned it was on the rebound. Too bad, dad was in awe of her and she could have asked for and gotten better from him. Easy for me to say now.

Being middle was a funny place to be. I suffered, but in many ways being middle in my family made me strong. I am convinced there is a scrambled genetic stamp comprised of moma's stuff, and dad's and my own eccentric baggage swirling around inside me. The swirl creating a throwback or forward – maybe even an outcrop, a new mutation that has nothing to do with middle-ness, but only to do with me and the ability to survive in spite of being less than the flavor of the month around my house most months.

Middle kids need what I call saviors. Thank God for mine. My grandma (dad's mom) loved me unreservedly – as the under dog maybe, but she was there. She touched me, held me, said I was cute and spent hours, and I mean at a time, playing hide the thimble, store, whatever I made up to do she adapted her day around. I think she must have championed me to my folks. Mom didn't like her much, thought her meddlesome (she probably was) and dad, well who did he like? (Including himself).

Another savior lived in a big house in the country. She said I was soft – called me Softy. The parents shipped me off to her a lot in the summer. Her daughter and I had some super adventures, but Helen King was really my friend. The memory of her hand brushing my face and calling me her softie is still right there. One of the most potent forces in my tenuous clutch to growing up somewhat uncracked. Another name she had for me, and of which I just thought, was Saddo, which I always believed had to do with Sara. Hmmm could she have known what a very sad little girl I was? Oh, I think definitely.

There were others. Teachers, lots of teachers. I had a highly developed and very honest sense of the absurd, the theatre. Some teachers in my very staid little Republican town were fine tuned to kids with imaginative talent. They were supportive and were my best listeners. I got B's when I didn't work and A+s when I pushed. So the teachers (most of whom were distant cousins) pretty much liked me. (I hadn't caused any of their breasts to fall off.)

My fantasy life was richer than rich, it teemed with curiosity. I took apart anything that rattled, couldn't put it back of course, but I usually found the rattle. I convinced my older sister to help me pick at the wainscoting around our great room because it was pieced oddly in one place. We figured there were diamonds (at least) behind that panel (no diamonds just wall).

This sister's room was sacred, not to be gone into by me. EVER, if possible. Her sailor boyfriend sent her Dentine gum by the carton (from the PX I guess) NOT TO TOUCH. Not even to ask, it was HERS. Of course my bedroom was not forbidden to "the baby." I had a doll as an ornament on my bed, which I really didn't want bothered. But "who's the biggest baby here?" I was asked. Luckily I really loved that little baby – the interloper. But I did feel frustration and anger and great sadness because I knew that equity was not a word my folks knew the definition of in my connection.

My folks brought attention to my body changes by making fun of me. I remember when my breasts began to bud and knowing attention would be paid and commented about, the brunt of many a bad joke, I stood in my bedroom smashed against the heavy oak door to my closet thinking I could just push myself into the door, become part of it and not have to endure the hurt of the negative comments. I did not want breasts, I had gotten used to being tall and skinny and unacceptable the way I already was. To have to hear about the new and unimproved, no doubt, me was just about all I didn't want to have to cope with.

So, middle aside, I had my parents' expectation that I failed and their subtle and not so subtle messages that began the day I was born and Georgia hearing these messages and reinforcing them with her own brand of devaluation to make sure I heard them, ain't it a wonder I'm here?

And boy, don't I whine a lot? It is only to say that middle is hard in any family, but when the middlest has a particular "function" to perform and fails at it, boy. Well that's enough about middle in MY family.

Except to say. From time to time I can pull out that baby, that little girl, that gangly teenager and say, "don't be sad anymore. You made it. You are standing in the light, kids. And it's good." ~Sara

Milk. I'm not sure if we sold any of the milk produced by the cow dad kept during our very young days or if we used it all. I remember moma making yummy butter and a butter paddle. Gosh what a lot of work. First she used a big bowl then came a big glass jar with paddles. She would turn the handle. I got to take a turn, but early in the churning, as I was a little girl and the churning got really hard toward the full-blown butter stage. We churned until we couldn't turn the handle. Then she dumped the big glob of daffodil colored stuff into the old bowl. The stuff looked sweaty and beady with no real form. There was the paddle again which she used to manipulate the glob till the sweat disappeared. Then it was truly butter. She did what with it? Into the old ICEBOX (as opposed to refrigerator) - I can't remember what was done with the finished butter. Only the process. I guess we ate it. Lots of butter making I'll tell you.

Maybe we had to have a cow because I spilled so much of my milk at the dinner table. That was a mealtime event for me most evenings. We would sit down and dad would look at me and say, "Well, I guess you will spill your milk." Well, hearing his command I did – spill my milk. OH, boy.

There was delicious buttermilk, cottage cheese and lordy, lordy, cream thick enough for a cat to walk across. (And one did once, too.) I don't think one can buy cream like that today. Life then was just a bowl of black raspberries with that marvelous leathery cream over the top. YUM. ~Sara

Momma. As the eldest I had the longest time to get to know the woman I called Momma. Some people have said I look a lot like her; perhaps when I was younger that was true. She died when she was fifty-eight and I am seventy so that isn't true any longer.

A few have said I act like her; I find that hard to believe. I was a woman grown with children of my own before I realized she wasn't perfect. What made me aware that she was flawed I cannot recall. I do remember how shocked I was in finding she had a fault.

I think part of my awareness of her deficiencies occurred as my sisters and I have begun discussing our personal relationships with her. Part of my awareness deals with being willing to look at things about her that I knew but had willed myself not to see as imperfections.

Elizabeth Georgia (nee Bell) Rawlings was fourth of a family of seven children – a middle child who didn't have the archetypical psychological definition. Her oldest brother, Dale, was born just two years before her. Because of this, she was allowed to date early, double-dating with Uncle Dale and his girl "as protection" for her teen-aged innocence.

I have the feeling that she was popular in high school. She was the only cheerleader at her school in Elko, NV; customs regarding cheerleading didn't include stuff like the Dallas Cowboys' cheerleading extravaganzas.

Her best friends in high school were Marchand Newman and Oma Harney, and Momma told me many stories of their adventures. The only snippet that I can remember is Oma saying to her friend, Betty-Bell, as Momma was called, "I always know when you're dressed up. Marchand's always gets her hair marcelled but you don't bother except when it's time to look special." I wonder if Oma Harney had no marcel combs, didn't know how to use them, was being catty about Marchand or was simply giving Momma a compliment.

In the 1920's, marcelling was elaborate wave-setting accomplished by pushing curved combs into one's hair, having first wetted it down with "wave set," a kind of gooey fragrant semi-liquid. This created deep artificial waves across one's whole head. Momma kept her combs for many years; I can see them if I close my eyes. They were about six inches long and the teeth were about an inch deep.

There's a delightful high school story about a ten-day camping trip with horses in the mountains around Elko. With Uncle Dale as protection and plenty of adult chaperones, some time in the summer after her sophomore year, Momma was in a lovely summer party.

One evening after pitching camp and before the evening meal, some of the group were playing rough, wrestling, chasing one another, just "horsing" around. Momma, like most of the group, wore boots and jodhpurs along with a pongee shirt of her brother's. At one point, one of the chaperones approached her and took her aside. "Betty-Bell, nice girls don't have their waists hanging out of their trousers." I could feel Momma's embarrassment years later when she told me, but she did think it was funny, just as I did.

She was a whiz at algebra and when, years and years later, I was pulling almost failing grades, she couldn't understand why I wasn't doing as well as she had. She was involved in drama and debating, belonging to the National Forensic Society and I still have her key. She read a dramatic presentation of Madame X when she was a senior getting a silver cup when she took first prize at the state level. Alas, the silver cup is lost.

All three of her daughters inherited that dramatic characteristic and Sara, in particular, has used it with great accomplishment, performing and directing internationally.

Momma wanted to be married so she could have babies and when she and Daddy were married on August 31, 1929, she could hardly wait to produce me on December 29, 1930. Times being what they were, baby schedules were strictly kept. When her baby cried ten or fifteen minutes before she was supposed to nurse, Momma told me she would sit crying, too, her dress soaked with milk and praying for the time to go quickly before all the milk leaked out.

After we'd moved to Illinois from California, I remember her singing to me. She would hold me on her lap in the big old green upholstered oak rocker while I pressed my little hand against a small mole growing on her neck. I could feel the vibration of her larynx as she sang "Red Sails in the Sunset" or "Dance with a Dolly with a Hole in her Stockin'" or "Bobby Shaftoe."

Though she quit singing the songs when I was older, I was rocked in the green rocker on occasion until she became ill with the cancer that killed her and I was 36 years old. I'm happy to say Annie has the rocker but it's shrunk over the years. Have you noticed how that happens with precious objects? They seem to shrink as we age.

Momma became an increasingly accomplished seamstress. There was little money in the 1930's but people gave us cast-off clothing. With ingenuity and creativity Momma ripped seams apart, pushed patterns around and devised lovely wardrobes for herself and her daughters. It was said that the Rawlings girls set style in town.

I think I was in second grade the fall Momma made me a brown tweed coat with a fur collar from someone's hand-me-down. When Christmas came, there was no new doll, but my old one lay in her bed in a brand new doll coat, just like mine, with a fur collar, patch pockets, and all.

I was thrilled and squealed with my pleasure. "Just like mine! How could Santa Claus make it?"

"He didn't make it. Mrs. Santa Claus made it."

"Oh, I didn't know there was one."

"Do you know who Mrs. Santa Claus is?" asked Momma, and thus I discovered in a loving way one of my first adult realities.

Momma began early on to adapt to the Rawlings ways. When they still were living with her in-laws and her father-in-law's mother, the young matron had little to do. She was in a strange land with no one familiar but her husband and her babe. No doubt getting mail was very important to her. One day, probably bored, she sat in a pair of pongee pajamas playing solitaire. In came her father-in-law, swept the cards from the table, "Those clothes won't be worn in this house and those things of the devil are gonna get burned."

Keeping peace was important to her. She joined the Baptist Church, became more fundamentalist in her Christian thinking and strict and severe in discipline.

One time in my early years, I was invited to a birthday party and somehow the date of the party got mixed up. I went to Carol Jean's house, probably with a gift, and we played all afternoon but there was no party. When I got home, it came out that there had been no party.

As punishment, she took me to Carol Jean's the real day of the party and made me watch from the car all the other children playing outside at the games, hearing their laughter, seeing the presents and the refreshments being served but I was denied the party.

Another time, I went overnight to Great Aunt Grace and Uncle Arthur's for an overnight visit. As she was helping me undress, Aunt Grace noticed welts on my legs and wanted to know what had caused them. Momma had switched me with a lilac stick.

There were other instances of what I know now were unjust punishments but originally my mind felt whatever Momma did must have been right.

She taught us manners – how to set a table properly, when to say "please" and "thank-you," how to write thank-you notes, and how to respect our elders. We learned to say "excuse me" in all sorts of situations. If we borrowed we always returned the loaned item, whether it was a cup of milk from Nannie or a garment to use in a play.

By example we learned that women do not need to wait for a man to use a tool to repair a sewing machine, hang a picture or a curtain rod. Women could keep books, invest money and create savings accounts. Sometimes she took employment if she felt someone needed her talents and abilities; usually her skills involved sewing and tailoring or nursing or taking care of babies.

In her later years, I felt we had crossed a bridge from parent-child to adult-adult. It's an aspect of our relationship that I treasure. I was 36 when my mother died and we had had that closeness for what I remember was a very long while.

Two examples of our adult relationship come to mind. One was a day when I was home visiting. Sophia Loren had just instigated her petition to the Vatican for dissolution of her first marriage in order to marry Carlo Ponti. Elizabeth Taylor was on her umpteenth husband. Both stories were in the news and Momma said, "Those women are just whores." I disagreed, stating that Loren was playing by the rules while Taylor had the morals of an alley cat. We bickered back and forth and finally Momma said, "I guess you're right, Sis. Maybe I'd not mind knowing Sophia Loren." That was an adult statement, not a Mother-knows-best pronouncement.

One of my sisters had made a marriage of which our parents did not approve. The other sister, married too young, was going to have her baby much too soon after the wedding. I had made what they deemed to be an approved marriage and my first baby did not appear for five years.

As Momma and I re-hashed once again the unfortunate events causing her so much pain, she stated, "You've gone through so much with me. It seems silly not to let you smoke in front of me like you were a little girl sneaking around." I'd been admitted to adulthood, able to make my own choices, good or bad.

Another facet of Momma's personality was her deep and genuine faith and spirituality. It doesn't jibe with the punitive side of her, but both were strong parts of who she was.

All the years of our growing up, we read at least one chapter of the Bible each night, followed by made-up prayers. We always said grace at meals. We learned many verses and a few whole chapters of scripture. Some I can still quote. I close my eyes and see her in her favorite walnut and cane-backed rocker.

She is in front of the living room windows with the morning sun streaming through her colored glass collection onto her back as she reads her daily devotions. She led an adult Bible class at her church for many years. People often came to the house seeking help or comfort from Mrs. Rawlings.

When she was in the hospital waiting for death, different clergy she knew came to visit her. They came back to be ministered to by her; there were at least six of them with whom she prayed during her last days.

When I was married to my second husband, he gave his definition of a gentleman: a person who never intentionally hurts another. Momma didn't know his definition but in thinking back, she taught us that a lady is the distaff side of a gentleman... wish she had taught me better.

She died the day my younger son became two years old. He's now 36 years old and I still miss her with her beautiful dark brown hair and snapping brown eyes, with her generous mouth and its broad grin or deep throaty laugh. For me, she was wonderful, warts and all! ~Georgia

Music. The hymns at church form the background for my earliest recollection of music in our family. Church was not a sometime thing for us. I might be allowed to stay home from school with a minor complaint, but one did not miss church unless a raging fever registered on the thermometer, preferably accompanied by vomiting. So the hymns were weekly, fifty-two times a year, and later, twice weekly or more, what with choir practice and concerts.

The other musics of our lives rang their own notes – Mother's radio, playing atop the refrigerator, accompanied more often than not by my mother humming or singing; my sister's record player (a square box about the size of a small suitcase, spinning hard black disks at a rate of 78 revolutions per minute) playing tunes from the forties – "Stormy Weather" was a particular favorite; sheet music for the piano, an old upright on which someone was always practicing, playing, or just noodling, mostly solo, sometimes a duet, often with vocals by the pianist or family passing through the room. Some of my great aunts played the organ or piano "by ear" – just sat down in their dim parlors, these white-haired, crisply groomed, slightly scented ladies with lace-up black shoes, and played rippling tunes, hymns or old ballads, or a minor classical piece, to my eternal amazement and deep envy.

There was school music – choral music, duets, quartets, octets – music for Spring concerts, Christmas concerts, graduation concerts, piano recitals, singing or playing for various ladies' clubs or church groups. We grew up humming, singing, old songs and new: "I'm Looking Over A Four-Leafed Clover," or "Mairzie Doats" or "Bewitched, Bothered, and Bewildered" (which Mother one day sang as "Bitched, Bothered, and Bewildered" which embarrassed her dear Baptist heart no end).

When Georgia started dating Paul, her first husband, he brought a new dimension of music to us. Paul played violin with the Springfield Community Orchestra, and to my five-year-old ears, his playing was the music of Heaven itself. I remember one time learning all the words of "O Little Town of Bethlehem" and then singing it to Paul's accompaniment – standing in the kitchen in front of the refrigerator, a homely duet. Paul was a classicist and introduced me to his dearest friends – Bach, Beethoven, and Brahms – and I became a weird kid that at 14 preferred Tchaikovsky to Elvis and Beethoven to practically anyone. But Mama loved Elvis, so we heard a lot of him on the radio. Other influences saved me from becoming a total music snob, including the discovery that Paul also loved Glenn Miller and his explanation that a lot of great music existed outside the classical group.

But the music closest to my heart, then and now, was the voices of my sisters singing in harmony as they washed and dried the dishes after supper in the evening. Silly songs, love songs, hymns, and strange country rounds unknown to the rest of the world. And I listened to my big sisters and wondered – how did they know when to sing up and when to sing down to make the notes blend so beautifully? My big sisters, in harmony over the soapsuds. ~Anne

N

Nannie. The most important person in my growing up years was my dad's mom. We called her Nannie, her name was Anna. My paternal grandmother, who was born in 1880, was almost 6' tall, which was really something for the time. She twinkled and she always smelled either of freshly turned earth or cooking. Her garden was dug and planted with the help of grandpa and comprised all good things to eat as well as gooseberries, ick. Her cooking was by pinch and handful and wonderful. New potatoes and new peas in a cream sauce that was never the same twice so always a new taste surprise and the only way I ever liked peas.

I remember her with a mop of white hair that most of the time strayed from its pins and flew around her head like a halo. Probably was a halo, she was surely my angel. She loved me unconditionally.

Nannie was never too busy to stop doing whatever she was doing to play with me. In the middle of cooking, canning, sewing, baking - it stopped or she found a way to involve me in her project. I first learned to sew on her old treadle machine. Rather than tell me to go away, she sat and showed me how to use the dern thing. Boy, was that a chore for both of us. Her patience was astounding. Aside from the many things I learned from her (I can make gravy in three languages) she "played" with me for hours on end: hide the thimble was a big pastime. Her house was more compact than ours, old fashioned cozy. Complete with big old overstuffed horsehair sofa and chair set. Lots of good places to hide a thimble. Sometimes she would use her turn at hiding as a lesson, though it never felt like she was teaching. She would put the thimble in plain sight and just as I became frustrated with not finding it, she would say, "look up" or "sometimes things are right in front of our eyes." "you're trying way too hard, just be easy." Hours of concentration on me.

She treated me as a person always, not a funny looking kid who was always underfoot and in the way. We invented games and played dress-up. We talked about school and life and things in general.

She kept me many times from Dad's wrath. Once I remember I walked through mud so thick it pulled my boots off my shoes. In great distress, I stopped at her house, which was just across the street from ours. She cleaned my boots, my shoes. An unspoken rescue. She just remarked, "it'll save your mom a big job," but we both knew she saved me from Dad's wrath. There were lots of that kind of "no big deal" rescues. I spent a great deal of time with her. I was allowed to be anywhere she was - cooking, laundry, planting, picking. I was special to her as she was to me. I remember once playing "Old Maid" with Nan, I was situated so I could see her cards in the mirror behind her; she thought I was looking at myself, I was looking at her cards, awful me, but she thought I was cute enough to want to peek at myself. What a revelation. To be thought cute by someone.

Nan commented about God in a way I've never heard anyone speak. It was as if He'd just been there, having finished growing a beautiful crop of rhubarb or asparagus – as if we had just missed Him as He stuck a rainbow across a wet blue-gray sky – as if He'd been there in the night to ease a fever or pain or a bad cough. There was never any Bible thumping or preaching – He was just there, lurking in the smell of the lilacs that grew on the bank of Nan and Grandpa's property, in the sweetness of watermelons, refining our sense of right and wrong, helping us define who we were to become. We read the Bible to learn about how Jesus conducted his life, what the Christian tenets are.

Nannie was curious about life and people, she wrote poetry that was GOOD. She wrote about her sisters, about love and thankfulness. I can't remember an unkind word from her mouth. Nan walked the hills of our very hilly little town selling greeting cards and embarrassing our father. I think she did this to socialize rather than for any money she might have made. Pennies on the box, I reckon.

My mom thought her nosey and I bet she was. She poked her nose into mom's business I am sure. It was the times and the place, some of it. And Nannie wanting to be helpful and part of her son's family life. Moma came from a much different place with many sibs and families too busy with their own business to meddle in others.

Nan was a marvelous storyteller, but her stories were never gossipy or hurtful, just the facts, ma'm. She was for the underdog and had a clear vision of just who the underdog was. When the details of my first marriage were being discussed, rehashed and dissected, her response to how she felt about it was "well, you know, all cats are gray in the dark."

My Grand grandmother, I was always visible to her. ~Sara

O

Order. There's <u>order</u>, as in "put down that book" and there's order, as in being tidy.

Momma and Daddy didn't really order us to do things as much as they gave us instructions about how things were most efficiently done.

Nannie wanted to borrow a cup of milk. I was asked to carry it across the street. The cup was brim full and I kept watching the milk slop over the edge, drop by drop, as I inched along. Daddy came along and said, "Don't look at it and just walk normal." In a way it was an order, but I spilled no more milk all the way across the street when I did as told.

Momma didn't say we <u>had</u> to iron a shirt in any given way but she did say the dampened shirt would be easier if we did the collar first (on the wrong side), then the yoke, then the sleeves and then the fronts, and, finally, the back. I've tried ironing in a different order. At least with all cotton or silk shirts, it makes a difference. Try it.

When it came to orders, both of them were more interested in getting the job done in a proper and expeditious manner. Ordering for its own sake rarely was exhibited. "Do it because I said so" is a stock parental phrase but we didn't hear it as often as some kids did. Maybe there was respect.

As to the <u>neat</u> part of order, WELL, we had two role models. Daddy had countless tin cans on a ledge above his shop bench. In them, were screws graduating precisely according to size, all the wood screw cans marching along, and then the metal screw cans in the same fashion. If someone upstairs needed something from the basement, Dad could be lying on his bed and tell where the item was. Dowels stored overhead in the shop were calibrated from large to small diameters. Boards were marked with chalk at their ends so Daddy knew the length of the piece of lumber before pulling it from its overhead bin.

His machinist's tool chest was a thing of exquisite beauty. Drawers as shallow as an inch were lined with bright bitter-green velour in which tools nestled in their neatly formed nests. It was a mysterious and extraordinary place from where all his knowledge of precision seemed to emanate.

Daddy's dresser drawers and clothes closet were in tidy stacks and in rows that rarely deviated. Then there was Momma. She was fanatic about cleanliness but neat? Clutter helped her thrive, I think. She sewed; she had two dressers filled with fabrics she might use some day and maybe she had a catalog of them in her mind. When we wanted a new dress or jumper or slacks, she had to go through all the drawers. "I know I've got a really pretty piece of grape-colored wool knit. Wait till I find it."

When she needed to do grocery shopping, she had to go through all the cupboards, open boxes and cans to determine whether she was low in supplies. This, despite the blackboard Daddy had hung in the kitchen for keeping track of foods that were needed. Once she asked me to clean her dresser drawers. She had some leftover wallpaper with which to line the bottoms so they would look pretty and clean. I decided to put things in orderly stacks, all the brassieres in one drawer, panties neatly piled next to them. Slips and half-slips all in the same drawer and her stockings tidy in a box in one drawer instead of some in each drawer.

When I was finished, I called her to come inspect. She smiled her big happy grin as she looked and then deliberately took her hands and rumpled up everything. "That's the only way I can find anything, but you did a beautiful job." Oh, Momma! So much for order of all sorts. ~Georgia

Outhouse. Georgia is speaking on privies, but she is the "old one" as she refers to herself, and what does she know??

Anyway, my memory of our outhouse is that it had three holes, she says only two. Well, somebody's had three. Hmph. I remember the huge horse flies - never mind. I remember seeing spider webs woven over the smallest hole and in the corners. I was always fearful a spider would "get on me." We used Sears and Wards catalogue pages for the necessaries –

the slick pages wouldn't do the job. I hated going at night and in the winter. We had "slop jars" under our beds for emergencies. Once mom was using that facility, dad was working in the basement and I guess the noise was really amplified where he was - anyway he pounded on the ceiling/floor with his hammer and mom jumped a foot. They laughed for days over that one.

I can remember in our part of the world and time outhouses were the norm as was tipping them over on Halloween. Nannie had an outhouse, the Petersons had an outhouse. Most of the houses in town had outhouses. Some were so easy to move the Hallowe'eners would carry them as far away as two towns over, leaving just the hole in the ground. Not nice.

There were outhouses with windows, with curtains on windows and some with a proper roller for toilet paper, even with a light to guide one's way. One I remember was wallpapered – same paper as their living room.

I always had a comic book or two stored somewhere near our sitter for contemplating. I was accused of going to the outhouse to avoid chores: hmm. Could that be true?

As in everything dad did he made the house as perfect as he could complete with flagstones from the back of the house to the outhouse door. That was dad. I remember all of this with great nostalgia – no accounting for our memories. ~Sara

p

Parties. Other than holidays and a few large family meals, there were few formal celebrations in our house or in our immediate circle. A handful of occasions were memorable.

Faintly, I remember the golden wedding anniversary of Nannie and Grandpa, fifty years together; celebrated in all formality with the most beautiful white-tiered cake I'd ever seen. I was 7, dressed in a new woolen suit, and since the serving of the cake seemed too long delayed, I decided to go play in the tall forest of Grandpa's late asparagus bed. When I returned in the midst of the cake cutting and picture taking, everyone dressed in their best, women with fresh hairdos and corsages, I was covered from foot to curls in asparagus seeds. I can't remember if I actually got any cake.

The next memory is of my friend Bambi's seventh birthday party. It was a pink party, all the little girls in pink dresses, dressy shoes in white or black patent leather, a large round table with a pink tablecloth, pink cake, strawberry ice cream, pink balloons. Children's parties were often elegant in those days, and I have a photograph, 8 by 10, of those little girls around the table, my hair in braids around my head, the other girls in long curls or neat bobs, ribbons, ruffles, and bows. What fun the mothers must have had.

A tenth birthday was usually something special in our family. Mine, on March 29th, was a roomful of little girls, all in party dresses, their best party socks, and shoes. Mother had made my dress of a pretty spring plaid, pastels of pink, blue, yellow, and green, and the colors were reflected in the linens and napkins on the big dining room table, in the cupcakes and candles. We played guessing games, sitting primly on chairs ranged around the formal 'front room,' and prizes were given out.

There was Sara's sweet sixteen party, with her navy blue and white dotted-Swiss dress and high heels, looking like a grown, lovely lady to my eyes, grown-up teenagers playing cards with the adults in the front room again – an evening party, lasting well after I was sent to bed.

But the special party – the party for no reason – was my bridge party. One of the young married women of the town, to raise a little extra cash, offered bridge lessons for teenagers, and for the better part of two years, six or eight or twelve of us gathered at her house or one of our own homes to play bridge. We were fanatical, playing once or twice a week, often until two in the morning on weekends. Since we were so well chaperoned, parents made no complaint about the late hour. (My lessons were paid for in babysitting for the bridge teacher, a nice thing for all.)

One day, Mother suggested having a bridge luncheon at our house. Fine, I said, thinking, sandwiches, cokes, and card playing would be fun on a Saturday afternoon. Well! The girls arrived, dressed in neat skirts, pretty blouses, hose and heels. Three tables were arranged in the front room, with score pads, pencils, little nuts and mints, decorative napkins. One player was late, and we were short, with only three at one table. No matter: Mother sat herself down and made a fourth, and swept the board. "If you could play bridge, why didn't you teach me instead of letting me take lessons?" I asked later. She brushed it away. I can't really play, she said. I just followed along. Ha.

The latecomer arrived, mother disappeared, we played a game or two, chattering in our pretty clothes. Eventually, lunch was announced. In the dining room, the big table was laid with the best china and silver, tablecloths and napkins. And the entrée was chicken a la king, served over the lightest, flakiest, tastiest savory pastries, all cut neatly into shapes of diamonds, spades, hearts, and clubs. I think the dessert had a card theme as well. The girls exclaimed and twittered and complimented Mother endlessly. And she was pleased, and proud, and found it fun to make a special kind of young-lady day for my friends and me. I was astonished and speechless. I wish she were here now, so we could talk about it. I think she could have had a lot of other happy parties had life been just a little different. ~Anne

Pasture. Our pasture was some over an acre, I guess. Our house was not in the country, but in the city, pasture and all. I knew every detail of our pasture, every blade, every thistle. I became intimately familiar with this-tles by stepping barefoot on one. Many an adventure was had in that open space. To the south was another folk's property, but we crossed the fence each spring to collect the morels that grew in the quiet dark damp of the other folk's pasture. They knew not either of our trespass or of the mushrooms.

That part of not our pasture was good as there was a tree that had fallen - age, rot, lightning? It formed the quiet mushroom place as well as a place for sitting and watching the mushrooms GROW almost before our eyes. We used the tree to sit and think up new adventures as well.

There was a dry cistern in the back part of the pasture. We threw our tin cans and broken other stuff in there. This stuff was on top of the stuff of other generations. Years later as an adult I rescued some of these good-ies as well as some layers down. Things like coffee cans, crockery, bottles, and tin ware of all kinds. There was silverware and wooden ladles. Just lots of goodies. These treasures went with me to flea markets and brought some cash to the coffers.

There were buildings in our pasture, an old barn, some sheds, and a long galvanized watering trough. The trough caught rainwater even though there was an old pump to splash out water for the cow. There was on old stump with a big old salt lick for the animals. Once I tried it – it was just salt.

I explored the barn, not a big barn as barns go. There was a place for hay, though, and feeding troughs, a place to milk and a space to stand and watch the cow as it chomped on the grain dad spilled. There was a three-legged milk stool hanging on the wall when dad wasn't sitting on it. From time to time I would discover a nest of kittens in the barn. Small barn as barns go – many adventures for an imaginative kid.

110

The brooder house was in constant flux as dad had so many husbandry projects. Pigs took over once. I remember the big sow and her "pups" – that lasted about 23 seconds. Sows can kill ya – did you know that? In that building we had sheep and some goats all at different times of course. It ended up being storage. Critters got in as well to make nests and babies.

There was a long building that housed chickens and sheep and whatever. Egg laying nests were big in this building. There were a dozen layer "holes" at least and one could jump a foot if a hen was disturbed during the egg laying process. What a lot of clucking and fussing!

The pasture was a grand roaming place, a nature place, and a place I wish I could have provided for my young'uns – a wide open grassy plain with a few mysterious buildings that kept me busy for all those years. I learned about foxes and moles and plants and oops cow pats. There was ever a new season and ever a new adventure and I did 'em all for at least 15 years. I can see me running through the grass, playing with my dog, whooping – whooping was not allowed where it could be heard as it might upset the neighbors – so whooping was a very special activity in my pasture.

Though what seems to be activities that were conducted over and over, there was always a new wrinkle, a snake to scream about a fox in living color – once a cow (not ours) fell from its pasture, down the bank and onto the tracks – gosh what a day that was. Just think, it never got old, our pasture. ~Sara

Petersburg. Petersburg is a town of roughly 2,000 people, the county seat of Menard County in Illinois, in the midst of good farming country, a prosperous, comfortable rural community of country farmers and dwellers, tradesmen, and professionals. In our time, it was a Southern town, much more Southern than anyone would think of a place only 200 miles south of Chicago. Speech was drawled, meals were heavy with creamy gravy, attitudes were entrenched, city folk were viewed with suspicion, church attendance was mandatory, and no stores were open on Sundays.

Petersburg was where we lived, except for a few years spent in Vallejo, California, where Dad worked just before and during the War. We lived in Vallejo, but Petersburg was our home. We lived in an old white frame house on three acres, at 521 North Eleventh Street, on Irish Hill (why Irish we never knew). Before dial phones came into existence in the mid 1950's, we had a party line and had to crank for the operator, and our telephone number was 415 Ring 2. Yes. Or ring rang ring two, as I said when I was just learning to talk.

In this small town, everyone knew everyone else, and knew most of their business as well. Acquaintances and relationships spread beyond the town, through most of the county, and beyond, to other counties and other towns. The town square had two bars, two drugstores (with soda fountains), a dry-goods store, doctors' offices, and various establishments around a central courthouse. There was a library, a post office, three gas stations, two veterinarians, a woman who raised canaries, two piano teachers, eight churches (but no synagogue), three beauty parlors, two funeral homes, and the usual assortment of eccentrics, drunks, bridge clubs, and the DAR.

It's a pretty town, Petersburg. Often called the village of seven hills, it is nestled in and around the Sangamon River valley, and comes as a relief from the flat farmlands through which you approach it. From part of the hill where we lived, you can look over the town and glimpse the river, and there used to be a white bridge over the river that gleamed through the fresh greens of spring and the reds and russets of autumn. The houses for the most part are handsome, old white frame structures with front porches, some large and imposing, others more modest, nearly all well kept and freshly painted. Other houses are of stone or brick, large or small bungalows, still with porches, and some are mansions, high on the hills, that used to be or still are occupied by the doctors or lawyers or wealthier landowners of the town.

Sheridan Road runs out of the town toward the west, past the foot of the main hill road to our old house, and curves in and out among small hills before climbing to the flat farmlands beyond the town. The road is called Snake Hollow, not because it hides snakes, as I used to think, but because of its shape, snaking through the shaded hills before reaching the sun again.

The Sangamon River, made famous by the poet Edgar Lee Masters (whose cousin Edith was the high school librarian from our father's time and into ours), created rich river bottoms around the town and provided fresh catfish. It also flooded its banks every few years, creating problems for those who lived on its banks and excitement for the rest of us who lived safely out of reach.

New Salem State Park, a historical reproduction of the village of New Salem where Abraham Lincoln lived, is two or three miles out of town to the south and was an important place in our youth, for picnics,

112

trail walking, plays, family reunions, and the like. Between the town and the park, an artificial lake was constructed in the early 1960's and people started building homes there on the water; gentrification had, in a small, slow way, begun.

But the scenes and stories in this book take place in the older times, the 30's and 40's and 50's, when the town changed little from year to year, where we knew each other and each other's families, where the seasons marked the most significant changes in our lives, the potluck suppers at church had their place, and the movie theater showed films three years old, until it closed in 1958. There were dark country roads, taken as short cuts between the small towns, and used as Lovers' Lanes, farmers' ponds with mud bottoms where we went swimming without needing to ask permission, county fairs with ferris wheels and barns full of livestock and farm boys, beautiful horses parading in the ring, and tents full of cakes and pies and flowers that won prizes.

There were long winter nights, dark and cold and white with snow, and long summer days, hot and humid, full of insect hums and bird song, springs with their hope and morel mushrooms, and autumns with their color and piles of leaves before burning.

Our parents' ashes are buried in the cemetery there, an old cemetery with big old trees. In the spring, the grounds are filled with the red shoots of hundreds of peonies and the grass is dotted with tiny pink starflowers. We don't go back much any more – our friends have scattered, the old house has been sold and remodeled, the land divided, most of our relatives are dead now. But Petersburg, the way it was and the way we were in it, remains with us, unchanged in memory. The long hill up to our house, its banks filled with blue and yellow wildflowers or heaped with snow; the churches, red brick or gray stone, with their stained glass; the schoolrooms, smelling of chalk and polish and filled with sunlight; the neighbors and friends met on the square, to stop and talk with for an unhurried time, friends met after school or at night for a Coke and gossip. We belonged there. It was ours. It still is. ~Anne

Peterson Girls. I was only eight or nine months old when the Peterson Girls became an integral part of my life.

It's only in retrospect that I can see them so clearly. They lived on a farm west of Petersburg that originally spread over 2,000 acres. It was, maybe, a federal land grant handed down from "Aunt" Onie's grandpa, maybe even her great-grandpa. She married Hardy Peterson and they had at least six children: Esther, the oldest girl, then Mary, Lois, and Jane. Dale was the youngest, surviving another child who died at birth.

That's the past history. Daddy and Dale were buddies as boys. Dale went to college, Dad left home at 18. They trapped and hunted and adventured together when they were young. The bond was still there when Emery brought Elizabeth and their baby girl back from California to live in Petersburg at the beginning of the Depression. Remember The Fire in <u>Eldest</u>? We went the Petersons the night of The Fire; I only found this out recently from one of the Peterson Girls. Remember when I found out I was the eldest? It was Lois who told me that Sara had been born.

One hot summer afternoon Momma sat in the front room reading to me. We were interrupted by a neighbor who had a message (we had no phone). "Uncle" Hardy had been baling hay and his new slick-soled shoes slipped him to his horrific death in the hay baler. He had loved me mightily and would stand me on their lace-covered dining table IN MY SHOES to recite a poem he'd taught me:
"I like peaches, I like pie,
I like a little girl just sooo high!"
and he would raise my arms sooo high.

All my children and grandchildren learned this poem when they were tiny. Still makes me think of Uncle Hardy. Though I don't think any of them stood on a lace-covered table in their shoes to recite it!

One time Momma said that after my nap we would go to the Petersons. I'm not sure whether this was before or after Hardy's death. When I woke from the nap, it seems as if no one was in the house. Having been told we were going to Peterson's, I left home, went to the bridge north of our house, down the embankment, and walked the railroad tracks to the next bridge, southwest of town and close to the Petersons. I knew the trains went that way so that was the way I went. Talk about FRANTIC!

Maybe FRANTIC isn't the operative word for another early remembrance the includes the Petersons, but…We were coming back from visiting there. Momma had Sara on her lap (the baby safety seat of those days) and she turned to me and said, "is your door closed?" Being oh, so grown up and responsible and remembering the big people opening and slamming car doors while cars were in motion, I attempted the same. Of course, I began exiting the vehicle. Momma kept the car on the road, kept the baby in front of her, and grabbed me by my dress hem as she pulled the car to a stop.

Dale later married a woman who was an English teacher and taught all the Rawlings girls. All three of us admired her very much, but she had little in common with the Petersons. Dale was not able to be a devoted son and a devoted husband at the same time, so he and his family were not close. He was postmaster in Petersburg for many years and when I returned as an adult I often visited him and his family. It was an awkward situation, as I knew there was little friendship between Dale and his sisters.

Aunt Onie, after her husband's death, kept the farm going with workhorses and later with tractors. Hardy had had a blacksmith shop and Jane, the youngest daughter, could shoe a horse, make machine repairs, and many other skills related to farm life. She could also make a coconut cake fit for a queen.

There was a dairy business with Lois in charge of the operation: feeding cows, milking, bottling, cleaning equipment, and then delivering twice daily to customers around town. Their cottage cheese is a remembered delicacy – a faintly sour, salty tang never to be duplicated in my life so far. Lois also scrubbed the kitchen floor every day before processing the fresh warm milk that was never pasteurized.

The Petersons had pigs and sheep. They had geese, ducks, and chickens for which Onie baked huge pans of corn-plus-other-grains bread. They always had lots and lots of barn cats and Lois always had a Boston bull dog. One would die and another would come to take its place. They also had a big dog when I was little, named Sharpie, maybe a collie mix.

The best part was that I was allowed to go to all the barns and pens, down the lanes, and into the gardens. I was allowed everywhere except the grain barn – it was dangerous – and there were so many places to go and things to do that I never needed to visit the grain barn. My visits were always too short, no matter how long they lasted.

Esther taught third grade at First Ward School, and it was a thrill to me to be her student when the time came. In her supply closet she had hung a Chicago Tribune cartoon, which was my first glimpse of "Injun Summer," printed every autumn by the Trib until it became politically incorrect. You can guess who I think of every fall.

Mary was a schoolteacher, too. For many years she taught at a one-room country school, often having to plow her way through the snow and keep the stoves stoked, as well as teaching as many as eight grades in a school year. Later she transferred to one of the town schools and taught second grade.

Mary had a small floral business and her own flower garden supplied much of her material. It was a gorgeous place for a little girl to wander, though I couldn't pick the flowers. Mary made my first corsage, a pale lavender creation of many irises that I wore to my eighth-grade graduation exercise. I think it was the loveliest corsage I've ever had.

Sometimes my time was spent inside. I can remember having afternoon tea while sitting next to Aunt Onie at the end of the big dining room table, me in the high-chair and her to my left, since she was left-handed. As she sipped her good strong tea, she would write "Peterson" on the cardboard discs used for capping the milk and cream bottles. I had my tea, liberally laced with milk and sugar, from a precious child's teacup of white porcelain. We usually had bread and butter with a little brown sugar on top. The bread was home-baked with wheat flour from their own wheat, the butter was home-churned, and my bread was cut into one-inch squares for a little girl.

There was a darling tiny old-fashioned upright piano, having maybe two and a half octaves that I could play. I expect it was an itinerant sales-man's demonstration model. How I wish I had those dishes and that piano!

When I was little I slept upstairs with Lois (I called her Low-dee) in her pretty cozy room on the south side of the house. The room had its own pot-bellied stove. As I got older, I slept in what had been Dale's room at the bottom of the stairs. In that room was a white bearskin rug with its head as part of the rug.

There were many times I'd go home from a visit with my fingernails painted RED. Momma didn't like it and told me so but I guess she never asked that they quit, and I did love being fussed over. I was held and cud-dled, tickled and teased. I was the little girl for the Peterson girls that none of them ever had. Their love for me was an active one, though none of them ever said, "I love you."

When I think of them I am a little girl again, traveling around the farm, chattering about new lambs or a garden I've planted next to the privy or fondling baby ducks warming behind the big kitchen cook-stove.

Onie-Hardy-Esther-Lois-Jane-Mary-Dale. They are alive in my memo-ries, just as my parents and Nannie and Grandpa are. Mary, 94 and Lois 92, live on the farm where they were born and they will always be the Pe-terson <u>Girls</u> to me. ~Georgia

Popcorn. How do you like your popcorn? Double butter? Light? No but-ter? Lo-sodium? No, no, no.

You like your popcorn popped in a three-cornered aluminum kettle, probably requiring two or three kettles full.

Wait, I have to go back. This was pre-World War II and the United States was still depressed so, along with all the sweet corn in the garden, enough popcorn was grown for a year's eating.

Early in those growing years, Daddy decided big yellow-kernelled popcorn produced too many "old maids." "Old maids" are the un-popped kernels at the bottom of the bowl that sometimes break teeth, in case you didn't know.

He did plant different varieties from year to year so we ate white, and red, and black popcorn. Of course, when popped it all became white with different colored centers.

After harvesting, the corn was dried and on Sunday night someone, usually one or more of us girls, would stand on the unheated glazed back porch to shell enough corn for the evening's eating. This was done by rubbing two ears together, the kernels dropped into a pie plate or other shallow pan.

After blowing vigorously to remove the chaff, it finally was ready for the popcorn kettle. Sometimes the chaff dropped to the floor and some-one swept it up later.

We were never allowed to eat in bed – except for popcorn. We had Togstad bowls, big red enamel covered bowls heaped high with fluffy homegrown popcorn lightly sprinkled with salt. No butter, thank you, nor artificial flavors found in the popcorn shops of today. No one had ever heard of a popcorn shop back then.

One deviation was at Christmas time when Momma made popcorn balls – delicious sweet confections colored red and green. She tried making chocolate popcorn balls once in a while, but they didn't hold together as well as the red and green ones, and they didn't taste like popcorn, be-sides.

Popcorn is considered a healthful food for cardiac patients. It is a good source of fiber. Popcorn, for me, is a wonderfully comforting food, appropriate for a Sunday night supper with a schoolboy apple and a glass of cold milk.

To read a favorite book with popcorn at my side is a pleasure I dearly love even at the age of seventy-one. ~Georgia

Prisms. We had bits of glass all over our house. Things that dad had taken in payment over the years when he did work for people and they couldn't pay. Mom filled old bottles with colored water, which reflected from the high east windows onto the tall walls of the "front room." We were all fascinated by the bouncing color and our ability to control the bounce. On the days she changed the water or added a new bottle I would "help" which really meant watching the colors flit and change as she moved them around to suit.

But the best was when I was sick; mom would hang a real glass prism from the big window in my room. As the day evolved the color and length of the rainbow would entertain me for hours. Mom would come into the room from time to time and move the wee bit of glass that would cause the rainbow to dance about all over the walls and ceiling. This is a silly thing to put into our dictionary, but I feel the prism rainbows gave me a deep appreciation for colors and for the wonder of the *arc en ciel* itself. Whenever I see a rainbow I am filled with joy and awe. This is a very good thing. ~Sara

Privies. This really tells the story to the youngsters, doesn't it? "What's a privy?" the grandchildren want to know.

Well, it's not those funny toilet-y edifices in parks with their indoor toilet seats and the stench of chemicals, and with concrete floors often moist with something unmentionable – or maybe it's just water. I do not want to know!

Nostalgic, cutesy pictures of hollyhocks surrounding privies with crescent moons cut in a wall come to mind, possible with a shuttered window and a window box filled with gay summer blossoms. Our privy had none of those amenities. Ours was an unpainted outhouse with the door facing the street and was a two-holer.

A respectable privy was a small shed built over a hole dug in the earth and with a wooden box inside that was the height of a chair. The top of the box had one, two, or three holes, and a wooden floor in front of the box.

The first privy we had was sort of in the middle of the back yard with a stone walkway leading to it. A purple martin birdhouse I won at school for getting all A's kept sentinel nearby.

When I was a very little girl, I always went outside in my nightie in the dark if I needed to use the privy. Momma asked me, "Are you afraid in the dark?" NO, I wasn't but I often thought maybe she was.

Some people had three-holers, with the third one cut smaller for children. The hole was always cut at an angle so that when sanded it would be satin smooth for our bottoms. The wood never was painted in the places I used.

Some privies had lids for the holes, though ours did not. The lids were usually just square boards, tipped up as necessary, but I've used a couple of them that had hinged lids – very upscale, don't you think?

As for having a two-hole "privy" meaning private or personal, it seems to be an oxymoron. We sometimes visited the privy with a sister or a friend or Momma; today I never am in a toilet with anyone! Further, we say we're going to the bathroom nowadays when we really mean we're going to a privy room, rather than going to take a bath.

Then there is that matter of toilet tissue. At our house, we used pages from old Sears and Roebuck catalogs, being careful to use the pages without color. Colored ones were slick. We crumpled them as we sat, making them softer to use.

The Peterson's privy had old dress patterns, which were, and are, made of tissue. Because one person who lived there worked in a dry-goods store, there always was an ample supply in a little wooden box. Of course, an occasional insect or rodent made for little surprises but it was better than the catalog.

As you'd expect, some privies had toilet tissue bought at the grocery store. Most toilet tissue was found in three-holers with hinged lids. That was really putting on airs!

I don't remember when our privy got moved behind the garage, nor why. Unlike those park things, home privies eventually filled so that may be the reason. A heavy layer of lime periodically was poured down the hole to diminish bad odors, in case you wondered, and I never remember a bad stench like those emanations I encounter in those nasty park places.

The convenience of privies may not be apparent. If a child is returning from school and suddenly is seized by an urge, it is the matter of a moment quickly to sneak into a privy. Going to the door of a stranger to request the use of a toilet is out of the question.

Conversely, in the midst of a rainstorm or a howling snowstorm, it was lovely when we finally had indoor plumbing. There was an old heavy red sweater with black trim that everyone used during those races to the back yard when the weather was fierce. Anything to avoid using a potty and, later, having to empty it!

Anyway, the privy had been moved to a more discreet spot and we began using "boughten" toilet tissue. It was a two-holer, really the seat that had been in the first one. By this time using it was a solitary activity. Momma wasn't needed to show proper procedure, sisters weren't welcome because they were sisters, and most of our friends had indoor toilets.

Maybe Daddy moved it because he loved to sit in the privy with the door open, looking down the fence-line, with a fenced pathway for the beef cattle traipsing through occasionally on the west side of the fruit orchard. Maybe in the privy he really was sitting on the throne of his kingdom that he loved so dearly. Although he installed a toilet in 1948 he used the privy until the house was sold in 1980 something. ~Georgia

Q

Quiet. I remember the quiet of our house. Oh yes, there was music, the radio playing, voices talking, singing, the sounds of my father's saw buzzing in his basement workshop, my mother's sewing machine, the Mixmaster in the kitchen.

But it was quiet.

Of a morning, Mother and I still full of sleep at the breakfast table, Dad already up and about at the household chores before regular work began – stoking the furnace, seeing to the livestock, quiet morning talk before the demands of school and work and chores.

Summer afternoons, so quiet you could hear the buzzing of the bees through the open windows, the drone of the cicadas ringing loud through the screens.

Sunday quiet was flavored with the remains of pot roast or fried chicken, each of us in separate rooms, reading or napping, unless company was there – quiet company, murmurings from the seldom used front room, low ripples of laughter from the women, deep chuckles from the men.

Winter quiet, warm in the house with the smell of baking bread, outside cold and white, the crunch of snow underfoot sounding loud in frozen air that carried sound a thousand miles. Washdays in winter, with the big wooden frame stretched over the furnace register, hung with pillowcases and shirts, drying so quietly, adding their humid comfort to the dry air.

Spring had a louder quiet, the windows up for the first time in months, busy breezes whisking through the house, curtains coming down for washing and stretching and rehanging, storm windows to be washed, screens to go up, daffodils making loud growing sounds beyond the fence in the pasture, their white bells ringing soundlessly and their scent in bouquets chasing the last of winter's chill from the rooms.

The quiet of our reading, the quiet click of Scrabble tiles on the table, the quiet whir of cards being shuffled or jigsaw pieces slipping into place. The click of the arm on the phonograph settling itself on the album, now wide LP's instead of my sisters' 78's, the quiet swell of symphony or chorus that grew louder – and we all directed, waving arms—before it sank into quiet again.

My sisters were gone, my parents were peaceful as they moved into their later years. We loved our solitude, our contentment, the sights and sounds of nature, our books, the days warm and cold, the nights dark and starry. We lay on blankets in the back yard during hot summer nights, Dad's voice blurring in my ears as I sank in and out of sleep until, softly, the blanket was folded and we crept quietly into bed.

My mother once said to me, "Why don't you call someone to come over? Why don't you invite some friends? You're always reading—don't you want to have some fun?" I knew even then that she was looking at my quiet life against the background of her own youth, busy, noisy with people, bustling with activity, and thinking that I was an odd duck, or perhaps she was fearful that I was being left out of things.

But I had enough friends and enough activity, and now I know what I couldn't have explained then: other people's houses were for parties and fun, for sleepovers and gossip and girl talk about boys and clothes. My house was for quiet, for dreaming my own dreams and thinking my own thoughts. Other teenagers did not belong there very often. It was a special place, my retreat from the noise of the world and from public demands. It was a place of quiet—home. I feel that way still. ~Anne

Quilting. One thing I've pulled up from my inactive file is a beautiful room full of women and quilts. The quilt in progress is stored on two long round rods, stood upright in some out of the way corner. We quilted in the winter when the ground was frozen, covered in snow, unable to produce.

The room is Nannie's dining room – not a huge room but bright with a western exposure through tall windows. The sweet smell of cooking permeates the space and lots of woman chatter, pleasant and jokey as the two long rods are positioned over the big oak dining table. Two sisters will arrange the quilt edge over the far rod, closest to the window. The quilt is rolled on the rod as the stitching is finished. Around the table each quilter has her own needle – some are long, some short – most of the quilters use a thimble and short thread no longer than 12 inches. Early in my inclusion around the table the reasons for the differences are explained. Bessie has small hands - she plays the piano at the Baptist church, you know - she uses a short needle.

Grace, who was 6'1" upright, used a middle finger thimble and a long needle. All sisters use a short thread and I am told long threads tangle – even though one stops to thread oftener, the short thread doesn't catch on itself and make knots. I can close my eyes and hear and see my grandmother explaining how not to tangle one's quilting thread.

The big fingers of Grace – I always thought about that. The needle, larger than the rest of the women's, moving in and out of the fabric more quickly than the smaller, neater hands of her sisters - graceful, deft and unhurried, but quick. She would finish her spot on the quilt and often not miss a beat in the conversation as she changed places with a sister who was not as quick to finish her rosette or block or whatever the pattern in order to move on – never did I hear words of "you're too slow" or "why can't you keep up" - never a put down, but exact acceptance of where each of us was right then.

It's a realization to be there now. In my head – in my young body – I can feel the acceptance, the inclusion. I wanted to be there – they wanted me.

The quilt pieces were from dresses and shirts and other quilts. Often the sisters would reminisce about this dress or that shirtwaist. They could recount the day, the place, the occasion and laugh or cry and explain at great length the feelings of that time - the taste of the potluck or the flirting with whoever was turning the crank on the ice cream maker and "how Bud's hair smelled when we danced."

I was taught how to hand sew to create what I now know to be a piece of art. Our old "homemade" quilts would fetch many dollars from collectors today. In MY time though these quilts were functional pieces used every night to cover ourselves for warmth. If a quilt was especially beautiful by the ladies' standards, it would be used as the "good" bedspread in the summertime. People quilt today to create art; we quilted then to socialize and create comfort. Gosh, I like this memory. ~Sara

Quilts. Of course one of the pleasures of simpler times was quilts. Everyone had quilts because no one could afford to buy blankets against our cold Midwest winters. All that was needed was fabric pieces, not necessarily with coordinated colors nor intricate designs. Many quilt makers had no sewing machine, and in fact, felt that machine-sewn quilts somehow were inferior.

Momma and Nannie both knew something about quilting, though each had different skills. I remember a decorative pillow cover Momma had using the "yo-yo" method. This consisted of circles of dull green, purple, and pink fabrics hemmed narrowly around the circumference with the thread then drawn tight. That created a pouch that was flattened and each was then whipped with black thread to its neighbor creating a hexagonally shaped pillow cover.

Yes, there was lots of work put into it, and yes, it was ugly! Another quilt, a "Sun Bonnet Sue" pattern, was badly worn and was used as a mattress pad. Waste not – want not was the motto of the time.

Nannie's quilts for the most part consisted of squares and rectangles in no apparent layout. What she did well was the actual quilting, the tiny stitches that fastened the backing through the stuffing to the quilt top. The ideal ratio was fourteen stitches to the inch.

Nannie had her own quilting frame, actually long boards three inches wide and ¾th inch thick that had been covered with padded pillow ticking. The padding was to anchor the quilt layers to the frame, which was held together by ornate black wrought iron quilting clamps at each corner. Many hands sat around that frame in Nannie's dining room stitching and visiting. Eventually, they went away, Nannie got old, and the frame went to the attic.

Years later I hand-stitched a queen sized "Grandmother's Flower Garden" quilt. It was put together with over 1,100 hexagons, one and a quarter inches per side, cut from remnants of Sara's and my little girl dresses that Momma had made.

I had found the remnants in what we called The Attic. They were stuffed in big flour sacks, pieces too good to throw away, too small for any practical use, even Momma's ubiquitous aprons.

Some of the fabric patterns weren't familiar. When the quilt was beginning to take shape and Momma was visiting with me, we pulled it out and as she identified them, I wrote down what she told me. She described how the garments had been made, and whether Sara and I both had a dress of the same style. She also identified a special print with a yellow background and white coin-sized circles, outlined in brown. She said it was her "hat dress" and we both laughed heartily when she explained. "She was wearing a hat," she had told me when she was pregnant with Sara. Good heavens! Children's ears must not hear "pregnant" spoken in polite company.

When the quilt was nearing completion, I decided that the quilt should be quilted on Nannie's quilting frame. When I went home the next time, I asked Nannie if I could use it. She said yes, of course, so I brought it down from her attic and she gave me the clamps (which I still have). She instructed me with clarity how to put the layers together and how to attach them to the frame. Her instruction was so clear, and then I asked, "Now when I begin to stitch, do I stitch at right angles to the frame, or along the frame?"

Her reply was, "You stitch from North to South. Of course, if you were Jenni (my oldest daughter), you'd stitch from South to North." I thought Nan had lost it for a minute, and then she asked a question. "Isn't Jenni left-handed?"

I was the one who had lost it. Nannie's quilt frame always had been set to face the west windows in her dining room. She'd always done her quilting in the afternoon to get the best sunlight and of course stitched along the frame, "North to South."

There were other quilts Nannie and Momma created, and others I made, as well. Come to think of it, this book, too, is a quilt, a quilt of our lives, snippets and patches, words woven together to create a covering of warmth and comfort, some parts not as lovely as others. Like other quilts, it has been folded away, put on the shelves of our minds for many years. Now, though, it's been spread out for everyone to see the handiwork, the creativity and the beauty. It is felt through reading, knowing how deep the fiber is, what the fabric has become, how ingenious the putting together of its pieces.

Quilts get hung on walls, spread across beds, used as mattress pads or padding when moving furniture. This quilt is for none of those uses. It is precious and to be put around your soul as a solace if you need it, or as a chuckle if you are tickled. ~Georgia

R

Reading. There was no television in our house. Even though by the time I was 12 or 13, TVs were relatively commonplace in the homes of my friends, my father refused to have one in the house. After a teacher assigned homework which required watching a Shakespeare play on television (I watched it at a friend's house), my mother, I believe, tried to persuade Dad that television might be a requirement. He dug in his heels, however, and refused to be persuaded. We didn't have much money but there seemed to be money available for records and, always, for books.

One Sunday, when I was five, I had a tantrum after church because I couldn't read the verses in the hymnal. Most of the first verses I knew by heart, but second and third verses, or an unfamiliar hymn, put me in the position of having to stand silently while the rest of the congregation sang on. Sermons were often boring, but I liked to sing – thus, the tantrum.

Never one to wait for someone else to provide a solution, my mother, that same afternoon, brought out books from some secret hoard – spellers, primers, vocabularies – and introduced me to phonetic reading. Within what seemed a relatively short time – a week or a month – I was reading on my own. After I asked Mama for the 99th time the meaning of a new word, she threw on my bed an unabridged dictionary, five inches thick and almost half my weight, and taught me how to use it. There was no stopping me at that point, and if nothing else was at hand, I read the dictionary.

Somewhere in this time frame, certainly in the same year, I was diagnosed with rheumatic fever. In those days, the treatment involved sulfa drugs and lots and lots of bed rest. Over the next two years, I alternated between being in bed for months at a time and having limited activity, but did not return to school until I was eight. A tutor came to the house occasionally, more than one in fact, to teach me the basics of writing, arithmetic and other elementary subjects, but instead of practicing my penmanship or working on my sums – I read.

Lest tears come to your eyes at the thought of this poor, pale, invalid child, like those in Victorian novels, I assure you that, to this day, I look back on that time as full of happy memories. For my mother, who for

124

some time was sure I was going to die (I learned later), it was an anxious time and a time of great labor and patience – a child to keep in bed, to wash in bed, to feed, to massage, and often to provide bedpans when doctors felt that even bathroom privileges were too much activity – bless her for all of that.

But my memories include a pet canary who had the run of the house, who was finger-tamed and sat on my books to peck the pages as they turned; a kitten sleeping on my bed now and then (not with the bird out of the cage, of course); dear friends of my mother's who brought me small dolls with complete wardrobes, surprise packages and treats of all kinds, the old encyclopedia at my disposal, coloring books, modeling clay, finger painting, and, of course, books. Books by the hundreds, perhaps by the thousands. Books for breakfast, lunch, and dinner, books before and after naps and before going to sleep. Books lent and borrowed and purchased and taken from the attic and dusted off.

Early in this time, a woman whose daughter had had the same illness lent me their collection of Oz books. Now, of course you know that there is a movie called The Wizard of Oz, and you may even know that it is based on a book by L. Frank Baum. You are among a smaller minority if you also know that Mr. Baum wrote not one, but 14 books about Oz, and that after he left this world to go to Oz personally, a number of other authors picked up where he left off and produced dozens of other Oz titles.

I did not see the movie until I was in my thirties, being a purist. Now I have seen it many times (what do you expect with all these grandchildren?) and I agree, it is a lovely, charming, wonderful film. But – it is a musical, the lion is not real, and its ending is entirely wrong. The point is not that we find happiness in our own back yard (of course we do), but that Oz exists. It exists, as the editor wrote to Virginia, like Santa Claus, to delight the minds and hearts of children. Not believe in Oz? Why, you might as well not believe in Santa Claus!

If you don't know the Nome King or Jack Pumpkinhead, you don't know Oz. If you haven't met Button Bright or the Hungry Tiger or the Shaggy Man, you're missing the point. If you don't know that Ozma is the princess of Oz (and that Dorothy is a princess, too, and lives there now), then you haven't a clue.

Excuse the digression, but Oz is a serious subject and taken much too lightly by most.

Reading was why I was never really lonely, even though I had few visitors, and very, very few visitors my age. In 1949, experts knew that rheumatic fever was not contagious, but not many adults wanted to take a chance, particularly with their children, and so my friends were those I met by reading.

Reading was not, for me, a simple pastime, nor an escape from a dull reality, nor something I did only when nothing better was at hand. It was an activity that, in our family, was not only encouraged but expected. Every one of us read, and the evenings and Sunday afternoons were often still and quiet, each of us in our own room, lost in a book. Stacks of books, closet shelves full of comic books, poetry, plays, cereal boxes – if it was printed, I read it.

Because of my early reading, I discovered too soon and before I was ready about the common non-belief in Santa Claus. A few days before Christmas, when I was six, Georgia and Paul were home for the holidays, and I was to sleep in the attic while they were given my bedroom. I was reading the current issue of Life magazine, and there, over several pages and in full color, was an article on all the department store Santa Clauses – their costumes, their beards, their participation in an evil conspiracy to delude trusting children. I went into strong hysterics at full volume. Sissy and Paul spent an hour or more trying to convince me that the spirit of giving was the real Santa, and when that didn't work, they spent another hour claiming that Life magazine was printing lies. Well, I was sad that Christmas and it took the family another year or two to restore my belief in Santa Claus, a belief that my children and grandchildren have been careful to protect (now, don't tell Mommie – she still thinks he's real). Really.

Reading allowed me to be different people, in different times, in different places. I rode horses and dragons, camels and mules, sailed on ships and submarines, slid down rainbows and traveled to the Moon and Mars and distant galaxies. In books, I could be a dog or a horse or a rabbit. I could wear the guise of a kindly sorceress or a wicked witch. I lost my glass slipper and pricked my finger on a spindle; I ate a poisoned apple, and danced holes in my slippers. I slid down rabbit holes and stepped through looking glasses and sipped things that said, "Drink Me." In charming parlors, I drank tea and learned to curtsey, I rambled in shrubberies and dressed for country dances to which I rode in carriages drawn by horses and driven by old coachmen, who told me to mind my slippers, miss.

There is no end to where I've been, what I've done, whom I've met, what I've thought. You lose yourself in books, they said. Oh, no…I find myself in books – and I find you – and you – and you. ~Anne

Religion. My mother was the driving force behind our religious life. Which is really odd, as while her family may have been somewhat spiritual and may have been churchgoers, I am not at all sure they were "religious."

As mom was plunked down in her own personal Bible belt (my dad's family) her religion may have been due to osmosis and a place to be in her head to find comfort in a not so comfortable place. I remember my dad's dad sitting for hours reading his Bible, but he was dour and unhappy. Whatever he sought in the Scriptures seemed always to elude him. Nannie, as we called my dad's mother, was happy, joyful and without a doubt about God. Neither her God nor my own moma's was punitive or fearsome. He was easy to know, great to lean on and always there for us all if we called.

We started as Southern Baptists with dad's bunch, but as Mom became more into the actual activity of church going, she was uncomfortable with the rigidity of the tenets as well as the view of God toting up our transgressions for zappers at His whim.

I was baptized by immersion at seven and it was right and I was ready. It's one of the childhood things that is etched in my memory. I remember a pink gauzy dress and wetness. Walking down several steps and a huge, pool-like area to the water, which was at the back of the pulpit and covered over with a large board when not in use. Our minister was waiting waist deep in the baptismal pool. There was no feeling of fear. It was exciting and mysterious. I was full of awe and wonder. I was dunked in the name of the Father, the Son, and the Holy Ghost – and then there was mom with a towel ready to enfold me. She was so happy for us. I remember getting rubbed dry and lots of dad's aunts around. Lots of joy and celebrating. There were other people there for their baptism – I am so grateful that I had this type of baptism. It took.

When we lived in California, we moved on to the First Christian Church or the Disciples of Christ depending on to whom you speak. Then when we came back we did not return to the Baptist church. Moma became active in Iscah, which, as I remember was adult Sunday school. Through high school I attended Sunday school and sang in our church choir.

As an adult I began to realize that church seemed very political and full of lots and lots of "hats." I began to think that the ladies came to church to outdo one another's hats. Lots of socialization with not much to do with "Good Works" as mom referred to things done "with a glad heart" for other people and on the "QT," as she put it.

I took my kids to church all through childhood and beyond. We went to a very prestigious church in Hyde Park, in Chicago, for a few years, but I finally threw in the towel when the Sunday school superintendent forbid three little black brothers to come to Sunday school because they took the (empty) collection plates home "because they were pretty." The stupid man declared them thieves. My position was more than slightly different, needless to say. The last and final straw was one year at the Christmas pageant, the mother of one of the angels came to church in a satin off-the-shoulder cocktail dress – it was suggested that she was inappropriate. I still ache for her discomfort. What did Mary Magdalene wear to wash Jesus' feet? Three piece suit and sensible shoes? I lost the argument, trying to convince them it was OK to wear whatever so long as they came to church.

I have always been uncomfortable with lots of talk about what's done in the name of God and what needs to be done – lots of committees that socialize rather than do. I have been involved in many churches – Baptist, Christian, Anglican and Catholic – to the extent my kids went to avoid our awful local grammar school. I find that I am most comfortable where there is warmth, humor, goodwill and openness. The people who visit persons with AIDS, hold boarder babies, read to the blind – these folks are my true heroes. All these things with no pomp and fulfilling every circumstance.

My own evolution as a spiritual being comes, I think, from all the miracles bestowed on me in my life. I have risen above, plowed through, circumvented so much bad stuff that couldn't have been avoided other than with some intervention from Himself. The greatest miracle is my personal evolution; from skinny, scared, unsure kid to "on my way and still going."

My view of life has evolved kind of like an artichoke – freshly steaming - sitting on the plate, with each leaf there's a choice and if we are lucky and play close attention we get very few of the sticky ends between our teeth. As we age and bite off each leaf of our personal artichoke, it is more tender, better. We are less likely to get the sticky ends if we've paid attention. At the end is the soft delicious morsel that is pure enjoyment, the reward for plowing through the sticky ends successfully.

So while I am not a churchgoer, I reckon I am religious and most certainly a spiritual person. And I am glad. Thanks again, folks, for the stuff you got so absolutely right. ~Sara

Rhubarb. We had rhubarb in the garden.

Anyone who sneers at rhubarb must not have seen it grown nor had it as a child. Massive, enormous, gleaming leaves of dark green (that are poisonous – did you know?), suspended on stalks twelve or fifteen inches high of a brilliant ruby pink. Where the stalks come out of the ground, they widen a bit and are of a lighter silvery rose.

Outside, these stalks are cut carefully from the leaves, taken in and washed, cut up into one-inch pieces, then stewed with a little water and quite a bit of sugar into a delicious, though admittedly gummy, mass. You can put a dab of cream on it if you like, though it's just as good without. Or it can be put into pies or cobblers, or combined with strawberries, or perhaps raspberries, served as a sauce over ice cream, or dabbed on toast or, better, hot biscuits. Rhubarb was canned or frozen for a summer treat in the dead of winter, sometimes spread on French toast, or put on bread warm from the oven.

My father must have loved to grow rhubarb, because we had tons of it, enough to eat, can, sell and at the end of the season to give away.

And while friends, neighbors, and acquaintances may have been polite about the green beans, strawberries, and raspberries we donated, they would line up to buy the rhubarb. Calls would start coming in two or three weeks before the rhubarb was ripe, with requests to "save us some." Lists had to be kept.

Other gardeners begged for Dad's secret growing methods, and the only thing I ever heard him say was "Lots of manure." I don't think they believed him, silly things. I saw him pile it on every year. ~Anne

S

Scooter. I look at the scooters zipping around the streets in the new phase of toys. HA these are not scooters – some of 'em have motors for heavens sake. HMPH.

When I owned a scooter in Vallejo CA it was a scooter! It was red like a fire engine and had hard rubber white-walled wheels. It had black rubber handle caps and a brake pedal that I worked by sliding my heel back and pressing down. A tongue of metal pressed the back wheel and I stopped! The footrest part was maybe 8" wide and it went like the wind – Sara powered. We lived at that time at the bottom of a very steep hill on the other side of which was almost the Pacific Ocean, I thought. This hill was tall, big by anyone's lights, even an adult's.

For some reason known surely not to me, I went to the top of that hill one day and rode to the bottom - no I flew to the bottom. Such freedom, such exhilaration, such absolute power. So I continued to fly whenever the chance presented itself. At some point my big sister discovered I was doing this on a regular basis and made it look pretty easy. She also told her friends – one of whom wanted to try it and did, but poor thing, used the brake too sharply and went butt over braces, broke her arm, her glasses and her spirit. She braked at the intersection "just in case." She didn't quite have the knack, the trust. I never did this. I was stupid, or I had lots of faith, as moma used to say.

Georgia told dad at some point what I was up to but wonder of wonders - Dad got such a kick from my flights. Such pride - now why was that? I was not allowed to swim, roller skate, ice skate or ski, but the scooter was ok and the down hill ride was even better. Maybe because I mastered it before he knew what I was up to. That scooter and that ride in some peculiar way helped me realize there was some nugget of independence, some trust in my own intuition that helped me find who I was to become. To say nothing of the pride in me on the part of my dad and sister. How interesting, the things and events that shape and sometimes even save our lives. Scooters are excellent. ~Sara

Secrets. All families have secrets. We had ours: those secrets from the outside world, which probably in that small town were no secrets at all, and only the most insensitive or perhaps the most nasty of individuals would bring up a topic that anyone else would know should remain undiscussed. We had secrets within the family, too, secrets from each other and, sometimes, secrets each of us knew that we could not admit even to ourselves, even when we were alone at night with our thoughts and dreams.

Daddy's first marriage was such a secret. I was sixteen, and we had recently indulged in a stereo hi-fidelity system, installed in walnut cabinets built by Dad. Once or twice a month, he would sit in the front room, listening to a test record that happened to be the sounds of trains – old trains, the steam and puff of locomotives, the hiss of brakes, the clank of cars coupling and uncoupling. Through the miracle of modern sound (modern for that time), the trains could be heard moving from one side of the wide room to the other.

I had given him that recording one Christmas, and I had never seen him so pleased with a gift, he actually blushed and was speechless. All my life I had heard how he loved working on the trains in his youth and it must have been a good recording because he listened to it and would describe the types of engines and the activities taking place, only heard in our front room, but seen again in his memory.

And one fine day, with the sounds of the trains rumbling through the house, my mother, at the kitchen sink, murmured almost to herself, "He must be thinking of his first wife." At first I thought I had heard wrong; then I thought I would faint. Mother brushed it all aside. "It was a long time ago, he was young, and she was older than he was, it didn't last long." Later, I confided in my sisters during their visits home. "Oh, yes," they said casually, "that was Charlotte." And why hadn't they told me, I demanded. "It wasn't important. It was a long time ago, long before he met Mama."

So it wasn't a secret at all, really. They just forgot to tell me. But I was shocked. I thought from time to time about that young man who wasn't my father yet, and this older woman who was his wife, and if they loved each other or if one of them loved more than the other, and how it had ended, and what had happened to Charlotte. It gave my father a new dimension, and I looked at him, looking for that strange young man that dwelt in his past and listened to the sounds of trains.

Mother's broken heart over her first love, Swede, was a sort of a secret – the kind that everyone knew but no one discussed. Sara's meeting and dating Walker was a true secret. She hinted to me about it once, lying on her bed with me, telling me of how it was to be a young teen-aged girl in love, with a boy with eyes like warm chocolate and big strong hands, and a sweet deep voice. I remembered that, later.

I learned secrets as we wrote this book – that Uncle Lynn had been in prison, for running bootleg liquor during Prohibition. Even more shocking, I learned that for all of five minutes, Dad had considered going in with him on this – to put food on the table, to protect his brother, to find a way out of the heartbreaking struggle for work during the Depression years. Thank God it didn't happen.

One of Mother's sisters, Augusta ("Gussie"), was retarded, as they said back then. She lived with her oldest sister, Aunt Kathryn, all her life, and was capable enough to be prized as a baby sitter throughout the neighborhood. The only time I met her, when I was nine and she was forty, she was the best playmate I could imagine, like a slightly older sister or cousin who ran and giggled and played games but was responsible enough to know how far away from the house we could go and when to be back for supper. This was not really a secret, but it was not a topic for casual conversation outside the family, either.

And poor Aunt Marietta, Mama's younger sister, the prettiest, the sexiest, who was an alcoholic most of her life, married and divorced and remarried. I met her too, when I was nine, her icebox full of root beer, her jolly husband, and her pretty teenaged daughter who took me fishing off the pier. It was a good visit because she was on the wagon and the family had hopes that this time it would stick. Poor pretty Marietta, who was found dead in an alley twelve years later, "in mysterious circumstances." I heard nothing more about it.

There was a morning when I was six or eight, when urgent whispers arose in the kitchen and I was rushed over to Nannie's to spend the day, while Nannie occupied me with games and stories in the front rooms of the house – not in the kitchen or the sewing room, which faced north toward the bridge. Years later, I heard the secret – that Mother, glancing out the kitchen window toward the bridge, saw the body, hanging from a strut over the railroad tracks. An unfortunate young man whose name I've forgotten, who had endured more than three dozen painful operations following a serious war injury and could not – could *not* – face another.

There was another time, another morning, when I was rushed away to Nannie's, but not before I heard the phone ring, early, heard Sara on the phone, and heard her scream. The murmurings and then my enforced exit. One of Sara's most loved high school teachers, a talented, kind man who encouraged her abilities, had shot himself – victim of a small-town discovery of his homosexuality. I thought of this later, when I had a teacher who encouraged my abilities, who was talented and bright and funny, who made no bones about who and what he was and paraded on Petersburg's square on Saturdays wearing lavender shorts and a dainty striped sailor's sweater. Well, his contract was simply not renewed and he was gone. I felt a wrench when I learned only six years later that he had died in a car accident, with a companion.

I had my own secret that no one knew. One day when I was fourteen, a big girl for my age, I was visiting Uncle Lynn at Nannie's house across the street. We were alone in the house. I often went to see Uncle Lynn, to learn magic tricks with cards, or watch him draw, beautiful black ink sketches. One hung in Nannie's living room in a frame, of a sunset or a sunrise, the sharp black rays of the sun spreading over a country land. That day as we sat talking, my uncle's arm crept around the back of the sofa, and he touched me. Touched me as an uncle should not touch a niece. I said nothing, but I felt embarrassed and sad and moved quickly from the sofa to a chair, and found an excuse to leave not long after that. I was breathless and a little frightened, and when I got home, Dad was standing in the big front bedroom, doing something. I went to him in a hurry and pressed against him and put my arms round his neck and hugged him as hard as I could. He was so safe. What's this all about, he said, hugging me back, but I could tell he was puzzled. I just needed a hug, I said, I just love you. Well, I did – I loved him enough to never tell him that his brother touched his daughter – touched all his daughters, as I discovered later from my sisters. Poor, lost, sad Uncle Lynn. My sisters thought nothing of it. Certainly it wasn't the first nor will it be the last such event within a family. Certainly it was mild and almost harmless as such things go. I took care not to be alone with my uncle again, and life, as it always does, went on.

Yes, we had secrets. Our family had other secrets. Did you think I was going to tell them all here? Not at all. Some secrets are not for telling. ~Anne

Sewing. The rooms in our house changed use periodically. There was one room that had been used for dad's spice sales, which we called the Togstad room and still do when we speak of THAT room in our house. This room was from time to time a bedroom. It was the wee interlopers space for a time. We had a card table set up in the room for working jigsaw puzzles, but it was finally to become mom's sewing room

Our mother made George and me twin dresses a lot. Keep in mind the fact that we were 4 years difference in age, just never mind all that, she dressed us alike A LOT. The difference was only the color of the print. I don't think we minded this. Hmmm wonder why not?

Remember now, mom was a good and true church going Christian but she did cuss her way through lots of dressmaking. Why she continued to do it I'll never be able to answer. Maybe she just wasn't going to be defeated.

I remember having things of my own as I got older, not twinned. One coat in particular I wore till I resembled a refugee. I found the collar edge quite delicious and chewed it to a nub, yumm.

There was a beautiful silk blouse with ruching across the top. It was autumn orange and way too good to wear. Along with this beauty was a skirt of off white summer wool that was too good to wear as well. I do this even today – have clothes that I don't wear cause they are too good. An occasion never seems to come that quite lives up to THAT particular dress.

Mom's expert dressmaking landed her a job at the local dry-cleaning establishment (part time). She learned to tailor men's suits and to do invisible weaving. Dad wasn't wild about this deal, mom working for money and away from home. I think she did this though after George and I were gone from the nest.

Anyway she made me at least four prom dresses in one season. One was an emerald green satin strapless number with a lace shawl so as not to be too racy. Another was a piqué material in white with roses all over it. She shortened it a bit to make it tea length and added lace at the bodice. And there was a magenta colored number of satin as well. She loved her satin, did my mom. She made my 8th grade graduation dress of sky-blue see through something or other with a yeah, satin under skirt. She made gloves to match. Little half gloves with lace around the edge.

I brought home some funny patterned material one day and sketched out how I wanted a skirt made up. Nothing to it. One day. No cussing. All my classmate girlfriends had poodle skirts, I wanted something different. This was a time when for whatever reason I was called Mert so mom made a black circle skirt and sewed different colors of rickrack around the

bottom that spelled out Mert. Needless to say we called it my Mert Skirt -
what else? For my 16th birthday party there was a navy blue dotted Swiss
dress with a huge full skirt and an organdy collar. (whatcha bet it had a
satin underskirt?) Big collar – white. She had probably 5 yards of satin
ribbon that was to be a cummerbund but time ran out so I just wound the
ribbon around my waist, voila, cummerbund. To this day if my sisters and
I need to return to that time or that dress, any one of the three of us
makes this insane movement with our hands as if we are winding something around our waist and right away we are back to that party – 100
years ago

For my high school graduation I wanted a REAL dress so we found
this perfect thing. It was way too short. But, never fear mom found
some fancy accordion pleated pink satin, which she sewed to the bottom
of the underskirt making a lovely peek through slip affair. The dress material was a navy blue flocked pattern kind like the burned silk of today.
It was delicious.

She made George's bridesmaids' dresses and she made christening
gowns. She made Anne's costumes for school plays. Slacks to fit the
length of my long legs. And though she cussed through lots of this I believe she got great joy from doing this for us. We sure loved our stuff that
looked like no one else's. Wonder where she learned to do this sewing
stuff. ~Sara

Sisters. Remember in the beginning of this book was the word abet? And
it was good. Without that word I could not be writing the things about
sisters that are so necessary to the pathways of this family landscape.

As middle child and not best placed in the hearts of my parents, I
have always felt weighted by much of my siblings' responses to the messages sent to them about me.

From the very beginning of my memory I heard stuff like, we should
have thrown her out and raised the after birth. With this fundamental
message, how the heck could an older sister value a sickly sib?

George was happy that I was here (in the beginning) but as time pro-
gressed it fell to her to take care of me and she was not best pleased by
the task. A tall, thin, sickly wraith floating close, always, seemingly, in her
peripheral vision, never to escape for even one bit of alone time (or so it
must have seemed). Here was this person to be gotten out of the parents
way - a reminder of a something sent for to perform a specific task and
failed that very impossible task...

For four lovely years she had been the apple of the eye of the world,
given whatever our parents had to give and suddenly she was responsible

for this – sister. Her resentment was palpable surely. But George had better fish to fry and didn't miss too many chances to let me know. I think the knowledge of not being her favorite person was always there - lurking - but somewhere around nine or ten when she began to have friends she wanted to be with, the message from my parents began to take a shape that was not so nebulous.

I remember many things that were said to me derisive and caustic, both dad and Georgia were masters of the acid tongue. But aside from words there were other things much more hurtful – physical things. Once George and a friend removed a screen from one of the tall windows in her bedroom and then, convincing me to lean out, she and her friend put the window down on me. I remember the friend was really not sure of this behavior, I remember the sense of her discomfort in the whole procedure. The lowering of the window didn't hurt, mind, but I was trapped, for in our old house the windows were raised and lower by hidden weights in the side of the frames. This window had a broken cord, which meant that the window was either up braced with a book or rod or the window was down. Down it was this time on me - half in the house and half hanging out in the outside. So here's me not quite understanding the whys of this and wondering if I was to be left there. The picture of a turtle on its back comes to mind. Not nice.

Once at an afternoon movie (a very rare treat) a friend of George's who was sitting in a seat in front of me crushed my probably nine-year-old toes in the fold of the seat – then blamed me for having my feet in the seat. Gosh, did that hurt! As usual George did not come to my rescue and I left the movie house, I remember toes hurting to say nothing of feeling devalued and soul hurt. Crying? Oh, yeah. The sis came after me, I think she knew she had crossed a line, saying "sorry" and "come back." I would NOT return. Someway I remember having a little power that day, she was gonna be in BIG trouble was part of it and I could control that – and I was NOT gonna let her off the hook by returning to the movie. Also, a part was not to be a victim that day. I remember the feeling of not being at her mercy being very important. That feeling was what I thought to be a miracle.

There was much real garbagey garbage in our relationship. I was so needy, and so in her way. The truly sad part in this scenario is how much I admired her and really looked up to her. I never could understand why I was so very undesirable, and I never stopped trying to be her friend. Such a loss for us both. Anyway I loved my big sis just bunches despite her whatever of me. I remember at one time I was in a speaking contest; she was helping me with interpretation. I heard her tell moma that she wished her diction was as good as mine. I was 12 – I can still remember that gift of her approval. "She pronounces "just" the right way," (she said); "I had to be told not to say jest instead of just," she told our mom. My God, at 67, I can still feel the thrill (and that is not a good enough word) of having Georgia approve of me. Lord.

During all the growing up time and whatever went on through it, I tried to get in a better place with my big sis. Not to be. Once I asked why she could not love me and her reply was perhaps you are just not loveable. Down her nose. There seemed to be a need to hurt me and I suppose it was the anger of having to parent me. Also remember I was in her way. Perhaps you are thinking – such whining, why didn't she just tell her folks. Ah, lest we forget - the folks were there, they knew, they sent the message in the first place that I was not very special – I could not have expected redress from that quarter. Life's like that sometimes.

Oh, from time to time we had our moments and when we got to-gether as big people, the shared history we focused on with Anne and others in the family were fun based, or trying to figure out what the heck our family was all about. (We never did.) (Maybe now, some.) We never got to be real friends or very close

One night George was visiting at "the home place" as 521 North 11th Street was called, I was doing my stint with the care-giving of our father and we were invited to visit Paul White, an old friend of our family (a guy who knew all of our family and liked us anyway). Well, Paul and George got pretty wet and at one time he said "It must be great to have Sara for a sister. She is so blah, blah, blah" – all good stuff and embarrassing but nice too. When we got home George says you know, Paul is right I am lucky to have you for a sister because you are all that blah blah blah. I just looked at her and thought, if you need someone else to point out that I walk on water it isn't very important and for the first time in my life probably 50 odd years, it did not matter that my big sis did not like me. Frankly my dear, I don't give a damn. Freedom.

The relationship with the interloper, that is to say Anne, and me was quite different. Little sister was my very own doll and I loved her to dis-traction. She was full of baby butterfly kisses and cuddled into crevices like something fluid.

I remember doing a diaper change one time and putting this huge pink headed diaper pin through her baby skin and God help me, pinning it closed. It still hurts to remember that. There was no cry, just a look of distress, which caused me to check the diaper. OH LORD. When I told this story during our writing she LAUGHED (the twit). I still find that memory so hard! She was loveable and I wanted her with me at every chance, even when I didn't want her I think I missed having the wee fat cherub in my wake.

I believe we are born with whatever nature we have. I am a nurturer, being the one to try and fix broken birds, and flowers and even dolls for heavens sake. That was not George's nature. Also Anne was MINE. Nothing as special as she had ever been given to me, so I reveled. I fussed and played and talked to her as I would a peer. I told her secrets the likes of which she could have had not one clue.

Ah but, I had a doll. One of the first ever made "live skin" dolls that sat on my bed – I really fought not to have ANYONE play with it not even Little Annie Roonie. One of the few things I denied her. She was however, allowed to play with the doll because as my father remarked, "who's the biggest baby?" I must say I resented this action, but after all who WAS the baby? So much of that "stuff" should go unreported I think. About that Annie Roonie business, if you are over 50 and Irish maybe you will remember the song of the same name. The last line going something like "little Annie Roonie is my sweetheart." So there in lies that tale. She was the sweetheart of us all probably. I'm surprised they shared.

George was only 4 years older than me. I was 9 years older than Anne. Better equipped in age diff to parent my wee sib – plus the parent message sent was WAY different. There were other inequities in our connections, Georgia's and mine, but they are hurtful and unnecessary to dwell on now. We, my sisters and I, are in such a better place - in a future dictionary maybe we can all address just that – sibling-ships. Just to say a couple things here – Georgia today loves me, of this there is no doubt in my mind and I mean she really LOVES me and as we were wading through some old memories with Anne not too long ago and during this process, I found myself patting and smoothing my evil ole sis's arm - something warm and fuzzy was dancing around in my heart and it was good. It was quite natural and very new. It is the book. It is the process.

Anne and I stayed very close for many years to the point that I probably smothered her – still playing mom, I reckon. We had a tiny bad patch when I moved to France and George moved to Galena – Anne later said she felt abandoned – I guess!

Recently both sisters have asked forgiveness for not being able to give me more support with taking care of dad. I can't say honestly that my care was any more than what I just do when there is a need. At the time there was a need and I was the logical person for the job. Plus now as I write, perhaps I hoped still to get dad's approval.

And now the young one has recently stopped killing herself at a job she once was in love with but which grew to suck her soul. She has been able to return to the calmer place she once occupied plus she fits it even better. The place that enabled her to be friends with her friends as well as her silly sibs. (She claims her sibs are her friends though so go figure.) So for the first time ever we are coming together where we all can laugh and cry and say honest stuff to one another, even very hurtful things, not the sweetest of our memories. Now we can say the things that were important either in helping us love each other or to get the actual take on what happened in reality, which at the time of the happening was not what was happening really. (Got that?)

One of our last writing meetings was even better than the ones before in many ways and I felt safe to say, "this book is way too fluffy, I need to write about Sissie and me, I need to address sisters. Right down to how Sissie became Sissie. And I can't remember, except that my mind sees Nannie's front porch and it is a beautiful day – me standing with the screen door open and calling, "where's Sissie." Everyone liked that and found it good and so it was. It is part of our history. We are lucky, our book is our healing and it is on going.

Now this abet thing. I always thought that word meant to help aid in a wrongdoing – hmmm not exactly. It also means to help get someone or something to a good place. So, use the book as a pattern, as a path to abet you in the process of healing a relationship that could use some work. Keep at it. It starts with the first word. Do it. ~Sara

Skates. The Christmas I was in 4th grade, I got my freedom wheels. Everyone had roller skates, and I finally had a pair, just like all my friends.

These were the OLD kind, not with boots attached, nor with wooden wheels suitable for the popular roller rinks of the day. My skates had a leather strap that secured them to my ankles, and clamps were affixed to the sides of my shoe toes by a key. One end of the key was a wrench. Its purpose, besides securing the skates to our feet, was to loosen or tighten a nut in the center of each skate so the size could be shortened or lengthened to suit one's shoe size. The wheels were made of heavy metal designed to take the hard pounding of sidewalks, with ball bearings inside the center of the wheels to make them go really fast.

Oh, how thrilled I was to have them. Our dining room was twenty-two feet long with wainscoting about 36" high, topped by a molding that jutted out about an inch. Wonder of wonders! Daddy's usual strict rules regarding care of property was relaxed, and I was allowed to practice on the linoleum-covered floor. Wheel marks were visible for years, but boy, was I good, thanks to the wainscot molding and the fact that the floor slanted eight inches from one end to the other, so I could even skate downhill in our dining room.

It was eleven blocks to school and I skated back and forth every single clement day. When we lived in California during World War II, the space between the elementary school auditorium doors and the public sidewalk was a wide, wide concrete slab. I wish you could have seen me then. I learned to race, to skate backwards, to couple skate with a friend, and roller dance with her. We were so great!

Later I went to a junior high school in California, again going on skates. The skates were much longer by then, and so was the route to school, but there was a lot more pleasant weather than in Illinois, so I didn't care.

One day, while coming home, I stroked my left wheels along the route and looked in horror as ball bearings rolled and bounced away on both sides of me. Removing the other skate to dangle by its strap next to its dead mate, I began to cry. All the way home I cried, broken hearted at the betrayal of a man-made pleasure.

After that, I went to the roller rinks with my friends. It was all right, but it wasn't the same. No more spontaneous little spins around the block or down the street. We had to plan our skating time with someone to chauffeur us, and with money in our hands to enjoy the skating.

Now I see the skateboards and they look dangerous. I see the in-line skates that include helmets and limb guards and thick padding, so they must be dangerous, too.

About twelve years ago there was a brief summer in my town when we had an outside rink. One could rent boots-with-rollers and go round and round to the accompaniment of an oomph-pa-pa loud speaker. Two colleagues, both younger than me, decided to go skating on July 4. I laced up the boots, staggered to the rink railing, holding on tightly. Soon I felt the impetus of rolling wheels beneath me, the speed increasing, and then I was off!! I was a little girl again, whirling along with the freedom of a 4th grader, and my 50ish friends looked in amazement as I swished past them. I'd like to do it again. ~Georgia

Sunday. *And on the seventh day, God ended His work which He had made; and rested on the seventh day* . . . Genesis 2:2

From the time I can remember, we worked, and we worked hard, from Monday through Saturday. Then Sunday arrived, the day of rest.

Dad did chores; usually just feeding and watering whatever critters were inhabiting the pasture at the time. Momma prepared the beef roast or Swiss steak or roast chicken. The meat either went into a low temperature oven or the refrigerator, the final cooking to be completed after church.

Then we went to church, all but Dad to Sunday school classes. Momma taught first to children, and in later years, to adults. We girls either were pupils, or in later years, helpers in the classrooms. After church, we stood around visiting for a while, and then we went home.

Uncle Harry Miller, husband of Nannie's sister, our great Aunt Bessie, rarely came to church without a grocery bag of goodies for Georgia Lee. Maybe Sara got some of the goodies later, but in the beginning the brown bag was mine, given to me after church.

In it were bananas, Juicy Fruit chewing gum, maybe unshelled hazel nuts from their bushes, or maybe ribbon candy. The ribbon candy began appearing a while before Christmas and was expected through most of the winter.

The bananas were usually overripe; the Juicy Fruit gum was my least favorite. Ribbon candy, however, is a delectable confection never to be tasted again in THIS life. Some of it was cylindrical, about a half-inch in diameter with an outer coat of a solid color, and sometimes with a hint of flavor (such as grape-ish with purple outer coat). Inside was a white core, often with a flower in the center or a decorative design. It was less than an inch long, and usually just sweet with little flavoring. The best ribbon candy, though, was about an inch wide, folded in accordion pleats and the colors of the church windows, which we had just seen inside the Baptist church. Mix its various strong flavors – cinnamon, wintergreen, lemon, cherry and orange – with overripe bananas and Juicy Fruit gum and you'll know what Uncle Harry smelled like, even if you can't see him.

Anyway, after the brown bag ritual, we went home to Sunday dinner. After we ate, "Be quiet – hush – sshhh" – or a hissing whisper: "your father's sleeping." If we had to use the toilet, we tiptoed and we didn't flush – might wake up Daddy.

We girls didn't sleep. We read, we wrote in our journals or to friends out of town. Mostly, we did the seventh day resting until Daddy woke up.

Neither of our parents cared if we played in the front yard or skated on Sunday. They didn't allow it, though, because it might offend the neighbors

After Daddy woke, we stirred around, the house began to breathe again, maybe chores had to be done or the furnace had to be stoked. Momma made food noises in the kitchen. Maybe popcorn was shucked and popped, or leftover roast beef went onto slabs of home-baked bread for sandwiches.

If Daddy was less acerbic than usual, he would let us snuggle onto his pillow and would read the *Springfield Journal* Sunday funnies to us. In remembering that activity I am most confounded at who/what my father was. He had a deep, velvety voice, with pipe organ overtones and it was very soothing to little girls, maybe others. (You know, I don't think he ever read anything but the funnies to us.) While he was reading, he would twiddle one of our ears. It was a caress, a safe feeling, and we loved it when he twiddled our ears. But too often, the twiddle became a tweak. It was a hurtful and cruel gesture. I don't know what Sara and Anne did, but I left the bed, even if the funnies weren't finished, retreated to another room, and forgot. Another Sunday was a week away, and maybe he'd just be loving then.

The point, I suppose, is that on Sundays we observed the resting instituted by God in Genesis. For many years, Sunday for me included having to work, what with five children, a big house, in later years a shop to run. Guess what, though – nowadays it's a rare Sunday if I do more work than it takes to get me to church, and in the evening to prepare a Sunday dinner. ~Georgia

Swing. *"How do you like to go up in a swing,*
Up in the sky so blue...."
Robert Louis Stevenson

We had a rope swing.

Actually, there were two: the first hung from a branch of the oak tree near the front porch. I was five or six when that was removed; it could have been because of my illness and no one was using it, or because Mama did not like the worn, bare patch of earth so near the front porch.

I must have been eight or nine when Dad reinstalled the swing from an oak in the pasture. The rope hung from a branch that was more than 20 feet above the ground – I'm not kidding. The seat was made from a board cut by Dad, with notches in the sides for the rope, a good heavy board, sanded to remove splinters. It weathered nicely to a silvery gray, so it may have been a piece of mahogany.

My sisters had taught me to 'pump,' and while Dad would give me a push or three once in a while, my swinging times were mostly solitary. That long, long rope allowed for a huge arc and the duration of the 'swing' from back to front lasted a good long time. Sometimes I stood up and pumped until the rope 'flopped' at its peak – the danger sign. Then I would sit quickly, mid-swing, and ride the high arc until it slowed, and then pump it up again.

Swing

There were days I would wind the rope around and around, then sit and dizzily unwind, then rewind in the other direction to balance things out. Sometimes I would take the board out and stand in the rope on one foot and swing high, pretending I was a high-wire artist. Sometimes I would swing up and jump out from six feet up (how did we do that?). Sometimes a friend and I would double-pump, standing up or one sitting on the other's lap, face to face.

And sometimes I would just sit, lazily twisting in the rope, toes digging in the warm bare earth, watching the lambs or the sky, or listening to a bird or the locusts humming in the hot summer afternoon.

The height of the seat was too low as I grew, and perhaps the rope stretched a bit, so I would knot the rope under the seat to make it higher, but it would come unknotted eventually. Then Dad climbed up his tall ladder one year and adjusted the rope so the seat was a bit too high at first, but just right in the years that followed. And I swung. I swung in the spring and in the fall, in the morning and in the afternoon, late, before Mama called us for dinner. I swung in the dusk and watched fireflies (lightning bugs, we called them) and glimpsed the high sickle moon through the branches above. Out through the gate into the pasture, avoiding the cowpats or sheep droppings, veering around a thistle or a bee, to the swing on the oak. I never learned to jump rope or roller skate, and my bike riding was always a little wobbly, but boy, could I swing.

Now the interesting thing about this is that the swing was on the south side of the house, but the kitchen windows and the sewing room faced north. So my mother went humming about her work while I swung, unobserved, unwatched, not fussed over, not told to be careful, you're going too high. I climbed trees, too, and fences, and got up on the roof of the brooder house and jumped off, wrenching my ankle more than once, and climbed high into the lofts of old barns with my friends and jumped down into piles of hay, and no one was watching and I was left alone. And I never got seriously hurt and I never fell out of the swing.

I think our parents in those days protected us from certain things – such as helping us guard our reputations by instilling manners and courtesy, forbidding swearing and foul language; they insured our cleanliness and neatness, demanded respect for authority, fed our bodies with good food and our minds with books and ideas, and kept our little souls on the path to an eventual Heaven. But mostly they let us be kids – we were free to explore, to climb, to swing, to risk life and limb, to pretend, to dare, all on our own, free of adult supervision and concern, free to discover our limits and dreams, and then to come in to supper.

I swung until I left home at 17 and if I ever find a big enough tree with a good branch arranged just so, I believe I'll swing again. ~Anne

142

T

Thanksgiving. Oh, boy, was Thanksgiving a great day when we were growing up. Christmas and Easter were much more subdued in those Depression years. Multitudinous gifts in glittery paper under a tall tree were dreams we did not realize during that time. Clever baskets with pretty pastel grass under a plethora of chocolate or marshmallow bunnies and chicks were not what the Rawlings girls expected. But Thanksgiving? Wow! Momma pulled out all the stops. Our dining room was twenty-two feet long and our table comfortably sat 14 people. Our family of four reached out and there suddenly were so many people – and so much food!

Excuse me, Thanksgiving is what you want to know about. Well, the Petersons arrived about noon. Dale never came. He had married and always went to his wife's parents for Thanksgiving. Lois and Jane never married but Esther brought her beau, Gene, and Mary brought her Bill. (They waited a very long while before marrying, long after I had.)

That puts the count at twelve (Annie wasn't born yet). Dora Turner lived with the Petersons and worked downtown at the dry goods store. I'm not sure why she lived there; she wasn't a relative. She was a diminutive maiden lady who was quite lovely looking. She, too, married late in life and came back to the Petersons when her man died after not many years of marriage.

That makes a good number for Thanksgiving dinner. Momma had been baking and cooking for days. So had Aunt Onie and her daughters, at least those who knew how.

Twelve wasn't enough, of course. Nannie and Grandpa were just across the street so they contributed to the bounty. Some years Uncle Lynn was home so that was 15. Annie got born, I got married, and then we had hardly enough room for our elbows to maneuver the silverware.

Momma had a white tablecloth of cotton damask that was so ample that after Thanksgiving dinner, we girls played Dungeons and Dragons (or the 1930s equivalent) under the table when the meal was finished and the adults sat around visiting.

As one might expect, the food was extravagant. Homegrown potatoes, beans and corn. Home churned butter and cottage cheese prepared from Peterson milk. Sweet potato, peach, cherry and/or gooseberry pies harvested from our gardens and made with lard piecrusts. Light yeast rolls and cloverleaf rolls in abundance. Home-canned pickles, celery sticks in delicate cut glass trays, and some years, pickled peaches or crab apples. Waldorf salad always was on the table. That was Nannie's contribution. "Be careful whipping the cream, honey. It will turn to butter if you whip too hard."

Never, not ever, do I remember a Thanksgiving turkey until I was an adult. Of course we had dressing - with oysters for the adults – Yuk. Sara and I, maybe others, had dressing without any of those nasty tasting things.

Once I remember the Petersons bringing a goose, which was beautiful and a treasure. We oohed and aahed, but I don't remember its taste. We had meat, of course we did. Maybe it was roasted hens. Maybe it was roast beef. Maybe we didn't care. It was such a festive time. All of us enjoyed the chatter, the excitement of so many people exchanging pleasantries, food being prepared, laughing together as old and comfortable friends do.

Before everything was put on the table, meals were prepared for delivering to shut-ins that we all knew. It was an important part of the Thanksgiving ritual to give of our plenty to some who had less than we did.

After dinner, which always was leisurely and lasting longer than any other meal all the year, there was a lull in activity. Some, of course, washed, dried, and sorted dishes to be returned to the various homes and cupboards.

Sometimes we walked over to Miss Flora's. She was a maiden lady who gave piano lessons and did needle work to make money. When we went we always took a plate of dinner rolls and pieces of pie. We also took money so we could buy a potholder or an embroidered tea towel.

Another activity was sitting together and sewing. Momma usually embroidered but the Peterson talent ran toward knitting. Every year, Esther tried, in vain, to teach me to knit. Again and again she tried. Again and again it was a failure, but she always brought the extra knitting needles and a bright red skein of wool in hopes that that would be the year.

When it was time for them to go home for milking, I often got to go with them to stay overnight. Mary taught at a one-room schoolhouse in the country. The Friday after Thanksgiving, I got to go with her. Country kids had fewer holidays than the town kids but they got out earlier in the spring. When it was time to put in crops there was no time for schooling.

At any rate, that always was a fun time with the novelty of children of several ages learning in the same room. Sometimes I knew the answers to questions older children had to answer and I felt so smart

The school is closed now but it still stands. All the children are gone, grown, and many have died. Memories don't die, though, and Thanksgiving and the Petersons always are linked in my memory of growing up. Who today even owns a table that seats that many? ~Georgia

Thunderstorms. My mother was terrified of thunderstorms, of the crash of thunder and the glare of lightning. Perhaps her Kansas birth brought an innate wariness of severe weather, tuned to the danger of cyclones. She did her best to shield me from her fear and succeeded in part, for though I knew she was afraid, I loved the storms.

When high winds blew, I would run out to play, to dance in the wind, to flutter long silk scarves above my head. A heavy rain would call me forth in warm weather to skip in the rain, to drink the torrent, smell the ozone, and sometimes wash my hair.

My bed was very near the window. In winter, I would open my eyes and see snow piled on the sill. In spring, robins chirped on the fence across the drive, in fall squirrels sat to nibble at the upright corncobs my father placed at intervals on fence posts. In summer, the window was open. The lower frame pushed up, allowing ten square feet of space for summer air to enter through the screen. It was often hot, so hot we spread sheets on the floor and slept there with fans blowing air across our damp bodies. But in bed, through sleep, I heard a crack and rumble, felt a bright flash against my closed eyelids and, even before I opened my eyes, my heart leaped – thunder, lightning, rain, and wind. They swept me up into a winged weightlessness, one with the elements.

My eyes opened to the night, to a scene through the window of roaring wind, huge old trees blowing wildly, rain whipping through the open spaces in the pasture. Thunder grumbled and crashed, lightning seared the universe, and I was filled with joy.

A step at my door, a tall figure moves around my bed to the window, pulling it down. Not all the way, I mumble. Silly kid, you'll get wet, my father murmurs. Leave just a crack, I say. He leaves the crack, leaves the room. I think, in a minute, I'll get up and push the window wide again and float on the wind and ride the trees. But I fall asleep to the rumbles, muted now and fading, and when I awake, the sun is shining on a clear, wet morning, the birds are singing, and the perfume of bacon and coffee mingle with the air of summer after storm. ~Anne

Togstad. That's an obscure word. In all the years I've been rattling around no one but the Rawlings family finds it a familiar word. We had a Togstad room. Momma had Togstad bowls in her kitchen and Togstad vanilla on her baking shelves.

After Emery had brought Elizabeth and their baby to Illinois to live in his parent's house, he had to find something to do. There were no round houses where he could work as a machinist. He sure couldn't work in an office. He needed money to take care of his little family.

Somehow he got enough together to buy a $30.00 Model-T (or Model-A) Ford. With transportation he could drive all over the county selling Togstad products – women's toiletries, herbs, spices and cooking extracts. The company was based in Kokomo, Indiana and was similar to Rawleigh or Watkins products, though not as long lived.

Daddy told us that the day of "The Fire" he had received a big shipment of Togstad goods. They'd been ordered for anticipated Christmas sales using his postdated check. After "The Fire" he went to the basement to see his merchandise in a soggy mass and utterly destroyed. What a disastrous day that was!! Because Daddy was a go-getter of a salesman the company was lenient and he eventually settled his debt.

After we moved into our own house in 1933, one bedroom was devoted to storage of the Togstad products. Dad quit selling for them in the late 1930s. Even though it was Annie's bedroom for a while and, later, Momma made it her sewing room, the north bedroom always was called the Togstad room.

As for the Togstad bowls, well, let me tell you they were some bowls. They were given away as "premiums" when customers bought a certain amount of merchandise. They were made of enamelware; Momma's were pale yellow with a light green stripe around the lip. I had three of them for many years, one a red one with a black stripe that I'd found in an antique shop. They held six or seven quarts of whatever – like popcorn, which always was dispensed from a Togstad bowl. Like cucumbers, sliced and soaking in brine to be made into bread and butter pickles. Like mixing dry ingredients for potpourri bags tied with pretty ribbons…

Like one perfectly awful time when Daddy's cousin, Norma Jane, had picked a Togstad bowl full of strawberries for our supper. She washed and hulled them and then asked Momma about sweetening them.

Momma told her to use saccharine. (Sugar was rationed and it was wartime.) Norma Jane didn't know that powdered saccharine wasn't the same as powdered sugar. She sprinkled LOTS of sweetener on the berries, stirred them well, and then tasted THE most NASTY bitter berries in this world. Poor young thing! Poor us, too. Nobody had berries for supper that night.

You may not know the word Togstad but it afforded dignity for my Dad and kept my parents' heads up high when money was scarce. It's a solid-sounding word. ~Georgia

U

Uncles. Most of my uncles, the ones I knew and that I remember the best, were of the Great variety. They were the brother of my grandmother and the husbands of her sisters.

My mother's three brothers were far away and I remember them chiefly from an extended visit I made with Mama when I was nine: Uncle Jim, a professor, courtly, slightly austere, gentle, quiet, and kind. He and Aunt Rita had no children and were not, I sensed, quite comfortable in my presence. But they were pleased that I could curl up in their study and read for hours, thus preserving the serenity of their household, and rewarded me the following Christmas with a huge volume entitled "The Family Mark Twain." I still have the book, tattered, with its covers half off and the stitching loose, but I cherish it, in spite of my later discovery that "Family" in the title meant that all the Twain works of the best pungent irony were omitted.

On that same long-ago trip, Uncle Dale, in Nevada, introduced me to the mysterious joys of ham radio and we spoke one evening with a man in Australia. Uncle Dale and Aunt Ruth were quite comfortable with me, have two grown daughters of their own, but my recollections of him, other than his kindness and genuine interest and attention, remain those of a child – that he had a wonderfully funny face with ears that stuck out and that he owned a dry-goods store, an actual store with his name on a sign over the door. Such power and glory were quite beyond my experience and he remains a semi-mythical, though entirely benevolent, figure in my mind. For many years following that trip, Christmas brought reminders with boxes of fresh pine nuts from Nevada, the thin brown shells crunching easily between the teeth, the savory, alien flavor of the nuts bringing a breath of Western mountains to the Midwest.

Uncle Woody, married to Aunt Kathryn, was an in-law uncle, a volunteer fireman who won my heart when he took me to ride the fire engine through town. Because he also had the entire approval of their enormous gold tomcat – 36 inches from nose to tail, at least 30 pounds, and victoriously battle scarred but patient with my stroking hands – I knew Uncle Woody was a "good 'un."

Uncle Benny, Benjamin, Jr., named for Grandpa Ben Bell, was fair and round faced and amiable, with a thin blond wife and two boys slightly younger than I, but who intimidated me by simply being normal boys – boisterous, noisy, and far too active.

My father's only living brother, Uncle Lynn, was "away" and came into my consciousness when I was twelve, when he returned to live across the street with his parents, my Nannie and Grandpa. From him I learned the frightening realities of alcoholism, what D.T.'s actually meant, and what a "funny uncle" was. A sad, brilliant, weak man, with gifts wasted and mourned. A fall on the ice during one of his "episodes" resulted in a broken hip and a long convalescence – a dry spell, since he had no way to obtain liquor. This was his period of rug braiding, beautiful creations, large and of subtle colors, that people bought from him. We had one for years, spreading its glory across the dining room, a comfort to eye and feet. I lent him my old canary to keep him company while he braided, and the little yellow bird hopped, chirping, along the woolen strands as they lengthened. He made my uncle happy and stayed with him for several years until he succumbed to a bird's old age of twelve years.

Uncle Clark – Clarkie – was long dead, at six, from diphtheria, when my father was only twelve. Now I understand why my grandmother's face, always so pleasant, so smiling, so kind, still carried that faint shadow that I now know comes from grief.

The great-uncles were another tribe entirely – my grandmother's brother Frank, and her two brothers-in-law, Arthur (married to Aunt Grace) and Tom (married to Aunt Ethel).

I remember little of Uncle Arthur, from two or three dinners at their house out in the country. They had an actual icebox, not a refrigerator, and the food was always good. Uncle Arthur had a round face, and a lot of white hair – or perhaps he was partly bald – but he put a chair for me under his prized grape arbor and let me eat all the grapes I could hold – deep, blue-black Concords, with the silver bloom on the skin and the taste of paradise.

Uncle Tom took me fishing once, in a boat on a little pond. I can't remember that we caught anything, but we laughed a lot and he gave me a pocketknife – a boy's gift and treasured by me, who was allowed only to be mostly a girl. Uncle Tom, spritely, elfin, and merry, who was always so happy to see me and let me know I had a special place in his heart.

Uncle Frank, Nannie's own brother, one of two brothers among five sisters, the gem of my collection. (Uncle Ed died years before I was born.) Uncle Frank would appear now and then, unannounced (back then we all felt free to visit without calling first), with gifts of his home-made sausage or fresh milk from his cows, perhaps eggs when we no longer had chickens, or a gallon pail of sorghum molasses.

He was tall, taller than my father who was six feet two inches, and even as a child I could see the Elmore family resemblance between them – only nine years separated them in age. And their voices, alike and yet so different – both deep and rumbling, but my father's words were crisp, clear, sometimes almost sharp, sometimes snapped out.

But Uncle Frank's voice sang – an instrument played by a lost tribe, with a deeper rumble in his chest and throat and a higher register through his nose, combining to make chords of his words, though half his words were lost. He mumbled, swallowed his words, and gulped in his throat, or hid his meaning behind an embarrassed deep chuckle. When he appeared, and stood for a few minutes in our kitchen (never anywhere else in the house) in his blue farmer's overalls and heavy boots, I sensed an irritation and an annoyance, unspoken but there, from my parents. Why? I couldn't understand it. Uncle Frank was a country wizard, a traveler with charms, his incantations tickling my eardrums and reverberating in the area 'round my heart, bringing gifts for our table.

He fiddled and played the guitar at family reunions, singing old songs, untunefully and garbled, in his unique voice. When my mother lay dying, he came to her bedside in the hospital, saying he didn't know what to bring or do or say that would be suitable to the occasion, but thought he would play a tune on the fiddle to cheer up Elizabeth.

My parents stopped him after a few bars, saying it was disturbing to the other patients. Truthfully, they were embarrassed – embarrassed to own to this great rustic untutored fiddling mumbling shambling overalled farmer who was so ignorant he didn't know any better than to bring his gift of fiddling, of music, of love – to a hospital room and a dying woman.

My shame is not for you, Uncle Frank. May God bless you. ~Anne

Postscript: I learn only now, as we are writing this, that the nurses at the hospital came running at the sound of fiddling and, all twittering and thrilled, begged Uncle Frank to come play in the main room of the floor, where other patients and their visitors could hear him. And he did. And then Dad was pleased, and proud, and people complimented him, and Frank, and everyone said what a Good Thing it was. But children know a Good Thing instinctively, without anyone else's approval, and Uncle Frank was one of them.

ν

Vallejo. What a pretty name! What a culture shock to come to that city as a ten-year-old fresh from Illinois cornfields. Momma, Sara and I arrived the summer of 1941 because Daddy was working at Mare Island, a Navy shipyard. He had gone there sometime in 1939 seeking better pay than his work at Caterpillar provided. Momma wanted us to be there with him.

Vallejo is just across an inlet of water from Mare Island and is an old town, established in 1850, and at one time twice the size of Sacramento. When we got there, Vallejo was on its way to another boom-time.

Our parents found us a little stuccoed ticky-tacky house. Two bedrooms, kitchen with a dining el, long narrow living room with a fake fireplace and an attached garage. It also had a bathroom, such luxury!

They may have shipped some household goods from Illinois but they brought no furniture. I wonder how they found furniture but I don't think they bought new things so maybe friends of Daddy and maybe Momma's relatives donated. They found a piano somewhere and a teacher who came to our house so I could continue my piano lessons.

Oh, we did get one new piece, an unfinished dining room table. Long before the days of antiquing kits, Daddy knew the formula for turning that humble table into a handsome "cherry" finished piece of beauty.

Momma must have been thrilled beyond expression with that table. In 1941, she and Daddy hosted the Thanksgiving dinner with <u>her family.</u> It was the only time in her married life that HER family sat at HER table for a holiday meal! Daddy thought they were keen folk so a good time was had by all. That year, we did have a turkey. It was prepared and stuffed at home but baked at a neighborhood bakery, conserving gas during wartime.

The table wasn't nearly long enough, not like the one back home, but with card tables at the ends and Momma's good table linen it was a respectable table. By that time, they had bought china and a silver chest filled with lovely silver plate so, by golly, Momma's family saw she knew how to orchestrate a feast. Way to go Momma and Daddy...

Very soon after we had found a place to live, Sara and I began second and sixth grades at Curry Elementary School, not too far from home. By the time Christmas came, America was into WWII. Along with learning new Christmas carols, we learned how to put on gas masks stored in the cloakrooms and how to place our bodies under our desks in case of bombing attacks. We were issued dog tags and thought it was all a lark.

Mare Island was a hive of activity, building new naval craft, repairing disabled ships (both American and foreign). Daddy went to work under tight, tense security. He also put in his time as an air raid warden in our neighborhood, searching for windows uncovered by blackout curtains or for enemy planes in the searchlight-streaked skies above him.

We girls got acquainted with the soldiers detailed on our school ground. They were guarding one of the many barrage balloons scattered around town as part of the Mare Island defense system. Momma didn't want us to talk to the soldiers -- "they might do something" (never specified) but they were fun to talk to and made us laugh. Now I know what Momma thought, but I suspect they were just lonely, bored, and enjoyed the diversion of the school kids traipsing by five days a week. Momma never knew we talked with them.

Another adventure was taking buses to go downtown. The main drag was called Georgia Street, like my name. I loved going to the library just a block or two off the bus route and in the middle of the business area. It was a huge building, as I recall, but it may just have been a little bigger than the Petersburg library, which wasn't very big at all.

Coming home was also an adventure. The sailors from ports all over the world prowled lower Georgia Street. There were bars and cafes, arcades galore, and girls waiting for busses who looked older than their years. Shhh! Don't tell Momma but I talked and laughed with the sailors as well as the soldiers at "our" barrage balloon.

By Easter, April 5, 1942, Sara and I were in a car headed back to Petersburg. Submarines sighted off Santa Barbara, too many air raid drills and blackout curtains made our parents nervous. We were safer back in Illinois with Nannie and Grandpa.

The man who owned the car, Doug Evans, had advertised for passengers from Vallejo to St. Louis, MO. He was interviewed and approved by Momma and Daddy. There were also two women passengers, so off we went to southern California and then across the southern route (old Route 66) of the United States. Is that called faith?

Doug chain-smoked...ugh! We stopped for car repairs in one spot and I drank my first (and last) Dr. Pepper. My, that's nasty! In Texas I had my first tamale, wrapped in real cornhusks from a vendor's cart. What a never-to-be-forgotten taste thrill. Where is that vendor now?

How the grown-ups worked gas rationing stamps and paying for Sara's and my expenses I never asked. We must have stopped to sleep but I have no remembrance of it. It was a long trip and a tiresome one. Uncle Lynn met us in St. Louis driving a borrowed car.

We stayed with Nannie and Grandpa who had rented their house, and we were living with them in our own house. Being in our house was comforting but after several months we wanted to go back to California; we missed our parents.

Just a little before Nannie took us back by train, we got a letter from Momma in which she included a swatch of fabric. She told us she was making herself a maternity dress and did I know what "maternity" meant. Oh, my goodness, yes, I knew what maternity meant, and the embarrassment I felt that those two old people had been doing what they undoubtedly had been doing. Oh, dear, oh, dear. I wasn't quite twelve years old, for goodness sake. What did I know? By the time we got back to Vallejo it was so glutted with people involved with the war effort, as well as the military personnel, that it was swarming with all sorts and conditions of men – and women.

Schools were so choked with kids from every state in the Union, that there were two shifts. When I began junior high, I was in the morning section from 7 or 7:30 a.m. to 1 or 1:30 p.m. The afternoon kids got to sleep in late but went home after normal supper times.

My class was self-contained, that is, unlike junior high schools then and now, where kids go from class to class – math in Mr. Brown's room,

English in Miss Jones' room, and science in the lab – I got stuck with Miss Faire Barry.

What a witch she was. At first we were six students: John Gorman claimed to have been to reform school before coming to seventh grade; a very intelligent little girl had skipped two grades but her mother arrived like a whirlwind after learning we were having coed sex education. (The child didn't know the meaning of the word SEX!)

A black boy seemed a normal sort. Another boy was a Negro albino being raised by an older sister who was not – talk about an underdog! Betty somebody-or-other was a girl who lived on lower Georgia Street behind a back curtain of a shooting arcade with her dad and an older sister. From Betty's stories of her and her sister's escapades entertaining the troops, I doubt she needed sex education.

As for the albino boy, Faire Barry's dislike for him was almost palpable and all of us were afraid for him. The prejudice mounted until one day she accused him of theft, hit him backhanded, and knocked him into the black board. He went wailing from the room, returning later with his sister. Such a screaming match – pretty scary.

By the time this had occurred, our class had swelled to over thirty kids so we all learned a lot that day. It's also when I learned true meanness: John Gorman had stolen the money the albino boy had been accused of and after a week or so told us he'd done so, laughing as he told it. "What a dumb old teacher," he crowed. That was also the year I learned to smoke, more's the pity.

After Annie was born, we moved to a slightly bigger house where we only lived for a few months before coming back to Illinois. By then, there was rationing of gas, meat, sugar, and maybe other commodities that I don't remember. We guarded our ration books more carefully than our money.

One day Momma went to the neighborhood meat market. As the butcher was serving her, he said, "Somebody left their ration book a few days ago, somebody from Illinois." "Oh, I'm from Illinois," said Momma. "I wonder if it's someone I know." The butcher laughed, "Illinois is a pretty big place." Momma wiped the smile off his face when he showed her the book. A friend from Fancy Prairie, IL (too small to show on a map) had been visiting us and had used her meat stamps to buy a meat treat before she left for home. Maybe she left them on purpose?

I won't tell you about baby-sitting a baby whose father had a twenty-four hour leave in San Francisco and about going to the famous old Mark

Hopkins Hotel. The naval officer took me to dinner before he and his wife went out to dinner. I ordered milk and a bowl of coleslaw for $0.15 "to save him money." I won't tell you about having to stay home from school when Momma developed milk fever and Mrs. Sauerwein, the woman hired to care for Annie (the interloper) and Momma, could only give us half a day's help. I won't tell you about learning to dance with Uncle Clark to the tune of "That Old Black Magic." I won't tell you of painting on nylons from a bottle because hosiery fibers were needed in the war effort.

Lotsa funny things happened in Vallejo. We were there for just a few months over two years and I learned more in that time than many people learn in a lifetime. I was ten years old when we came and not quite thirteen when we left for the last time. ~Georgia

Values. Our parent's values were very evident to us as we were growing up. Almost every thing had a value. Friends, money, honesty, integrity, moral fiber, manners - oh just name it. It was important to value others' opinions of us – to do our best and then some, to look our best, to be our best- we were after all Rawlingses.

Value meant giving our word and keeping it – as kids we were taught the value of a promise and a handshake. A promise made was surely a promise kept. I can remember wanting to date a fellow and dad said the guy was dishonest in his business dealings. No dates with this guy.

We were to hold our endeavors valuable inasmuch as we did the best work possible on any project we undertook. Once I did some signs for a pancake supper and the signs were far from perfect. The man who asked me to do them told dad they were lacking. Dad was embarrassed and I heard about it big time.

Our things had value i.e. our clothes – we were expected to change after school and to hang our dresses up properly. Most of our dresses had been made by moma so they had extra value due to her efforts. What we changed to were not scrappy things – maybe older, maybe faded, maybe a hand-me-down or something we wore to school till it wasn't good enough – quite - to go to school. We were never allowed to "dog-ear" a book, no matter how old or tattered it might already be. We could not make the smallest mark in our textbooks. Boy, have those times changed.

We would get reprimanded severely if we put our feet on anything other than the floor. Other people had to sit there. We had always to figure in the other guy and how our actions would affect him. We were not in a vacuum living just to suit ourselves.

Dad taught us to value our land, our property as it gave us food. Our animals were valued – dad cared for the livestock as if they were people. He spent hours keeping the hen house clean and safe from predators. The sheep were always shorn in a timely manner. He said they might become ill in the heat. He milked our cow at the same time every night in order to keep her comfortable and her udder not over full. Our dog Dan was most definitely a family member, dad kept him in excellent health, watching for fleas and ticks. I remember dad holding the dog between his knees and working out a fat tick. His hands moved gently and swiftly, pulling the tick from Dan's ear with a tweezers. Dad explained that he had to get close to the ear skin and pull gently in order to get the head of the tick out so Dan's ear would not be infected.

People were treated with respect, even if not always deserving. One kept friends close and ignored their flaws. I can't remember ever hearing my folks gossip about anyone (except Aunt Bessie and that's a whole other story).

One time I took ONE Hershey kiss from a store. Mom found it in my pocket, not fit to eat, but we went back to the store to say sorry. She returned the blob to the store owner who did what the heck with it? I imagine a pound of the things cost a nickel, but it wasn't mine to take. I write this with awe as I realize how really good our parents were and how these values are mostly lost. This loss is not a good thing. ~Sara

Victory. So the book is finished, but of course it is not. For we keep seeing things that come up in the now of our lives.

Anne and I were sitting, tinkering with "the book" – the punctuation, spelling, tiny changes. She cleared her throat, a portentous sound.

"There's something we have missed," she said.

"Oh," I said.

"Well," she said, "I keep reading our book and hearing "Sisters" and "House" that you wrote, hearing the gut wrenching pain and wondering where were we? Sis and I haven't visited this and our readers are gonna say where were these girls as their sister lay bleeding on the linoleum?"

Well, that's an interesting concept; let's take a look.

In the first place my pain is much more evident as it is written and read about than it was during the time it was going on. Anne's and my relationship during our growing up years was very different from Georgia's and mine. Anne says today that she was aware of Dad being mad at me what seemed to be all the time; but she didn't hear the message of my inadequacy. I, like George, was expected to manage my younger sib and I have a big feeling there were times when I felt drowning seemed a good option. The tragedy of my big error – not saving our mother's breast – was not as keen after all those years so it wasn't drummed into Anne so blatantly. George, being a totally different personality had her own agenda re MY drowning so what she saw and heard suited her. May not have been consciously, but nevertheless THERE.

George heard the messages but surely did not realize how damaging they were or that she played a big part in the reinforcement of the process to make me invisible. She had been the apple of the eye of the world for four years, told she walked on water AND parted it and then here I come along wanting all the air in the room. Plus needing to care for me. I am glad the Sangamon River was blocks away.

We have passed this; the book has shown how insidious negative messages can absolutely destroy a person. Georgia was aghast about **Sisters,** not having an inkling about some of the things that hurt me so, she was young you know. Just following the folks lead and really wishing I would just not be there for her to have to mind.

If you listen to **Cards, Chickens, Evenings** and even **House, Middlest, and Sisters,** you hear a glimmer of something even stronger than happy. There are, here and there, expressions of joy, joy for being seen, being an actual 3-D person, something touchable, not smoke.

Through the evolution of writing and listening and looking at the words, I see for myself a victory of life. My big sister probably never hated me; she's having real trouble forgiving herself for whatever her part in my pain was. She is working hard toward that victory.

Because I compensated so much I have a sense of humor that turns almost any adversity on its head. I see stuff pretty clearly, I have friends, and I take risks – all victories.

The three of us have come through the raising we were given to such places it is awesome – even to us. Little town, more than slightly rigid. We left that town to do some really remarkable things, all victories.

Even if there was a current of overwhelming pain it was years before I knew why. So I could not have expected my sibs to recognize it either – the whys – so Annie how could you have known and besides which it is all over now and I and you and George are settled into our skins pretty well and it is ok.

And yes, that is me on the back cover. I am bald due to chemo – just one more victory, for I am well now. ~Sara

W

Walker. Moma and daddy always, always taught us to be kind to everyone. To be careful of feelings, mindful of the other guy. We were taught God loved us everyone, and further more equally. We were never allowed to use words in rhymes that were derogatory or down putting. Everyone who came to our front or back door was treated with respect and kindness. From the hobo needing food to the banker and his wife in to buy furniture, all were the same.

During the war years when we were in California, dad's very best friend was an Italian man. He and his wife would come to the house often for meals and an evening of conversation. The gardener next door was a Japanese gentleman – and he was in every sense. He went about his work with a quiet dignity that dad remarked on. He laughed with us kids though and we never felt threatened. One day he just disappeared. Dad said he had been incarcerated "for his own good." Dad's rage was palpable, as the gardener was an American citizen born and raised in America. Dad spoke of this often for this man was not the only one to come up missing.

One time while still in California, I asked mom if Sally could come over to play after school – sure, she said. Sally was a very dark "colored" girl as we still said then. We had great fun – she came often and this was in the forties. Mom never remarked – ever – about Sally's color.

One time I watched dad as he rubbed a picture of an Indian woman who appeared in the National Geographic. Tears were streaming down his face. Later I looked at the article and it was about the plight of Native Americans still held behind barbed wire and living in quiet desperation. Across the top of the page dad had written in heavy black marker "man's inhumanity to man."

When the last room of our basement was dug one summer the people who came to dig were black men, four as I remember. These men were of a family who built culverts, moved houses, and seined for catfish in the Sangamon River. Their women folk fried fish every Friday night outside in the summer inside in the winter, home made spaghetti and cole slaw, huge slabs of homemade bread and butter. People lined up to buy their Friday supper. Some of us were lucky enough to be friends of the family and get all these goodies for free and oh don't forget the fruit cobbler to make ya weep.

Back to the digging of the basement: when lunch time came – dad and the crew (truly a crew for dad worked side by side doing his share of the digging) sat in our back yard eating their lunches dad eating with them and moma serving the men ice tea or freshly made lemonade. I was nine at this time lurking around the edges watching, listening learning how to not treat people differently.

At the dinner table dad would often speak of the strength of these men, their professionalism in doing their job, the conversations among them. He commented that there was no carping or complaining rather lots of fun and laughter. The men told of other jobs and things that went wrong or went very right. Guy stuff, workmen stuff. We heard the respect for these men in dad's recounting his workday with them.

As children if we passed someone who was different, on crutches, in a wheel chair, disfigured in some way, mom would say "don't stare it isn't nice. People know they are scarred; they don't need you to remind them by staring at them." This was with kindness always, not rebuke – just teaching.

When I was in Jr. high mom had to take me to Springfield to the doctor a couple times a week and once in a while we would have a treat. She took us once to the Abraham Lincoln Hotel coffee shop for a hamburger. We sat, we ordered. The waitress had a big white mug sitting on the sink counter which she hit with a hammer breaking it into a million pieces, chips flying everywhere. Mom hissed in her breath and said, "Why did you do that?" The waitress said, "A nigger drank out of it." Another hiss and a whirl of stool, me gripped by the coat sleeve and we were out of there. Mom mumbling things under her breath and between her teeth – "Abraham Lincoln indeed, he's turning in his grave." I can't think when ever she was that mad.

And so it went, being taught by demonstration to never hurt or compartmentalize other folks.

A few years later I was away at school, having won a Summer Theater scholarship at the University of Colorado in Boulder. Moma wrote often and told me newsy stuff. Things of little consequence really, just to keep me from being homesick which I never was. But anyway, in one letter she wrote that one of the young men who had helped to dig our basement so many years before had been hospitalized with a ruptured appendix and was not expected to live. For some inexplicable reason this news made me very sad.

I knew this young man of course from digging our basement, eating fish at his sister's, from his nephew with whom I went to high school. I knew him from his legendary prowess on the basketball court. I knew him for his kindness to me when I waitressed at the local restaurant where everyone from the crème de la crème of our town to the truckers took their meals. I was 14 or 15 and had long legs that went all the way up to my arm pits and was pleasant enough to look at I guess. Anyway the guys would never dare to be ribald with me as the young man would check them very quickly with – hey, she's a kid, watch your mouth. She's Emery Rawlings' daughter, ya know. And such.

One of his nieces was married to a Harlem Globetrotter, another niece was away at school in Washington DC and from time to time during fish fries and visiting in general, I would be lucky enough to be in the company of the basketball big guys, folks from Brown and Howard and the inclusion into that family as if I was just OK and not some young white girl in the way – it was phenomenal.

Sometimes I would pass by on the long way home from school just to chat and perhaps get a piece of something fresh out of the oven or off the stove. There was always lots of laughter and fun. No one seemed to recognize the fact that I had a knobby nose or was way too tall and gangly. They never poked fun at one another except in the most loving way. There were rarely hurt feelings and if there were they never lasted. There were no sexual connotations to conversations, just warmth and good nature. In front of me anyway. I guess thinking of this guy not being around and still a part of this made me sad when I heard of his illness.

When I returned from Colorado the young man was well and completely out of the woods. I went to a fish fry soon after and he was there with cousins and all the folk that were regulars in for the fry. There was talk of his near miss, of fish fries, basketball and jazz.

One time I was there and he and a cousin or two were going to a club in Springfield and they said did I want to go along and I said sure. I went. I'm not sure how or why I was allowed to go at night to Springfield to a nightclub, maybe I lied? Anyway that night was the beginning of a friendship that grew. The young man was popular, witty and easy on the eye. He was the baby of thirteen siblings and was doted on. He left school in his senior year due to his dad's illness, to help care for the family full time.

We all went to Springfield a lot to what I remember was called the Panama Club – might be wrong. Being there enhanced my education about "colored" people. I don't remember any mention of being used or mistreated or how wrong whites were. No militancy whatsoever. This was 1951 and 2. Sometimes I might say some gauche thing and be told quietly "I can't go there, we aren't allowed to…" This was very peculiar to me and I did not fully comprehend what that meant. I was still pretty young and was there, I suppose, illegally. I never knew that, I always felt protected and included.

I was certainly not the only white to frequent this club – maybe the youngest but not the only. I was just another person totally acceptable and my appreciation for jazz grew steadily. I learned about Muddy Waters, Count Basie, Coltrane, Gene Ammons, Bessie Smith – the buzz one got from a jazz organ. The conversations were mostly about music and folks danced to beat anything. Not me though, too awkward.

On one of those nights we drove home together and got caught in a rainstorm fit to flood the car. We pulled into the state park entrance to get out of the deluge. While we waited out the storm, the rattle on the old car pleasant and relaxing, not saying much, Walker remarked, "I love the sound of the rain on the car roof." "Me, too" says I. "I miss not finishing school, I liked literature and English. Did you learn the Brownings?"

My response was pretty sharp, something like "Huh? The poets you mean? Yeah -- How do I love thee? Mrs. P. still teaches that stuff." Oh, well that was just wonderful as Elizabeth Barrett Browning appealed to my young romantic self like nothing else. We sat till long after the rain was gone and just talked. He spoke of literature being a favorite and at the same time painful as the references to niggers were throughout Mark Twain's writings that were taught as classics in school and without commentary. He told me of feeling small and worthless in class when some things were read out loud and his classmates would look at him and laugh. He was the only black in the class. Wanting to sink into the floor when made fun of, made less of. I ventured the question about his nickname, which was Goat, and I had heard it was because he butted people as a child. He was vague. What he told me was his name was the same as his father's, John Walker. He was called Walker by his family. Never Goat.

Through the years there was a rather fierce rivalry between our high school basketball team and another town and one night after the game as I was walking home two local boys asked did I want a ride. I knew them, I took the ride. They took the long way home and on the way they both raped me, then took me home, dumping me at the driveway to our house.

My father literally fainted, falling on the floor and hitting his head on the bedpost bloody badly. Well the upshot of all that drama was NOT to arrest these boys – the folks figured it would be too hard on me to go to court. I'm not sure how I feel about that decision, not convinced about their reasons. Shame, etc. Anyway when Walker found out about this it was all his family and I could do to keep him from doing something stupid. He was wild.

Well, you see where this is going and yes we married after my senior year, quietly. His family knew, not mine. Why did I not tell them? It is not clear in my mind today why not. I was 17 – they might have said no. I'm sure there was some undercurrent of implausibility about our relationship, something sensed but not brought into the light of day and examined – I was just 17 remember. It was published in the paper, as were all notices of this kind – births, deaths, and marriage license sales. All that good stuff.

Some good soul called dad to tell him the news. He went into hibernation. My mother and baby sister were in California; he did not call her or tell her until they came home two months later. He did not want to spoil her trip I was told. I was also told lots of other things, which were very confusing to me. What happened to those learned lessons, of equality, never looking at different people differently? I never got the message that we treated everyone equally because we were better than they were, luckier to be us rather than them. The message was good treatment of our fellow beings was just the right thing to do. I was confused. How come my marriage was as wrong as it seemed to be?

Did this mean that all the things, the beliefs, the lessons I thought I heard weren't true or right? What? Whatever was true I was isolated from my family. It had to be ok and I was blessed to have Walker's family who loved me, mostly. I continued to learn the lessons of race and anger, of other people just hating me because I married a black man. I heard things for instance at the Laundromat, like "we don't do colored clothes" – this was to the young black woman behind me. Her response was "ok I'll take my colored stuff back home." "No, we won't wash *your* clothes." Can anyone believe how I felt? Here I am white and married to a black man - had they known? Lord help me even today it makes me ashamed and crazy. I can remember Walker's mom with whom we lived for a while along with several of his sibs and their kids, saying how come your folks are called white and mine are called colored? How come we can't be black if you're white? Oh I was so hurt for her, for them. Stella, it came, it was just too late for you.

I am by no means here to say this man was "Guess Who's Coming to Dinner" - he was not. He was just an ordinary human being, a man of great integrity in his work and dealings. He was basically good and very smart. He was to become a police officer in Peoria, one of the first blacks to do so. Because his test scores on the police test were so very high, he was made to sit not twice but three times and retake it. Not possible for HIM to reach such a score.

This, remember was early 50's – are we better now? I'm not sure, I hope so. I do believe though that Dad was more disturbed by what the neighbors were saying than the fact of the marriage. He was a good man and I do believe he was true to what he believed when he taught his lessons.

It took years; we sorta healed as a family. I went home eventually. All was forgiven. Maybe not my little southern, Republican town altogether, but dad and I got back to whatever we had before my marriage which wasn't stellar in the first place, but at least I was allowed to come to Petersburg, bring the kids and visit.

Once on the sidewalk in Chicago, my kids, the folks and I were walking five abreast making passing impossible for anyone coming toward us.

Someone did of course, a grizzled old black guy who stepped quickly off the sidewalk. Dad said "oh, no don't step away we are rude to be taking so much space."

When Dad was in his last days, living in a Jewish nursing home, chosen by me for the caring care of the elderly, I remember him reaching up to pat the cheek of one of the staff, an ebony lady, and saying, "oh, honey Black is so beautiful." She had snuck him in some beans with ham hocks and corn bread occasionally and was always fussing at his bedclothes – even on the day he died.

This is what is true. I know that in my heart.

Walker and I eventually divorced, not for any black/white reasons necessarily, but more for the usual man/woman/young girl reasons. For one, he was way too good looking for his own good and mine too – the ladies loved him. Racial times WERE hard and we were so very young, there was some of those stresses in the mix, but after the hurt abated, we remained friends through all his other ladies and wives (whom he referred to as my wives-in-law, each one as they came and went).

In Walker's last illness our son went to Peoria to care for him and be with him as my wife-in-law worked. He was grateful not to be tended by strangers and David was blessed to be able do this for his father. He called me a few days before he died that December and said, "Rawlings why aren't you here?" So I went. At his funeral with his family and our children and grandchildren, my wife-in-law and about 200 others we celebrated his life. It was a blessed time. ~Sara

Water. *"Little drops of water;*
Little grains of sand'
Make a mighty ocean
And a pleasant land."

Nannie told us she taught that to Daddy but that he said "p'eas-ant 'and."

The little drops of water were mighty precious when we were growing up. The first memory of water was a black pump next to the kitchen sink. The sink was just a zinc box with a drain and the water was cold, in winter very, very cold.

There always was a teakettle at the back of the coal-burning stove but in the summer the water was tepid, at best. Attached to the stove was a reservoir, not very warm in the summer, except on washdays. Washdays always were Monday; only slovenly folk didn't do their laundry on Monday.

Besides the reservoir for the laundry, there was the wash boiler which had to be filled from the pump. NO, it wasn't that far to cross the kitchen with a bucket of water but the wash boiler held enough water to fill the wash machine and two rinse tubs. Lotsa buckets of water got toted across the kitchen floor and spilling just made for more trouble. Don't slip – time out to mop it up!

Eventually, first one pipe with a faucet attached, and then two pipes with faucets came through the kitchen floor from the basement. Dad had figured out how to have hot water with the use of a tiny coal-burning stove in the basement.

That didn't mean we had a constant supply of hot water. On Mondays we had hot water for the laundry and when it was bath day, usually on Saturday but sometimes on other days of the week, we had hot water.

There was a small mirror hanging on the wall in the kitchen. Above it was a bare light bulb which was turned off and on by a brass chain. That was where Dad stood to shave. One night, Momma had her hand under the water at the sink and reached up to turn off the light.

That was pretty exciting! She stretched her full length on the floor, I began to cry because I thought she was dead, but Dad knew how to quickly revive her from the electric shock. Rule No.1: DO NOT MIX WATER AND ELECTRICITY.

About the same time that the hot water heater was installed in the basement, Dad decided that a showerhead would be a handy thing. His furniture repair/refinishing shop being in the basement, stripping off old varnish and/or paint was much, much easier with a showerhead to flush away the gooey stripping compound he had concocted. Of course, being the clever man he was, he also had a shower to cleanse himself, as well…and so did all of us!

It was pretty primitive, with pads of newspapers on the concrete floor covered with rag rugs. The faucets were marked H and C in blue carpenters chalk on the concrete wall behind them and there never was a shower curtain. Furniture stripper would have made short work of one.

Despite the cobwebs and the rough concrete and having to bring towels and fresh clothes downstairs, it was a big improvement over the baths-in-a-basin that we had had before the advent of the showerhead.

There are a couple more random thoughts about water. We had a huge vegetable garden and I remember Dad going out after supper with a bucket of water and a coffee can (the old squat-shaped kind) with nail holes punched into its bottom. He laboriously dribbled a coffee can's worth onto each tomato plant, each row of potatoes, beans and peas, returning to the house for another bucket of water, and another bucket, and another. Later, there was an outdoor faucet and a hose.

We never were allowed to "play under the sprinkler" at our house on hot sultry days. We were allowed, however, to bring up the washtubs from the basement and fill them. We loved playing in the tubs. None of our friends did that so it was a kind of special Rawlings summer activity.

We finally had a bathtub and a vanity in use by 1950. (The toilet had been installed in 1948.) A long time from a kitchen pump to a full bathroom wasn't it? Now the house has three baths but we don't live there anymore. ~Georgia

Windows. The house I grew up in was built just after the Civil War, though the legal abstract is not clear as to the exact date. Two of the first floor bedrooms had only one window each but all the others were bright with light and sunshine, admitted through hand-crafted long rectangular panes, four above, four below the sashes.

The living room and master bedroom, which comprised the front of the house, had four windows each, stretching from the floor to the 10-foot ceilings. The other rooms boasted two windows with their four-over, four-under wavy panes.

Looking through the south windows showed the pasture with the mammoth white oaks, the barn, the chicken and brooder houses, the incongruous long rows of old fashioned narcissus to grace the springtime view. After research as adults, we determined that originally a long sweeping driveway lined with flowers had approached the house. It hadn't been a pasture after all!

Looking north immediately next to the side lawn was an immense garden, mandatory during those depression and post-depression years of making do. Further away was the bridge under which the Chicago, Illinois Midland passenger and freight trains passed, and over which cars drove to the northern part of town called Irish Hill.

Momma kept the windows dazzlingly clean; it was almost an obsession that they sparkle. She used a vinegar solution with a rag to apply it and dried them with crushed newspaper. No Windex for her. In the master bedroom was a pot of hoya vine placed between the 9-foot double windows. It climbed up, across the lintels and back down to the
floor. When the dozens of clusters of pale ivory flowers bloomed, with their lavender velvety star-shaped centers, their perfume literally dripped to the floor, intoxicating anyone who could smell. We still have remnants from this plant – imagine!

In the living room's east windows was Momma's collection of colored glass sitting on sashes, on the sills, and on glass shelves hanging from the sashes. A few bigger pieces even were on the floor, only six or eight inches below the sills. How those windows twinkled with their breathtaking rich jewel-toned beauty!

At the west the windows faced away from the street and to the back yard. There were the chairs under the sycamore tree where Momma and Daddy sat on summer evenings. He drank his Tom Collins Momma had mixed, though she never had a glass. They visited about their day and maybe they reminisced about the past.

There were fruit trees planted in the back yard to be admired for their spring blossom and their summer and autumn harvests. There was the big walnut tree, disfigured at its base from countless ax scars incurred in dispatching chickens over the years. There was the clothesline where Momma made sure the underwear was hung in the middle with towels and sheets hung on the outside lines so people wouldn't see the bras and underpants.

The west windows in the dining room were the weather-watching station - torrents and floods of rain, hail big as tennis balls, lightning streaking and dancing across the vast western sky, blizzards of snow. Wide and deep vistas of farmland beyond our boundary stretched as far away as five miles with boundless blue sky or white or angry gray clouds towering overhead.

To try to describe the sunsets seen from the dining room windows is impossible. There is a catch in my throat as I remember the stunning beauty of them and I've not seen a sunset through those windows in over fifty years. ~Georgia

Women. We were a house of women.

Not only that, the extended family of grandparents, great-aunts, cousins, and friends were a circle of women as well. Much is said in these pages about Dad, about how he dominated our family, our emotional lives, our spirits. This was true; life was pleasant when Dad was pleased or at least when he was not displeased, and life was tense and unhappy when he was otherwise.

But as I look back, our daily lives, the operations of home, family, friends, activities, the tone of the home and the family, were established and maintained by the women.

And they were strong-willed, opinionated, fearless, and determined.

In our house, we were four women – Mama, two half-grown women, my sisters, and little me. Many scenes arise in my mind of half-naked women, drying themselves after baths or showers, darting around in their underwear to fix hair or makeup, drawing sheer nylons up their pretty legs (we all have great legs, thanks to Mom), working together at the thousands of chores that needed doing. In these scenes, Dad is in the background – quiet in his bedroom, reading, perhaps dressed only in undershorts and tee shirt, but still dressed, amidst all this femininity. He did not dominate at these times. He seemed to retreat, to leave the house to his women. I don't think he objected to the nudity at all, he may even have enjoyed it, but he was the alien, the outsider, and he was significantly outnumbered.

It's odd, the messages and signals and behaviors and attitudes we pick up as children and don't think about or interpret until years – sometimes many years – have passed. Now that I think about the man/woman patterns of my youth, I see different truths than I saw then.

As a general rule, women tolerated men – their demands, their tantrums, their edicts, their needs – and accommodated them as far as they, the women, thought reasonable. That far, but no further. If men stepped over the line of what women thought reasonable, well! That shoe didn't fit. None of the women in our circles were of the unreasonable variety; none of our women were spendthrifts nor were they indolent or neglectful of their duties to home, family, children, friends, church, and community. They knew their own worth, by and large, and knew their duty. Men were necessary and I think in most cases, they were loved by their women – but they had their place and they had better keep it.

I think now that women had their own distinct priorities, the things that were important to them, the keeping of their homes, the raising and care of their children, the cooking and baking and canning and washing, tasks that may have been onerous and repetitive but which they took pride in doing well. And doing well often under the worst circumstances, of having to carry water and wood and coal, of making soap in the basement, of churning one's own butter, of cold rooms in the winter and hot rooms in the summer. The burden of caring for sick children, often through the night, while men slept in order to have energy for their own work the next day. As though women could sleep the day away after being up all night.

So these strong, busy, working women felt rightly that men could go so far, but no further. It's very clear now. It's also clear that women of the time did not waste their time or energy in trying to change their men. Husbands were, after all, to be respected, especially in public, to be allowed to be the heads of the household, and to be looked up to as such by their wives, their children, their community. Men were not encouraged to help with chores or children, or to be in touch with their feminine side (what feminine side?), or to participate in conversations about their relationships. The lines were clearly drawn.

The real meat of life happened when women were together, when men were at work or napping or busy elsewhere. Women together were the backbone and the mind of the family and the community. Tales were shared, help was asked for and given, work was parceled out, the rules of living were established and confirmed. Women were allowed to talk about people and what they did and why they did it, about whether children were doing well or needed correcting, about easier ways to accomplish the endless work, about growing up, growing old, growing wise, growing tired. Problems were solved or at least sympathized with, support was given, prayers were offered; women laughed like girls and wept like them, too. Women quarreled more often with each other but that, too, was a lesson – it's possible to disagree and still get along, still love.

Our women had as much honor as men, honor in fair dealing, in truth telling, in charity and good works. This did not include bothering the men with every little detail – the cake that burned and was thrown out, the shirt that ripped in the wringer and would have to be replaced somehow, the wrongdoing of a child, the forgotten dish in the icebox that spoiled and was wasted. Men were not mindlessly handed ammunition for their role as critic – that would have been foolish. I suspect that men did not share everything with women, either.

I was always glad, from a young person, that I was female. Men did not seem to have as much fun as women. They did not get to giggle and laugh as much, their talk seemed to be confined to such boring topics as politics or work or repairs, and in many important respects, they seemed helpless – helpless to soothe a crying baby or sew a rip or put together a quick meal or make lemonade. They were dependent on the good will and generosity of women to get so many of their needs or wants met – I felt sorry for them. And they worked so hard and then were too tired to have fun, unlike women, who worked hard and got chores out of the way so they *could* have fun.

Now, the man/woman thing seems so cluttered and confused – Mars and Venus indeed! The men in our lives are just like us and want the same things – love, respect, comfort, security, family ties, and the time to enjoy it all. They are better at talking with women, though they still tire more easily and can only take a limited amount of the kind of talk women enjoy. They are less sure of what women really want and what their own roles are.

It may be heresy, but these things seemed to be simpler 'way back then. I've learned a lot from men and I love the ones in my life – they are special and different. I believe in equal pay for equal work, in mutual respect and mutual tolerance - but I still like my doors opened, my chair pulled out, my meals praised, and my new dress admired. And when I'm hungry for good, real talk about the important stuff of life, well, thank God for all the women. ~ Anne

Wood. When I was old enough to understand, I was told my father was a cabinet maker.

He also painted, houses and barns, funeral homes and churches, inside and outside. People would be on a waiting list to have Emery Rawlings paint for them, his work was so prized and respected. But painting was generally a summer job; woodworking and cabinetry were for the short winter days, when he could work in his basement workshop, warm from the coal burning furnace and the woodstove on top of which his glue pots simmered.

I often wandered down to the basement, a cellar, really – furnace and coal pile in the middle, beyond which to the right was the laundry room and storage cellar with all of the canned bounty from the garden, in shining quarts and half-gallons, with a rough shower in one corner. To the left was Dad's workshop, a long narrow space with a rough flat work surface, a wood lathe, different table saws, jigsaws, tools aligned on the wall, furniture waiting for repair, and wood – wood planks (often from walnut or cherry trees cut on our property or from the grandparents' trees across the street), stored flat on rafters arranged below the low ceiling; wood chunks, blocks, bits, long squared rectangles that would undergo the magic of the lathe and become beautifully rounded legs for tables, beds, chairs.

Near the flat worktable was a high stool or two and I would climb up on one and watch the work in progress. Now and then, I stood, to watch the work on the lathe (magical) or the dangerous operations on a saw, but the thing I loved was to watch my father's hands touching the wood. My father's hands had no doubt been beautiful in his youth – shapely, long, strong – but many years of rough work on machinery, with farm animals, and with woodworking had turned them sinewy, gnarled, rough, and often discolored from stains and varnishes. No matter – to me they were man's hands, true hands, hands that brought objects of beauty out of trees.

I would watch him planing, the wood curling back from the planer like my own long curls, but harder and springier; I would play with the curls and wonder how he managed to plane just so, and no deeper. I would watch him sanding, first rough sandpaper, then medium, then fine – a few strokes, then rubbing the wood with his bare hand to judge the feel. Sand, sand, rub, repeat. As the sandpaper grew finer, his touch grew lighter – and I realized, before I was very old, that he loved the wood. Sometimes he would take my hand and run my small fingers down the wood, showing me where it was still rough, where it was smooth and silky.

After staining, he would sand again, finer still, the color bringing out the variations of the grain. Often he would rub the wood with his bare hands, with oils, with varnishes, some composite of his own mixing, and the wood would begin to gleam.

Much of our own furniture had been made or restored by Dad and it was common for visitors, or customers, to walk through the house and say "I'll give you $xxx for that bureau (quite often a very high dollar amount) or that table or that wood-framed mirror." But nothing was ever sold from our house in my time. These were our possessions – things that were brought in because my parents loved and cherished them. No matter that an old bureau had been found in a barn and Dad had paid $5 or $10 for it, or carted it away for nothing. He had spent hours of loving work bringing the wood alive again, making the drawers slide smoothly, repairing ravages of time or damage, of insect or water, and it was more our own than anything that could have been bought in a store. The offers were $500, $600, higher, to my parents whose income was usually two or three thousand a year. No. It was not for sale.

I had few chores, but when I was nine or ten, I was given a great responsibility. I was to be allowed to polish the furniture in our house. I was instructed in this great task, not by my mother, who kept house but did not enjoy it, but by Dad. He sat me down in the "front room" – what might have been a parlor in an earlier era, seldom used except for company – a grand room of good proportions with ten foot ceilings. We faced a small oval side table that he had made of walnut. We had dusting cloths and a bottle of lemon oil (that I think also had a bit of turpentine and beeswax in it, but the formula is lost). The task was formidable – to polish and feed the wood, to leave a gleam but no excess oil, to not drip on the carpet or sofa. A few drops on the cloth, rub, rub, until the oil was gone; a few more drops, rub, rub, around the sides, down the legs. Another drop or two, rub, rub, all over. A clean cloth then, rub all over to remove the oil, to bring out the shine, to leave the wood feeling energized – and loved. Tables, chairs, bureaus, linen chests, corner cupboards. Our house had a lot of wood. I was then, after my lesson, left alone to continue. Conscious of being admitted to my father's special realm, conscious also that my work would be inspected, I spent perhaps three hours on the furniture in the front room alone. Not a streak, not a drop, not a speck escaped my notice. I worked, with anxiety and enthusiasm, determined to do a job that would be beyond criticism (not expecting any compliments, of course). Later, at the dinner table, I remember vaguely some comments from my mother that I was exhausted, that the job was too much for this recently invalided child, that I was overexcited, flushed, and would probably be ill. It was not important. My father's blue eyes gleamed from his ruddy face: his smile held no trace of sarcasm or cynicism. I had done the kind of job he would have done, and he was proud of me.

Once, when I was eleven or twelve, we visited the Museum of Science & Industry in Chicago. In it, among its other wonders, was a Hall of Wood – a long, curving, gently lit corridor on the sides of which were hung large polished planks of different kinds of wood: mahogany, ebony, pine, walnut, cherry, maple, oak, woods I had never heard of and could not pronounce. And there my father talked to me of wood, spoke of each kind, its hardness, its grain, its use, its beauty; he ran his hands, so gently, so lovingly, over each plank, feeling the wood, the living thing it had once been, and for him, still was. He had me touch the special ones, examine the grain, observe the knots. That day, I felt for the first time what adulthood might mean, to have a conversation with another being, sharing his soul, his knowledge, his love. I knew that my father wanted to pass on to his children this special gift, this almost lost art, this deeply felt connection to the wood of the earth. And in that hour, for the first time, I dimly realized that there would be a world someday in which my father would no longer live. So I walked with my arm in his and listened and smiled, but there was a ringing in my ears, and my feet somehow couldn't feel the floor.

Now in many houses in this state and in others, my father's customers or perhaps their children and grandchildren look at tables and dressers, beds, and bowls made or repaired by Emery. It is likely that underneath the table or on the back of a frame is written a date and "E. E. Rawlings" in his unique bold writing. In my house and in the houses of my sisters and our children are tables and frames and bowls, made by him, and signed. When I polish the wood of these things in my house, I think of his hands – I think of him. ~Anne

X

X. This letter, by anyone's dictionary is a hard thing. I can think of momma hating folks using Xmas when speaking of Jesus' birthday.

There was also Madame X which was a dramatic piece mom did in high school and later was made into a movie with Lana Turner. Mom won accolades and first prize including a ribbon and a loving cup in her declamation contest so there are some x memories. Oh, and lets not forget the Xes on the floursacks that didn't get made into dresses.

Bet you thought we wouldn't find an X, huh. Fooled you. During my sister Anne's and my sorta coming of age years (I should have already come of age, but no, and guess what I am still working on that), Anne had this boyfriend – big guy, funny guy and always telling us something funny or insightful – lots older than either of us. He ran a bar. OOPS!!

Anyway this was the time of Malcolm X and the other X bunch and we all were pretty thoughtful about 'llowing as how that might be right to call your last name X if you were brought into a land not of your choosing and not of your own last name. And we pondered and we were thoughtful and deep thinking and speaking of this social blight. We took it very seriously. Until Moms Mably came along with her funny and side splitting skit about Sara X, well, then the seriousness got lost a little and I became well, you know. Later Annie became an x as well. So there's your x file. ~Sara

Y

Youngest. If you were born eldest or middlest or one of many, but never youngest, I recommend that you come back as the baby of a family.

It's great! You can be as manipulative, spoiled, and sly as you please, and it will be all right – because you're just a baby (even if you're twelve). You may play with your sister's favorite doll and she'll be scolded for yelling at you. Then she'll forgive you and buy you a new comic book.

If you're enough younger than the next sibling, you won't have to wear hand-me-downs. Your parents may well be in better shape financially, so you'll have more stuff – pretty clothes, good food, toys and books, your own room. If you work it right, you can soon be an only child because your older siblings will be disgusted and move out as soon as possible, leaving an open playing field.

Your parents, having dealt with at least two children before, will have learned some lessons and will tend to leave you alone, say yes more often than no, and not assign as many chores (except during strawberry and green bean picking seasons). They'll tend to smile more indulgently and more often.

Everything above is magnified if you can manage to be a surprise, late-life baby. I recommend, however, that you not announce this fact to your sixth grade class on your birthday. The kids won't get it and the teacher will gasp, turn purple, and call your mother.

Depending on your timing, you can miss a lot of the hard times – the Depression, most of a war, the dog dying, your parents' early quarrels, and living in near poverty. The only drawback is that, in adulthood, your siblings will have long conversations about people, places, and events in which you played no part. They will thus ignore you or say dismissively, "Oh, you were just a baby."

The above covers the classic possibilities. Our family was, of course, nothing like this.

Being the youngest in our family, I had a child's-eye view of our lives. This was compounded by my nose being stuck in a book most of the time, unaware of conflicts and storms swirling above my head. This may have been pure escapism. On the other hand, my memories of childhood and youth are seen, even now, through a haze of golden summers, long and endless, of laughter and love, of good food and friends, of my sisters and parents as being my touchstones, the guardians and preservers of my safe corner of the world. When I was born, my mother was 36 and my father was 42. By the time I was nine, both sisters were gone and I was, at least on a daily basis, the equivalent of an only child, with the added benefit of having big sisters to visit. I was an aunt when I was ten, and when I was sixteen, Sara bought me my first beer in a nightclub in Chicago.

In those safer days, I was allowed from the age of six to travel alone by train to Chicago, to see Sissy (Georgia) and her husband. I was allowed to stay alone in their apartment for a few hours at a time, to play endless games on the back porch of their apartment near the el train. When I was ten or eleven, one of Sissy's neighbors taught me to ride a bike for the first time, and Sissy's first husband, Paul, taught me dirty limericks and rude rhymes. I was with Sissy when I wore my first bra (that didn't fit) to her church picnic, and I was also with her for a long time one summer when I was thirteen and Grandpa was cared for by Mama and Daddy in their home, until he became violent and had to be institutionalized – hardening of the arteries, it was called then. And I was with Sissy when I heard that Grandpa had died.

We were at Sara's apartment in Chicago for one Thanksgiving, maybe two, and I remember reading and dozing against Dad's shoulder during the long boring afternoon while adults chatted endlessly. I remember feeling so happy that we were there together and Daddy was mellow and wasn't angry with Sara or with anyone that day, and that we were a family together.

Maybe most of all, I remember when Mama had had cancer for almost 18 months, and one day at work, when I was not quite 23, a voice whispered "Go see your mother." And I called my sisters and said, I'm going down to see Mama this weekend, tomorrow." And they said, we'll go too, and Sissy said, I'll drive. And we all drove down, and sang songs, and laughed and cried and were silly. And we saw Mama, thin and wasted in her hospital room, and she saw us all together. And then she asked to see each of us alone, and she gave us her last wisdom and her love. We spent the night, and hugged Daddy, and left. She died within the week with Dad at her side. We went down again, all of us with our children, and the house filled with people, and friends came, and the ladies of the church brought coffee and food and cakes, and the wake was in our house. There was no funeral because Mama had left her body for medical research. A year later, we went back to a memorial service for her that she had written herself before she died.

And Dad lived alone and came to visit us for Christmases and Thanksgivings, and we went to see him. When he was 82 he had a stroke and Sara came home from France to live with him and care for him in Petersburg. I didn't go there very often, I was busy with a career and a love affair, and I was a total bitch. But we have gotten past that. Dad got better and then had more strokes and lived in nursing homes in Chicago for a while so I saw him more often. His circulation got very bad and he went blind in March and could no longer read. He died in December, 1987, on Pearl Harbor Day, the day after Sara and I sat with him and read to him. He knew us but he didn't know where he was and he kept looking for Mama. She had been gone for twenty years.

Dad left his body to medical research as well. On a beautiful April weekend, Sissy and Sara and I went down to Petersburg to take Daddy's ashes to rest with Mama. The ladies of the church, old now but just as kind as ever, arranged a coffee and cake affair after the memorial service. The old church was beautiful in its simple way and Sara read the eulogy.

We went out to the cemetery on the hill and looked at the spring flowers and prayed with the young minister and said our goodbyes. We didn't look at the old house, now sold and changed. We looked at the hill we had walked up so many times, and at the streets we had known, and at the town where we had lived and grown up. We said goodbye and we went home.

We've been back since, once or twice, for reunions or to see the few old friends that are left. We've looked at the old house and cried – it's all changed and remodeled and new, and the pasture has been split off and another house built there. The furniture shop sign is gone, of course, and so is the swing. The bridge is gone, and the railroad cut is filled up so it's just a shallow grassy valley. The house where Nannie and Grandpa lived is not much changed, but the gardens are gone and the old cherry tree and the lilac bush no longer exist.

So we think of all that was, and we remember, my sisters and I – Sissy and Sara and Annie. The Rawlings girls. I am two years older then Mama was when she died – and I am the youngest. ~ Anne

Z

Zest. In spite of it all, we three girls have a zest about us that includes questing still -- zest for wonder as in awe. The zest for embracing the ever-evolving evolution of our self-nesses. We are all zestful in the truest sense.

We are full of gusto for life and new adventures, ready to take it on, learn new stuff, take a risk, get knocked down, get up, even at our advanced years of 200 total. We are ready for the next – nay eager.

This must be because of our dictionary or maybe in spite of it. ~Sara

Dad's Eulogy

We're going to have your memorial today, Dad. I'll be reading your eulogy myself. I'm not interested in having someone laud you, saying what a swell man/father/husband you were. Me, middle child, caretaker and general stupid person, me who knew you better than you did – I will do the eulogy. I'm gonna do this – I will get through this. There's no one more qualified to say a few things about my father. I cannot eulogize him – in the true sense – he would hate that anyway, people saying words that weren't him. Somewhere though, floating about this church is some bit of him and, to be honest, some bit of that bit is enjoying these proceedings, as he might call them.

My father was rarely pleasant, he had few friends, and he was critical and acerbic. He was a loner, enjoying his own company and the company of books. His mouth was (usually) a line across his face that came down at the corners.

But I have seen this spring wire of a man stride across his land, determined seeming, scowling toward his errand – stop, cock his head, listening to something I certainly could not hear – see him bend down, stand again and that dear sweet – so much more so because it was so rare – smile would appear, see him stride back and into the house where he would open his hand to my mother, revealing "the first violet, Mom." The steely blue-gray eyes sparkling like two pieces of Cornwall sky come adrift to settle in his head.

I have seen this man whose stomach was his master decline lunch because a small brown cat had settled in a sunspot on his lap for a protracted snooze. There, my hungry father would sit until the cat freed him.

I have seen my crusty old father weep openly over the plight of the native American as portrayed in National Geographic, seen him weep, his body shaking, taking a black pen to write across the page, "Man's inhumanity to man."

I have seen him look up at an ebony black woman, a nurse, as she bent over him in his last days, to make an adjustment in his bedding, pat his face, something to make him more comfortable – seen his eyes still piercing blue, but seeing only shapes and shadows, and heard him whisper, "oh, honey, black is so beautiful."

Dad you are home, you no longer need to fight your two selves, wonder if you will ever get it all right. It is all perfect now.

174

I thought I had a handle on you Daddy, but I do not. You have taken your secrets to the grave, the secret of who you really were why so angry, judgmental, unaccepting – so gentle with the earth and with animals, sensitive, sentimental.

I may not have figured you out, but Daddy I've always known I love you. ~Sara

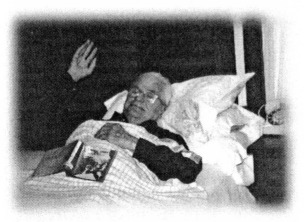

Epilogue

Somewhere, in an adjacent world, the house still stands, untouched, as each of us remembers it. The pine in front still bears the sign of "Furniture...;" a rope swing dangles from the oak in front.

On Mondays, washday, laundry hangs on lines in back, snapped by the wind and scented by the grass. The wrens still nest in gourds along the garage, and four-leaf clovers line the back door stoop.

The pastures stretch beneath both sun and cloud, now wet with rain or drifted high with snow, now studded with the flowers of spring or golden with the summer, each in turn. The lowing of a cow, the cluck of hens, a bleating lamb, and farther off, a barking dog, are heard from one day to the next.

Within the house, the ghosts of pantry or a pump shift lazily beneath the structures newly built. A star to dance on anchors kitchen floor, and ivy twines across the dining room. A rocking chair moves gently with a touch, and buzzing from below speaks from a saw.

A woman moves from door to sink, from stove to wooden table, its oval set for five. She hums and almost dances to the door. Unseen, she swiftly kicks her leg to touch the lintel at the top and laughs in triumph – still limber, and still young.

Again outdoors, the forms of children dart along the fence and through the gate, race through the grass to hide behind a barn, or watch the chicks, or call a dog to heel. Far more than three, the images are we, in all our ages – four or six or ten – playing in their solitudes or pairs, caught in their happiest times, the golden moments of our childhoods past, captured in an age long gone, yet ever present.

In that world, we live free, are cherished, loved – no stain lies on our youthful hearts, it is perfection on an earth that might have been, or is, or will someday be born.

And yet, through all our scars, through fault or blame, an echo of that place stirs in our hearts. Some moments from that world we lived, we carry still the rare and golden times that, some day, will expand to blot away the pain that haunts today. Meantime, they live for us, those spirits lovely and complete, attaining each to her, or his, maturity, to live at last in full ability, in joyous harmony, and with most kindly humor.

They see us now, and we will be there soon enough.

THE END

Printed in the United States
19176LVS00007B/241-417